LABOR'S GRASS ROOTS

ROOTS

A Study of the Local Union

BY JACK BARBASH

Professor of Labor Education and Economics,
University of Wisconsin

GREENWOOD PRESS, PUBLISHERS
WESTPORT, CONNECTICUT

Library of Congress Cataloging in Publication Data

Barbash, Jack.
  Labor's grass roots.

  Reprint of the ed. published by Harper, New York.
  1. Trade-unions--United States.   I.   Title.
[HD6508.B352 1974] \   331.88'0973   73-11839
ISBN 0-8371-7064-8

Copyright © 1961 by Jack Barbash

Originally published in 1961 by Harper & Brothers, New York

Reprinted with the permission of Harper & Row, Publishers, Inc.

Reprinted in 1974 by Greenwood Press,
a division of Congressional Information Service, Inc.
88 Post Road West, Westport, Connecticut 06881

Library of Congress catalog card number 73-11839
ISBN 0-8371-7064-8

Printed in the United States of America

10 9 8 7 6 5 4 3 2

LABOR'S GRASS ROOTS

CONTENTS

PREFACE

The principal focus of this study is the internal government of local unions. There are several *specific* local union investigations but this study aims at the development of a reasonably comprehensive scheme in which the whole range of local union behavior can be perceived. Obviously this attempt at comprehensiveness would not have been feasible if I had not had the incalculable advantage of being able to use other people's firsthand research. My specific obligations in this connection are indicated at the appropriate places in the text.

The internal government of local unions is part of a complex of organization and function consisting of (a) related units of union government, for example, the international union; (b) related functions of local unions, for example, collective bargaining; and (c) public regulation by courts and legislation. The local union cannot be properly understood unless it is seen as part of this complex, and for this reason I have sketched it in at relevant places in the discussion.

The method of approach has been first to convey a general impression of the local union in many of its varieties (Chapter I). This is followed by the scope and evolution of the local (Chapter II) and its formal constitutional foundations (Chapter III).

In the next sequence I deal with the main actors and institutions shaping the local: the membership in the union meeting (Chapter IV), the business agent (Chapter V), the local-wide leaders of the factory union (Chapter VI), the steward (Chapter VII), and the international union and its instrumentalities (Chapter VIII). The process of conflict and controversy in the local union is investigated in Chapter IX. The local union as represented in the attitudes of union members is examined in Chapter X. The meaning of local union government for theories of democracy is the concern of the concluding chapter.

The intent has been to present the main body of material in a matter-of-fact way with, I hope, a minimum of argument. I have reserved the concluding chapter for personal conclusions and judgments.

I am deeply obligated to a number of people and institutions. The

Trade Union Issues Project of the Fund for the Republic started me on the track with a financial grant. Graduate students Raymond Barrett, Alton Bartlett, Ronald Coyte, (Miss) Madhuri Gurnaney, L. A. O'Donnell, and Dwight Scarbrough rendered invaluable assistance in supplementing through direct investigation the stock of specific case studies available to me. Observers in various cities, whom I regret I may not acknowledge by name, permitted me to quiz them at length. My association with the School for Workers and the Department of Economics, both of the University of Wisconsin, provided me with important vantage points of insight. My late colleague and friend, Professor Selig Perlman, was a unique source of illumination for me as he was for every student of unionism who crossed his path.

Fragments of this work represent previous writing by me in *The New Leader; Labor Law Journal,* incorporating Industrial Relations Research Association proceedings; *The Practice of Unionism* (Harper, 1956); and *Labor's Public Responsibility* (National Institute of Labor Education, 1960).

The greatest obligation is to my wife, Kate Barbash, whose patient and skillful collaboration has made this enterprise practicable for me.

J. B.

Madison, Wisconsin
1961

LABOR'S GRASS ROOTS

THE LOCAL UNION IN MOTION
An Overview[1]

The purpose of this chapter is to let the reader see the local union as a complete enterprise. Later, the major working parts in the local union will be examined separately in closer focus.

FUNCTIONS

The five functions of the local union in the American labor movement may be classified as: (1) internal union administration; (2) collective bargaining and related activities including strikes; (3) relations with the labor movement; (4) legislative, political, and community activities; (5) member welfare activities. The first two classes constitute the hard core of union functioning. Local unions vary greatly as to their interest in the other functions although, as time progresses, local unions are probably enlarging their scope of operations.

The internal union administration can be divided for purposes of generalization under the traditional headings of legislative, executive-administrative, and judicial. The highest legislative authority in the local union is the membership, characteristically functioning through the union meeting and less typically through the referendum, as a supplement to the union meeting for the more critical issues such as strike votes, ratification of the contract, or dues increases.

The executive-administrative phase is mostly concerned with the regulation of disbursements and income. Here the chief movers are likely to be: (a) the local union executive board, which exercises the major executive-administrative authority between

[1] Since this is a summary chapter there will be no extensive footnoting of sources here but the sources can be found at the points where the illustrative material is examined in greater detail.

and subject to union meetings, and (b) the local-wide officers who may or may not be full-time officers.

The judicial function is exercised through the executive board and the union meeting, with the latter invariably as the court of last resort within the local on disciplinary actions involving members.

The collective bargaining class of functions is concerned with issues arising out of the collective bargaining relationship with management, and is carried on by stewards, local-wide officers, the executive board, and ultimately the union meeting. Collective bargaining as a total process is the negotiation of the agreement, the enforcement of the agreement including arbitration, and the strike as the fundamental sanction through which the union is able to bargain collectively.

The reach of a local's collective bargaining functions invariably extends to collaboration with other locals of its international union and with locals of other internationals. Within its own international, the typical local union is part of a network of relationships which include the equivalent of a district council or joint board, a region or district, or industry council. Its participation in these intra-international union bodies is commonly carried on through delegates elected by the local. By way of example: a building trades local in a large city will have formal relationships with a district council composed of local unions of the same international; it is likely to be a participant in a state council composed of local unions in the same international. A mass-production local union—to take the United Automobile Workers (UAW), with its highly organized network of internal relationships, as a case in point—is likely to be involved in an industry council (agricultural implements, aircraft), an employer multi-plant council (General Motors, Ford, J. I. Case, etc.), an occupational council (skilled trades).

The local union will also be involved frequently in collaboration with locals of other international unions. The most characteristic instance would be the local building trades council, composed of the standard building trades locals in a city. Other prominent examples of this kind of collaboration beyond the confines of the international union are the hotel trades councils in various areas, composed of locals of various internationals with interests in the hotel and restaurant.

The dominant agencies in the labor-movement class of func-

2

tions are the central AFL–CIO labor body of the city and the state AFL–CIO. (This, of course, applies only to locals of AFL–CIO internationals.) The city and state bodies are composed of constituent local unions with delegate voting strength in an established proportion to membership. The state bodies and the larger city bodies will invariably have one or more full-time officers. The state bodies are governed by an annual convention and the city bodies by a weekly or monthly meeting. Between conventions or meetings the affairs are administered by an elected executive council.

The main functions of the central bodies derive from their roles as the symbol of the total labor movement. The central bodies are most influential in legislative, political, and community-representation affairs; and, depending on the prestige, tradition, and size of the central body, in jurisdictional disputes, assistance in organizing, and collective bargaining.

Many locals—but the likelihood is not a majority—function politically, legislatively, and in the community on their own power. They may carry on this activity to further specific interests and to support broad programs. Legislatively, locals lobby in the halls of city councils and state legislatures. Politically, locals undertake to support their political friends and defeat their political antagonists. In the community, some locals will train "community service" representatives to help members in trouble. Depending on the situation, the "local"—as used in the context of legislation, politics, and community activity—may mean paid officers, part-time officers, or a special committee, or some combination of all of these.

When a local carries on the welfare function, it sees its interests as going beyond the representative function in the plant and extending to the union member as a consumer and as a social being. For the limited number of locals that carry on this order of function it may mean a variety of activities, including housing cooperatives, scholarships for members' children, health care clinics, credit union activities, legal representation for members, assistance in filing workmen's compensation, unemployment compensation and social security claims.

ROUTINES

The local union is always in a state of what might be called moving equilibrium. In its workaday existence, the local union

3

holds meetings in the union hall and on the job. It collects dues from members and spends money for a variety of per capita payments. It engages in bargaining with employers, it handles the grievances and complaints of individual members and responds to the vexations of individual employers. It sends delegates to all sorts of councils and to state and city central labor bodies. It passes resolutions in favor of or against particular legislation. It is doing these and one hundred other things. This is the normal life of a union. It is in motion.

There is enough detail for one West Coast UAW local to give us something of the flavor of a specific factory local union in motion.[2] Not that every local union conforms to this pattern, but the pattern of activity of the factory local is likely to be along the lines—if not with the same intensity—of this particular UAW local. The president of this large local writes, edits, and supervises publication of the local union paper, which is mimeographed and published weekly or so in one to four pages. If a grievance is unsettled at the plant, it is his responsibility to write it up for further negotiation. He supervises the two part-time secretaries in the office.

The recording secretary takes minutes of the official meetings of the local. In addition he holds office as secretary-treasurer of the county CIO council. He handles the major portion of the correspondence of the nonbargaining variety; the president handles the correspondence relating to bargaining. He participates in the bargaining procedure at the upper levels within the local and the local management, along with the president and first vice-president. He is generally regarded as the floor leader for the officer group and speaks frequently and "well" on the issues coming up on the union floor.

The first vice-president keeps the bargaining files and sees to it that the grievance deadlines are held. He frequently takes minutes at membership and other meetings if the recording secretary is absent. He spends much of his time in the local union office and tries to assist the president. At the local union office, inactive members ask for information; if they cannot get hold of the president, the girls in the office will refer them to the first vice-president.

The financial secretary takes care of depositing the local union's

[2] This is taken from James L. Stern, "The Role of the Local Union: Case Study of Local 844, UAW–CIO," unpublished Ph.D. dissertation, University of California, August 1954.

money in banks, the forwarding of the per capita tax to the international union, the furnishing of membership cards, and the maintenance of an up-to-date inventory of the local union's property. He is also involved in the upper echelons of the bargaining procedure. The treasurer cosigns checks; he deposits the money in the banks; and maintains a record of the finances of the local union.

In addition to these top officers, there are trustees who function as the purchasing agents and budget planners of the local. During one period the senior trustee was substantially involved in negotiating the construction of a local union office. A sergeant-at-arms introduces the new members and visitors at the union meeting, and helps the president in maintaining order when asked to do so.

For the membership, there are general membership meetings and departmental meetings.

The names of the committees indicate the scope of activity which is carried on. Thus, there is the executive board, a political action committee, a fair practices and antidiscrimination committee, a community services committee, a constitution and by-laws committee, a recreation committee, a union labor committee, and an education committee. If these committees are active at all, the committee, for practical purposes, is usually the chairman of the committee. The exceptions to the indifferent functioning of committees are the executive board and the bargaining committee which always function and for whose meetings there is usually no difficulty in getting attendance.

In its relations with its own international, its delegates attend the national convention of the international; there, among other things, they participate in the election of a regional director, who is the most important contact with the international. The local also participates in an intracorporation council made up of all the locals in a bargaining relationship with their multiplant employer.

The local is a part of the state labor body and the county labor body. (The local's recording secretary is also the secretary-treasurer of the county council.) He spends a good deal of time on county council business where he is active in political and community activities.

A typical day in the life of a business agent in a building trades union may look something like this.[3]

[3] From George Strauss, "Business Agents in the Building Trades," *Industrial and Labor Relations Review,* January 1957.

5

IN THE OFFICE:

Arrives at 7:30 A.M.

Deals with job requests of members already waiting for him.

Calls up two jobs to check that referrals have arrived.

Writes letter to out-of-town company—what about retroactive pay?

Promises older member to visit his brother in the hospital.

Two men laid off day before—want new jobs.

Answers telephone call from contractor—sends a man out to meet request for specialist.

Calls employer to find out reason why he refused to hire a referral. Finds out that man had a record of drunkenness; employer won't budge. Business agent agrees to send somebody else; warns member to "lay off the bottle."

Member comes in; asks business agent to step outside; wants a personal favor, a job for his cousin. Business agent says can't admit new members at this time.

Members come in to pay dues.

Issues referral to traveling union member from another local.

Union member asks a transfer card to leave town—his wife kicked him out of the house.

Agrees not to send men through picket line of another local union on request of business agent of same.

IN THE FIELD:

First stop: talks to a steward about new projects, to employer who asks for more craftsmen, to men who say they won't be satisfied with less than 20 cents an hour raise during negotiations—stops at office to pick up wages of man who got drunk last week and quit.

Stop No. 2: steward complains that boss has tied him down to one job so that he can't get around, says two nonunion men hired on another section of the project—business agent questions men about union membership, their evidence is vague—goes to the "boss," who agrees to let nonunion men go.

Stop No. 3: steward asks about negotiations, and after chiding steward for not being present at meeting, business agent briefs him—steward complains about foreman pushing men around —business agent asks for facts in writing, talks to foreman— foreman says steward has it in for him.

Stop No. 4: takes steward to lunch—discusses new processes— takes up complaints with boss.

Stop No. 5: new project run by large national firm which has agreement with international union to divide jobs 50 per cent locally and 50 per cent with its own men—business agent

6

tells superintendent these contracts are not observed locally
—superintendent says O.K. but asks that his foreman be retained.

OTHER DUTIES:

> Meetings in his own local, two to six nights a month. In addi-
> tion attends meetings of the executive board, the examining
> boards, etc.
>
> Participates in interunion functions, building trades council,
> central labor body, state district council, banquets for other
> business agents.
>
> Serves on "countless civic committees and regularly appears at
> community functions."

In one form or another these activities constitute the routine
of daily movement in the local union. In the factory union the
activity is likely to be more diffused but rarely involves in any
active way the majority of the membership. In the building trades
and other nonfactory types of employment, the work is more con-
centrated in the hands of the business agent and secondarily in
those of his assistants and the local union officers.

STYLES

Some local unions acquire a distinctive character. The individuality of the local may be derived from internal characteristics and conflicts, the special quality of its relationship to management, the impact of industry economics and technology, or
the manner of its involvement in the total community. What
follows is not a comprehensive scheme of union styles but rather
a suggestion of the inexhaustible varieties of circumstances and
experiences that give uniqueness to some local unions.

There are the locals—usually large locals—which bear the im-
print of a high-powered leader: a Harold Gibbons in Local 688
of the Teamsters stimulates busy participation, collectively bar-
gained health schemes, and intense political activity; a Harry Van
Arsdale in Local 3 of the International Brotherhood of Electrical
Workers (IBEW) creates elaborate organizational networks of
union within union, liberal arts educational programs; a Joe De-
Silva of the Los Angeles Retail Clerks uses his union's collective
bargaining power to remake the pattern of medical care.

There are locals which take their tone from the factional turbulence that prevails, for example: the Allis-Chalmers Local 248
of the UAW in Wisconsin; the building trades local unions around

the Paducah, Kentucky, atomic installation where the old-timers attempted to retain control against the influx of newcomers; or the wartime shipyards of the West Coast confronting the same kind of situation.

There are local unions whose internal life is given a special quality because of their running challenge to the leadership of the international union, as for example: the so-called "Dues Protest Movement" converted into the "Organization for Membership Rights" among the Steelworkers locals at the Irwin works of U.S. Steel in Pittsburgh and the Aliquippa works of the Jones and Laughlin Steel Corporation; Carl Stellato, president of the giant UAW Ford River Rouge Local 600 taking on Walter Reuther; the Hollywood local of the American Federation of Musicians (AFM), up in arms against the leadership and policies of James Petrillo, resulting in the international union ultimately taking the local out of the AFM and setting up a rival union.

The divisions within the international become translated into conflict for power within the locals, and this fact becomes the mark of local union distinction. The battle between Emil Rieve and George Baldanzi for control of the Textile Workers split many locals. Internal turmoil in the local with ideological wellsprings is seen between supporters of UE ousted from the CIO for Communist domination, and the IUE chartered by the CIO to wrest control of the electrical manufacturing industry from the UE.

The internal life of the local is sometimes so apathetic that vocal minorities dominate the governmental processes, not by design but by default. A TWUA local of printers and dyers in southwestern New England permitted itself to be dominated by a "politically ambitious minority faction composed of younger, more mobile males" until an international representative moved in to bolster the will of the inarticulate, older majority.

There are locals that have acquired a special style as a result of their accommodation to ethnic influences, notably the Packinghouse Workers locals and their Negro membership. There are local unions whose stock in trade has been the exploitation of defenseless ethnic groups as in the "paper locals" headed by Johnny Dio and their exploitation of newly arrived Puerto Rican workers.

The membership composition in some locals gives them a dis-

8

tinctive quality—Actors Equity, the Air Line Pilots, the professional engineers, and the Hollywood talent guilds, who come into public view because creative and professional people are not normally associated with unions. And even less so when these creative and professional unions function like orthodox unions, striking, picketing, haggling over jurisdiction, and fighting about premium pay for overtime and pensions—like ordinary workers.

The dominating fact in the existence of some locals is repelling invasion by rival union groups: the unsuccessful (on the whole) attempts of the affiliated unions to move in on the local independents in the chemical and petroleum industries; or the attempts of the local independents to withstand the attack of the Communications Workers in the telephone industry. Rivalry is also a vexing fact of life between locals of affiliated unions: Teamsters *vs.* Brewery Workers, Carpenters *vs.* Lumber Workers, Pressmen *vs.* Lithographers; or the ideological rival unionism of the UE *vs.* the IUE, or the Steelworkers *vs.* the Mine, Mill and Smelter Workers.

Rival unionism of another sort is in the daily order of life for building trades locals where the protection of jurisdiction from other locals is a central concern fully as demanding as protection of the worker from his employer.

Sheer size occasionally distinguishes a local union so that it is perforce almost a "little international." IBEW Local 3 with 30,000 members and Hotel and Restaurant Local 6 with over 20,000 members—both in New York—UAW Local 12 in Toledo, Chicago Teachers Union local in Chicago, Longshoremen and Warehousemen's Local 10 in San Francisco, Local 688 of the Teamsters in St. Louis are additional examples of situations in which massiveness is more than a difference in degree—it almost becomes a difference in the kind of local unionism.

For one thing, the large local union, when it is something more than a huge monolith, has the resources to extend the reach of local union interests beyond collective bargaining into large-scale welfare unionism of the kind noted previously in connection with Gibbons and Van Arsdale. In the case of IBT (International Brotherhood of Teamsters) Local 688, which is in a class all by itself, welfare unionism comprises a medical center plus drug, dental, and optical services, a 218-acre rest home and vacation

9

resort, counseling, classes, credit unions, bowling clubs, baseball teams, hiring halls, free income-tax service, and political ward stewards.

For many local unions the overriding fact is the quality of their relationship to management, or the manner of adjustment to the economics of the industries in which they happen to be operating. There are the celebrated "mature" collective bargaining relationships—celebrated in the National Planning Association's (NPA) Causes of Industrial Peace studies. For some of the locals the push to maturity comes from the management initiative, as was perhaps true of the West Coast "paper locals." For others the initiative comes from the union's side, as in the Amalgamated Clothing Workers. Local unions in the building trades and in the Teamsters are also prime movers in mature relationships. For still others "good" labor-management relations stem from the limited objectives and labor movement relationships, as in the oil-refinery independent at Esso's Bayway plant.

On another band of the union-management spectrum is the local union whose relationship to management is dominated by turbulence—the J. I. Case and Kohler locals of the UAW and the Textile locals in the South, all living on the margin of existence—are cases in point.

The local union as a fortified island apparently sufficient unto itself is the hallmark of the unaffiliated, independent local union. Its union life is contained within the plant, uninhibited or unenriched by external labor movement relationships except as occasionally it may maintain an undemanding liaison relationship with a coordinating council of independents in the same company. The independent locals in petroleum appear to function on this kind of narrow stage.

Somewhat further removed from this self-containment is the local union which is part of an international but whose interests are so inward-centered that the international is hardly more than a repository for per capita payments. Sometimes this isolation is enforced, as in the case of a UE local at Allen-Bradley in Milwaukee, by the stigma attached to the international union.

In another form of self-containment the union is almost a total community—or interchangeable with the community—as in locals in one-industry towns in mining and textiles. The union aboard ship is an enforced community for its members, especially, it would seem, for the unlicensed personnel.

Union-management "cooperation" of the collusive variety provides the underlying character of some local unions—which is really no union character at all—since the reason for existence of these locals is solely the personal enrichment of the "leaders" and of the employer who hopes to profit from the differential wage advantage arising out of the collusion. In these instances the local is a shell without organized government.

In another variety of collusion, the local union is not a mechanism for worker representation but a mechanism for elimination of competition among enterprisers, as in the juke-box local, where the strike power of the union is the sanction for allocation of juke-box territories.

Fundamental industry-wide change in technology, as in the railroad and textile industries, is the significant circumstance in the life of the locals; or the imminent plant shut-down as in some packing house, steel, and textile (again) locals. In these situations the temper of local unions is the accent on adversity.

The nature of the employer, as in public employment, confronts the local union with the need to find alternatives to orthodox striking and collective bargaining, and the resort to these alternatives—demonstrations, intense political and legislative activity, and slowdowns—gives an individuality to some local unions. The locals in New York and Milwaukee and Transport Workers in New York's transit system illustrate how public employment shapes the style of the union and encourages the emergence of "hell-raising" leaders.

Local unions of public employees do not always or necessarily live in crisis. Relations with public administrators are regularized by an approximation of the processes of private collective bargaining, as in the AFSCME locals in Philadelphia, and the prototype of stabilized union-management relations in the TVA.

Union relations in public employment are regularized via another route—the route of political accommodation with the public administrators, as in the history of the policemen's and firemen's local unions in New York City, for example.

Some local unions that deal with a private employer find the nature of their employer's business makes government everpresent in the bargaining relationship. This is the posture of the locals engaged in the atomic energy production complex. Whoever the employer is technically the Atomic Energy Commission defines the area of maneuverability for the parties.

11

The point of all of this can be put briefly: (1) Every local union except possibly the pathological types carry on a hard core of unvarying, routine, matter-of-fact activities involving their members, employers, and to a limited degree, the community at large. In these relationships small troubles are the order of the day. The members expect it and the leadership of the local generally takes these in its stride.

(2) For many there exists (or perhaps existed in the past) some dominating quality or style arising out of leadership, internal or external conflict, size, the quality of its collective bargaining relationship which gives the local a distinctive face. The fact that the local may have such a distinctive face should not obscure that whatever else it does it must function routinely.

2

THE LOCAL UNION IN
THE AMERICAN LABOR MOVEMENT

ORGANIZATIONAL NETWORK

The main line of labor movement government in the United States functions on four levels. From the bottom up these levels are in summary form at this point: (1) the local union; (2) the intermediate body; (3) the international union—for the most part a *national* union but called international in common usage; (4) the federation, i.e., the AFL–CIO.

The local union is the nuclear unit in union organization in the United States because (a) it is the point of normal contact for the average union member, and (b) it is (within broad limits) a self-sufficient unit of government. By way of contrast are the several removes which separate the member from the higher levels of union government. A direct union-member relationship also prevails in sublocal units but these sublocal units—the shop committee in a multiplant local, the department steward—are not, except in rare situations, self-contained governments. The local union can be differentiated from these sublocal units in that the latter are not typically organic governments.

The sovereign entity in the traditional system of trade union government is the international union. Within the limits imposed by law and voluntary arrangements the authority for internal management, collective bargaining, and jurisdiction is derived from the international union.

The organization chart of the typical international union will not, however, normally show an uninterrupted line from the international to the local. More characteristic is for the line to be broken by a level of government intermediate between the international and the local in the nature of district councils, regions, state councils, joint boards, joint councils, or conferences.

13

The common property of these intermediate bodies is that they are multilocal in character; or to put it another way, the constituency of the intermediate bodies are locals not individual members. The intermediate bodies vary (1) as to the nature of the tie that holds them together and (2) as to the degree of interaction with the constituent locals.

The federation, which here is equated with the AFL–CIO, is a voluntary association of sovereign international unions. The federation imposes certain conditions for affiliation, but affiliation is a matter of choice for the international.

The federation contains within it two types of subfederations, as it were: (1) the city central bodies and the state federations composed of the locals of federation-affiliated internationals in a particular city (or county or metropolitan area or state); (2) the departments of the AFL–CIO: Railway Employees, Metal Trades, Building and Construction Trades, Maritime Trades, Industrial Union, Union Label, and Service Trades. The departments are designed to bring together internationals with a common interest in the trade or industry suggested by the name of the department. The departments, other than the Industrial Union Department, include subordinate city and state councils which are the local branches of the national departments and are made up of locals of the internationals affiliated to the national departments.

A local union is consequently involved in a network of affiliations and superior bodies. The main line of a local union relationship runs to an intermediate body and to the national union. Lateral lines run to city and state federations and to local councils of the departments.

There are, in addition, local unions that have no organic relationship to a national union. These are of two kinds. There is the "directly affiliated local union" in the AFL–CIO for whom the AFL–CIO serves in place of the national union. The directly affiliated status is regarded as a transitional status until the local union chooses a permanent place in an international. For some locals the transition has become permanent, lasting as long as twenty-five years. There are 507 of directly affiliated unions with a membership of 108,000.[1] There are also local unions which are "independents." These are unaffiliated unions typically limited

[1] American Federation of Labor–Congress of Industrial Organizations, *Report of the Executive Council*, 1959, p. 35.

to the employees of a single plant or a single company and without organic relationship to any international union.

The United States Bureau of Labor Statistics estimated that in 1958 there were 78,110 local unions affiliated with national and international unions. About four-fifths of the locals were in AFL–CIO affiliates.[2] (This number includes something more than 4,000 locals in Canada.)

EVOLUTION

The local union has been the seedbed of unionism and the labor movement in the United States. The emergence of the local union is by common consent located in the closing years of the eighteenth and the beginning years of the nineteenth centuries. These early local unions were as much mutual aid societies as they were trade unions. George E. Barnett, in his classic essay has established four benchmarks in the evolution of the labor movement.

> In the earliest period—from the end of the 18th century to about 1815—the local union was the only form of trade-union grouping. . . . The second period, extending from 1827–1838, was marked by the rise of the city federation, or, as it was then called, the trades' union.
> The third period from 1865 to 1888 marked the formation of national federations.
> The fourth period in the structural history of American trade unionism—from 1897 to the present—has been distinguished by the increasing control exercised by the national trade union over the other forms of grouping.[3]

The emergence of the local association of unions—that is, what we would call today the central labor body—is generally attributed to the need for some multilocal instrumentality crossing national union boundaries to express the political and legislative goals of a city or state labor movement. It was the hours-of-work issue that brought together the earliest known city-wide associations of unions.

The widening scope of the product market or the labor market,

[2] U.S. Bureau of Labor Statistics (BLS), *Directory of National and International Labor Unions in the United States,* 1959, Bulletin 1267, p. 15.
[3] "The Dominance of the National Union in American Labor Organization," *Quarterly Journal of Economics,* vol. 28 (1913), reprinted in John R. Commons, *Trade Unionism and Labor Problems,* 2d series (Boston: Ginn, 1921), pp. 387–388.

DISTRIBUTION OF NATIONAL AND INTERNATIONAL UNIONS
BY NUMBER OF LOCALS AND AFFILIATION, 1958

| Number of locals | ALL UNIONS | | | | UNION AFFILIATION | | | |
| | Unions | | Locals | | AFL–CIO | | Unaffiliated | |
	Number	Per cent	Number	Per cent	Unions	Locals	Unions	Locals
All unions	184	100.0	78,110	100.0	136	62,910	48	15,200
Under 10 locals	19	10.3	79	0.1	7	39	12	40
10 and under 25 locals	13	7.1	201	.3	6	90	7	111
25 and under 50 locals	22	12.0	800	1.0	12	437	10	363
50 and under 100 locals	23	12.5	1,779	2.3	18	1,364	5	415
100 and under 200 locals	30	16.3	4,105	5.3	27	3,677	3	428
200 and under 300 locals	14	7.6	3,324	4.3	12	2,844	2	480
300 and under 400 locals	9	4.9	3,011	3.9	7	2,316	2	695
400 and under 500 locals	10	5.4	4,289	5.5	10	4,289		
500 and under 600 locals	6	3.3	3,318	4.2	5	2,770	1	548
600 and under 700 locals	7	3.8	4,501	5.8	7	4,501		
700 and under 800 locals	5	2.7	3,755	4.8	5	3,755		
800 and under 900 locals	2	1.1	1,749	2.2	1	860	1	889
900 and under 1,000 locals	6	3.3	5,755	7.4	5	4,815	1	940
1,000 and under 1,500 locals	7	3.8	8,511	10.9	6	7,214	1	1,297
1,500 and under 2,000 locals	3	1.6	5,289	6.8	3	5,289		
2,000 locals and over	8	4.3	27,644	35.4	5	18,650	3	8,994

Source: U.S. Bureau of Labor Statistics Directory of National and International Labor Unions in the U.S., 1959, Bulletin 1267

as the case may be, is commonly held to be the primary generating element in the combining of local unions into national unions. The continued dominance of the national union reflected the ascendancy of collective bargaining as against the social reform objectives of the central bodies.[4] The national associations of unions evolving ultimately into the AFL–CIO can be traced to a variety of influences, of which the need for national symbols of labor solidarity and the importance of national legislative representation are probably the most important. Intermediate bodies, not included in Barnett's scheme, arose out of a need to maintain a degree of economic liaison and common action among locals (primarily) of the same international.

There are two physical centers in which the governmental processes of the local union operate; in shorthand terms these centers are the union hall and the worksite at which local union members are employed. In the former the participants are officers and members. In the latter the participants are officers and members aligned on one side and the employer and his representatives aligned on the other in a collective bargaining relationship.

It is the worksite collective bargaining relationship that gives meaning and thrust to the union-hall relationship. A union hall which does not rest on an existing or anticipated collective bargaining situation has little significance in the American system of unionism.

JURISDICTION

The starting point in the local union's collective bargaining is jurisdiction. Jurisdiction as used here means the territory within which a union organizes and engages in collective bargaining, or to which it asserts a claim for purposes of organizing and bargaining.

In a general way a local union derives jurisdiction from its parent international. Significant deviations from the jurisdiction of the international are nevertheless frequent. In the locals comprising District 4 of the IUE, 72 out of the 154 plants were under the stated jurisdiction of IUE; 18 were in borderline jurisdiction;

[4] See also John R. Commons and Associates, *History of Labor in the United States* (New York: Macmillan, 1926), vol. 1, chap. 1; William M. Leiserson, *American Trade Union Democracy* (New York: Columbia University Press, 1959), p. 32 ff.; Lloyd Ulman, *The Rise of the National Trade Union* (Cambridge: Harvard University Press, 1955), chap. 18.

37 were clearly foreign to IUE's jurisdiction. The union organizers and officials admitted that "anyone working under a light bulb" is fair game.[5] Departure from the stated jurisdiction of the international is likely to be more prevalent in the amalgamated locals because workers in the smaller establishments are more concerned with the strength of the local union in the area than they may be in the formal jurisdiction of the national union.

In turn the international derives its jurisdiction from two sources in greater or lesser degrees. If it is an AFL–CIO affiliate, then its jurisdiction is a result of (1) the territory it is able to get legitimated by the federation and (2) the power it is able to muster in acquiring and holding on to its jurisdiction.

For the local union the jurisdictional "territory" has three, and in some instances four, significant dimensions. The local union territory is, first of all, a more or less specific geographic area—a city or a part of a city, a state or a multistate regional area. Secondly, the territory has job, craft, technological, or industrial characteristics. Third, jurisdiction may be based on the scope of the employer unit.

The geographic jurisdictions of local unions range from part of a city in the case of a large city to a multistate area. The local unions of the Operating Engineers frequently cover a state or multistate territory. For example, Local 542 of the Operating Engineers covers 34 counties in Pennsylvania and the entire state of Delaware.[6] Local 3 of the Operating Engineers covers northern California, northern Nevada, Utah, and the Hawaiian Islands.[7] Operating Engineers Local 139 includes the entire state of Wisconsin.[8] Local 459 of the IUE, although its base is the New York City metropolitan area, represents groups of people as far away as Milwaukee, Chicago, and New Orleans.[9]

More characteristically the geographic coverage of a local union is likely to be an area compact enough to be serviced easily—which means a city or county. In large cities the local's

[5] Charles J. Dempwolf, "Trade Union Organizing on the District and Local Level: A Case Study," unpublished M.A. thesis, Rutgers University (1956), p. 102 ff.

[6] U.S. Congress, Select Committee on Improper Activities in the Labor or Management Field, *Investigation of Improper Activities in the Labor or Management Field* (hereafter referred to as McClellan investigation), part 20 (1958), p. 7924.

[7] *Ibid.*, part 19 (1958), p. 7514.

[8] *The Milwaukee Journal*, May 25, 1958.

[9] Dempwolf, *op. cit.*, p. 89.

jurisdiction may be limited to a section of a city, as for example Carpenters locals in New York, or the Auto Workers locals in Detroit.

The geographic aspect of jurisdiction for seagoing unions departs from the pattern of most unions. There the unit of jurisdiction is the port branch. Members have no permanent attachment to a branch, but branch facilities in the major ports are available wherever the member happens to be.[10]

The second dimension of local jurisdiction is its craft, trade, or industry characteristic. This ranges from craft to trade to industry to multi-industry. Because this aspect of jurisdiction evolves out of a complex of practical considerations it is rare for the lines of demarcation to conform to the neat categories, say, of the U.S. Standard Industrial Classification Code. Cases in point:

PHILADELPHIA MEN'S CLOTHING WORKERS

Despite the fact that the Amalgamated Clothing Workers Union is an industrial union, the employees of the Daroff Co. in Philadelphia are organized in six craft local unions. This may appear unwieldy on paper but in practice "it works to the satisfaction of the union, the employees and management, all of whom are thoroughly familiar with the lines of jurisdiction and authority."[11]

SAN FRANCISCO HOTEL AND RESTAURANT INDUSTRY

Apartment and Hotel Employees Union, Local No. 14 of the Building Service Employees, covers handymen, janitors, porters, elevator operators, and doormen, etc.

Hotel Service Workers Union, Local No. 283, covers telephone operators, bellboys, checkroom men, maids and housekeeping workers, hat checkers. Office clerks are covered in small hotels only.

Cooks, Pastry Cooks and Assistants Union, Local No. 44 of the Hotel and Restaurant Workers, covers chefs, cooks, assistants, and helpers.

Waiters and Dairy Lunchmen's Union, Local No. 30 of the Hotel and Restaurant Workers, covers waiters, busboys, captains, checkers, cashiers, and countermen.

[10] Elmo P. Hohman, "Maritime Labor Economics as a Determinant of the Structure and Policy of Seamen's Unions," *Industrial Relations Research Association Proceedings* (1957).
[11] Richard A. Lester and Edward A. Robie, *Constructive Labor Relations,* Princeton University, Industrial Relations Section, 1948, p. 98.

Waitresses and Cafeteria Workers Union, Local No. 48, covers waitresses, busgirls, cashiers, hostesses, counterwomen.

Bartenders Union, Local No. 41, covers bartenders and head bartenders.

Miscellaneous Employees Union, Local No. 110 of the Hotel and Restaurant Workers, covers dishwashers, vegetable men, pantrymen, and bar boys.[12]

LOS ANGELES MOTION PICTURE INDUSTRY

The jurisdictional demarcations of the International Association of Theatrical and Stage Employees in the Hollywood film industry is divided among 17 unions as follows: prop men, painters, costumers, art craftsmen, scenic artists, laborers, story analysts, set designers, grips, sound men, makeup artists, cartoonists, electricians, cameramen, projectionists, film technicians, and film editors. Each of these constitutes a separate local of the IATSE.

An agreement between the Costumers, Local 705 of IATSE and the Property Men, also an IA local, provided that "the costumers shall work on military uniforms; military packs when not removed as part of the action of the picture; gunbelts and holsters worn by principal players; dummies used to represent principal characters; jewelry; and rain apparel. The prop men control sidearms (including swords, daggers, swagger sticks, halberds, maces, and spears); canes; packages and other articles that are carried; wearing apparel that has been removed as part of the action of a picture; flowers of all kinds; and safety equipment."[13]

THE PHILADELPHIA PRINTING INDUSTRY

Typesetting—Typographical Union

Platemaking—mostly under jurisdiction of Stereotypers and Electrotypers Union, but offset platemaking frequently under jurisdiction of the Lithographers.

Printing—letterpress printing under jurisdiction of the Pressmen & Assistants Union; offset printing under the Lithographers; gravure printing, Pressmen.

Photoengraving—Photo-Engravers Union.

Bookbinding—Bookbinders.

[12] Van Dusen Kennedy, *Arbitration in the San Francisco Hotel and Restaurant Industries,* Labor Relations Series (Philadelphia: University of Pennsylvania Press, 1952), p. 7.
[13] Hugh Lovell and Tasile Carter, *Collective Bargaining in the Motion Picture Industry,* University of California, Institute of Industrial Relations, 1955, p. 2.

Mailing—competition between ITU and an independent Mailers Union.[14]

The third dimension of jurisdiction is the scope of the employers' operations. This can range from one plant of a multiplant employer to a multi-employer unit.

For a declining number of locals there is a fourth jurisdictional dimension: the ethnic. The ethnic local is either forced or voluntary; forced, as in the case, frequently, of the segregated local; voluntary, as in the case of the kinship principle of jurisdiction in the Italian or Jewish locals of the Ladies' Garment Workers Union in New York, or the Italian or Irish locals of the International Longshoremen's Association on the East Coast.[15]

The prevailing tendencies in local union jurisdiction appear to be on the following order:

A. The city or local labor market area is the typical scope of geographic jurisdiction of local unions.
B. For the factory unions there are three significant variants with respect to the mix: industry, skill, and employer elements in jurisdiction.
   1. All the production and maintenance employees of a one-plant employer (single plant local).
   2. All the production and maintenance employees in one plant of a multiplant employer.
   3. All the production and maintenance employees of several employers (amalgamated local).
C. For the nonfactory unions there are two major variants in jurisdiction.
   1. In the building trades all the employees in a particular craft or trade of all the employers.
   2. In service industries all the employees of all of the employers (hotels and restaurants, retail trade).
D. The amalgamated local is probably more common in nonfactory employment than in factory employment, although it exists as well in the latter in substantial degree. It is more

[14] John W. Seybold, *The Philadelphia Printing Industry: A Case Study,* Industry-Wide Collective Bargaining Series, Labor Relations Council of the Wharton School of Finance and Commerce (Philadelphia: University of Pennsylvania Press, 1949), p. 9.
[15] Jack Barbash, "Ethnic Factors in the Development of the American Labor Movement," *Interpreting the Labor Movement,* Industrial Relations Research Association (1952), p. 70.

3

THE CONSTITUTIONAL BASIS
OF LOCAL UNION GOVERNMENT

The constitutional sources of local union government have normally been found in two documents: (1) the international union constitution sets out the provisions to which local union constitutions are required to conform; (2) the constitution and by-laws of the local incorporate the international requirements plus provisions unique to the local. To the extent that the requirements of the Labor Management Reporting and Disclosure Act are not already incorporated in the local union's governing documents, specific sections of that law in effect enlarge the constitutional commitments of the local union. (See page 45.)

There is considerable diversity in the scope and depth to which international union constitutions regulate local union government. The likelihood is however that LMRDA will enlarge the area of local union law regulated by the international and increase the number of internationals who will undertake to do so.

In the pre-Landrum-Griffin era almost all international constitutions set local standards in varying degrees. Most of these have fallen materially short of being a comprehensive scheme for local union government; the financial affairs of local unions seem to be most minutely regulated by the international. A minority of internationals—on the order of one-third by one estimate—standardize the bylaws of their constituent local unions.

The objective here is first to examine a small but (hopefully) representative sample of local union constitutions.[1] Where addi-

[1] This study is based on a survey of the constitutions and by-laws of twenty-two local unions in Milwaukee and Madison, Wisconsin. The constitutions were received in response to a request mailed early

in 1959. The locals in the survey and approximate membership in parentheses are:

Amalgamated Association of Street, Electric Railway and Motor Coach Employes of America, Division 998 (2,000)

Brotherhood of Painters, Decorators and Paperhangers of America, Local 802 (300); Local 781 (1,700)

International Brotherhood of Teamsters, Chauffeurs, Warehousemen and Helpers of America, Local 360 (400); Local 200 (6,000)

United Papermakers and Paperworkers, Local 356 (800)

United Steelworkers of America, Local 1343 (1,250)

International Brotherhood of Electrical Workers, Local 715 (165)

United Association of Journeymen and Apprentices of the Plumbing and Pipe Fitting Industry of the U.S. and Canada, Local 75 (1,010); Local 394 (305)

Hotel & Restaurant Employees and Bartenders International Union, Local 257 (220)

International Association of Machinists, Lodge 78 (1,677); Lodge 1406 (625)

International Union of Electrical, Radio and Machine Workers, Local 1131 (1,100)

Office Employes International Union, Local 9 (950)

American Federation of State, County and Municipal Employees, Local 171 (1,038)

International Printing Pressmen and Assistants Union of North America, Local 7 (450)

Amalgamated Lithographers of America, Local 7 (1,200)

International Association of Bridge, Structural and Ornamental Iron Workers, Local 383 (210)

United Brotherhood of Carpenters and Joiners of America, Local 314 (1,350)

United Mine Workers of America, District 50 (——)

Retail Clerks International Association, Local 1469 (——)

The sample was designed to represent in a general way: (1) most of the major categories of unions operating in the U.S. building trades, transportation, printing trades, mass production, service, maritime, public employment, white collar; (2) range in size of membership: 165–6,000. The sample probably overstates the importance of nonfactory local unions at the expense of the factory locals. At points in which it was possible to compare provisions in the sample with a broader survey, there appears to be a reasonably close correspondence. Accordingly, I believe the sample reflects general tendencies accurately.

I have deliberately refrained from using numbers in the text to indicate the frequency of provisions because I make no claim that the survey represents a rigorously designed investigation. The words "majority," "typically," "characteristically," "most," "almost all," etc., mean varying magnitudes of more than half of the constitutions. Words like substantial, several, few, very few, a small minority mean varying degrees of less than half.

Miss Madhuri Gurnaney, a graduate student in the industrial relations program of the University of Wisconsin abstracted the constitutional provisions and developed them in tabular form. I am responsible for the narrative analysis.

tional information bearing on local union constitutional provisions are available these will also be referred to.

The scheme for analyzing the constitutional framework follows:

I. Members
    A. Admission
    B. Retaining membership
    C. Disciplining members
        1. Grounds
        2. Procedures
        3. Penalties
II. The local union meeting
III. The local union officers
    A. Nomination
    B. Election
IV. The executive board
V. Collective bargaining
VI. The strike
VII. Financial administration

MEMBERSHIP

Workers are barred from membership by all the constitutions if they are also members in subversive organizations or in dual organizations. In most local union constitutions only United States citizens, or those formally expressing their intent, are admitted to membership. Members are universally asked to take an oath of obligation. Other recurring requirements for membership are a minimum age limit especially by craft unions, a period of apprenticeship and/or work experience, and "good moral character."

A majority of constitutions require admission to membership to be voted upon in the affirmative by two-thirds or majority of those voting. In some instances the application of a new member needs to be proposed or attested to by a member or members in good standing. Almost every constitution mentions a lapse of three to six months before a rejected applicant can be reconsidered.

The National Industrial Conference Board investigation of 194 international union constitutions is in general accord with the findings in the present sample with respect to membership admittance, except that NICB finds a substantially smaller proportion of the constitutions requiring admittance by membership vote.[2]

1. In 125 unions, the primary requirement is that the applicant for membership must be employed at a craft or in an industry under the union's jurisdiction. . . .
2. The constitutions of 27 unions provide for a "fraternal" system of admittance in which the applicant is accepted or rejected by a formal vote of the members of the local union which he wishes to join. . . .
3. Twenty-five unions admit applicants primarily through an apprenticeship training program in which the applicant goes through a period of on-the-job training. . . .

According to NICB "the most important restrictions" in international union constitutions are those dealing with communists and other subversives (156 unions), with the admittance of supervisors (35 unions), and with the admission of Negroes and other racial minorities (5 unions).

The primary qualification for retaining membership—that is, being in "good standing"—is the payment of dues and other financial obligations. Provision is universally made for a period beyond which a member may not be in default of his financial obligations, typically three months. The ultimate penalty for arrearage is summary expulsion with many constitutions providing for intermediate penalties before expulsion is resorted to. The intermediate penalties include withdrawal of union benefits, prohibition from attendance and voting at local meetings. A few constitutions specify removal from employment as a penalty. A small minority of constitutions provide for written notice of arrearage. Most constitutions do not mention notification of arrearage.

Most constitutions deal with the restoration of good standing. The general practice is to require the payment of all arrearages and the payment of an additional fee characterized variously as interest on the arrearage or as a reinstatement fee. Nonfinancial requirements for good standing are specified in a very few cases, as for example attendance at education classes and registering to vote.

DISCIPLINE

The recurring *general* grounds for initiating disciplinary charges are characteristically formulated as: disloyalty, slandering, falsi-

[2] National Industrial Conference Board (NICB), *Handbook of Union Government and Structure*, p. 54.

fying or using language detrimental to the association; activities bringing disrepute to the organization; any disreputable act; conduct unbecoming a union member; soliciting in any manner against the organization; attempting to create dissatisfaction or dissension among the union membership; allegiance or affiliation with any organization of any kind whatever; engaging in any course of conduct inconsistent with duties and obligations and fealty of union members; violating sound union principles; discussing proceedings of union meetings in private; discussing the affairs of the local with nonunion members; such other acts and conduct considered inconsistent with duties, obligations and fealty of a union member or violation of sound trade-union principles; questioning in any way the integrity of an officer, reflecting upon his public or private conduct.

Recurring themes in *specific* offenses include: "soliciting members to join a rival organization"; "coming drunk to the meeting or disturbing the decorum at the meeting repeatedly"; "failure to report immediately to the union any violations by the employer of the union wage scale or working agreement"; "working for less than established minimum union scale of wages or failure to live up to the provisions of the contract"; "accepting employment at a struck place where strike has been approved by the international"; "furnishing the list of members to unauthorized persons"; "deliberately interfering with any official of the international union in the discharge of his duties"; "working with nonunion men"; "embezzlement of funds"; "engaging in an unauthorized work stoppage"; "accepting employment without depositing travel card with the concerned local"; "encouraging in any manner any totalitarian philosophy."

Almost every local union constitution requires that the charges be filed in writing, typically with an officer or officers of the local. Only two constitutions require specificity in the filing of charges. The majority of constitutions do not state who may file; a substantial minority do. Of those that do, the prevailing requirement is that the charge must be filed by a member or a member in good standing. In one instance the charge must be filed by five members in good standing, and in another instance by a party described only as a "complainant."

The prevailing method of hearing is by the executive board of the local union. Next in order is a trial committee appointed by the president or the executive board. In only a small fraction of the constitutions is there a provision for general membership participation in the hearing or in the designation of the trial instrumentality.

The first decision as to the guilt or innocence of the defendant is rendered typically by the agency or instrumentality which heard the charges. In only a small minority is there provision for the first decision to be rendered by the membership meeting.

Recurring procedural safeguards for the defendant are: selection of any union member as counsel and the right to present witnesses; the right of cross-examination and notice of hearing are provided for in a few constitutions. Time limits are characteristically set for various stages of the disciplinary procedure. The local union meeting as the agency of last resort within the local union is commonly specified.

All constitutions provide for methods of appealing disciplinary actions. The first line of appeal is almost equally divided as among the international union executive board, the international union president, or an intermediate body. The agency of last resort within the international union is almost universally the international union convention. In one constitution the referendum is provided as an alternative to the convention, and in another constitution there is no appeal from the international union executive board "in all matters involving officers of subordinate bodies and individual members."

The penalties include reprimand, suspension, fines, expulsion, permanent debarment from membership, ineligibility to hold office, loss of membership, removal from the job, and debarment from holding office in the local union. In a substantial minority of stated offenses the penalty is related to the stated offense, but in the majority of offenses the penalty is discretionary.

Under international union constitutions, analysis of the disciplinary process indicates that prevailingly (1) the power to discipline rests with the local union, and (2) that within the local the power rests with the local union membership.

MEMBERSHIP MEETINGS

The union membership is the supreme authority within the local union. The significant exception is a delegate representation mechanism for large membership locals where a membership meeting would be unwieldy.

Provisions of 153 Union Constitutions Determining Which Local Union Body Has Power To Discipline Members

	Local Union Constitutions	
	Number	Per Cent
Total	(153)	(100)
Member is disciplined by his fellow local union members	78	51.0
Local union meeting investigates, determines guilt or innocence, and imposes penalty	11	7.2
Charges are investigated by a committee of local union members. Committee reports to local union meeting. Membership vote determines guilt or innocence and imposes the penalty	40	26.1
Committee of local union members investigates, determines guilt or innocence and imposes penalty	15	9.8
Committee of local union members *or* local union meeting investigates, determines guilt or innocence and imposes penalty. (Membership vote determines which method is used)	6	3.9
Charges are investigated by executive board (or subcommittee of the board) of the local union which reports to local union meeting. Membership vote determines guilt or innocence and imposes the penalty	6	3.9
Local union executive board or subcommittee of the board has power to discipline	44	28.8
Local union executive board *or* local union membership meeting has power to discipline	2	1.3
Local membership committee *or* executive board of local union has power to discipline	6	3.9
Local union has power to discipline (constitution does not give details on specific authority)	23	15.0

The supreme authority of the membership within the local, most characteristically expressed through the membership meeting, is asserted with varying frequency and specificity to (1) admission of new members, (2) disciplinary action, (3) financial administration, (4) collective bargaining—but not specified in the

*Constitutional Provisions Determining Whether Local Union or International
Has Power To Discipline Members*

	Local Union Constitutions	
	Number	Per Cent
Total	(194)	(100)
Local Unions or district organizations of co-operating locals may discipline members	89	45.9
Only international union has power to discipline	8	4.1
Local *or* international may discipline members	64	33.0
Other (complex provisions which set up original disciplinary bodies which consist of both representatives of the international union, usually vice-presidents, and members or officers of the local union)	9	4.6
No provision for discipline of individual members	24	12.4

Source: Adapted from National Industrial Conference Board, *Handbook of
Union Government Structure and Procedures,* pp. 68–69.
Note: Eighty-nine union constitutions, of the 194 covered by this study,
grant the local union power to discipline a member; sixty-four state that
both the international and the local may discipline members.

majority of cases, (5) striking, and (6) amendments to local union
constitutions and bylaws. Decisions of the union, whether by
the membership meeting or by other methods, are always subject to the authority of superior bodies within the international.
The limits of authority of local subordinate bodies—like the executive board, for example—are most explicitly set forth in relation to financial administration.

The interval for regular membership meetings most frequently
mentioned is monthly; for a very small minority, twice monthly.
In a few instances there is no information on the frequency of
local meetings. A very small number mention a specific inducement usually in the form of a dues rebate for attending the meeting, or specific disciplinary action—usually a fine—as a penalty for
nonattendance.

Every local union constitution except one makes provision for
special meetings. A majority of constitutions mention who may
initiate the calling of a special meeting. In a substantial number
there is no provision for special meetings initiated by the membership. The number of members required in most constitutions
for calling a special meeting is usually small, ranging from five
to twenty-five, with the former recurring more frequently. For
two large locals the requirement for calling a special meeting was

one-third of the membership for a 2,000-member local, and one-fourth of the membership for an 800-member local. There seems to be no relationship between the size of the local union and the number of members required for calling a special meeting.

Specified decisions require more than a majority vote of the membership in a large number of constitutions. Amendment to the constitution and bylaws of the local is most frequently mentioned as requiring an extraordinary majority. An extraordinary majority is frequently required in financial matters such as expenditure of monies over a stated maximum, assessments, fines, death benefits, and membership admission. A small number of local unions require a two-thirds majority of those voting for expulsion.

OFFICERS

Every constitution specifies that the president, vice-president, financial secretary or equivalent, and recording secretary or equivalent shall be elected by the membership. A very small minority of local union constitutions do not mention the election of trustees. The business agent or equivalent, where the office exists, is typically elected by the membership, although this is evidently not universal. In addition, most unions elect a variety of minor officers on the order of sergeant-at-arms—variously called conductors, sentinels, wardens, guardians, guides, etc.

Virtually all of the constitutions require that officers be members in good standing for a specified period immediately prior to nomination, typically between one and two years. However the full range is from six months to five years. Other recurring requirements for officer eligibility are employment in the trade (mostly in the craft unions) and attendance at a specified number of meetings.

Almost all of the constitutions require that nominations for office be made at a specified time before the election. A minority of constitutions require that the candidate be present at the meeting to accept nomination. A smaller minority specifies acceptance by the candidate in writing. Some constitutions specify a special election meeting with due notice. In one case the nominations come from a nominating committee designated by the executive board although additional nominations may be made from the floor.

All constitutions provide for a stated term of office. The most common is two years; one year is less common but substantial; successively fewer are three-year terms and four-year terms. In a substantial minority of cases provisions are made for terms varying directly with the importance of the office.

A large majority of constitutions requires secret ballots for the election of officers. A small minority specify election by referendum and a similar minority contains no information as to the method of election. A substantial majority of the constitutions requires a majority of the votes cast for election. A substantial minority requires only a plurality and in a few cases there was no information as to the percentage of vote required for election.

In the overwhelming majority of cases the election tellers are appointed by the president, the presiding officer, or, in one case, by the executive board. In a small number of cases the election officials are appointed in the above manner but subject to confirmation by the membership. In a similarly small number of constitutions provision is made for the election of tellers and the designation of observers by candidates. There are no provisions for determining the election results in a small number of constitutions.

Members of the executive board are elected in every case or at least provision is made for the election of officers constituting the executive board without specifying election of the executive board as such. The executive board almost always includes all of the constitutional local-wide officers of the local union. There is an equal division between executive boards composed only of officers and those composed of officers plus additional executive board members. Of those in the latter category the membership to the executive board is elected at large from the membership for the most part. In a small number of locals there is a provision that additional executive board members be elected from specified constituencies within the local.

The executive boards meet either twice-monthly or weekly. Almost half of the local union constitutions contain no information on the frequency of executive board meetings. A small number specify a monthly meeting. A similarly small number do not specify a regular interval but use the phrase "when necessary" or its equivalent.

A very large majority of constitutions provide that the executive board must report to the local union meeting, and a substantial majority within this category specify that the membership meeting must formally approve the actions taken by the board. In one local the executive board may handle only the business referred to it by the membership meeting or by the officers. In another local a two-thirds majority of the board is required for decision. Limitations on the scope of executive board authority are absent in a few instances.

A small number of constitutions prescribe that no board member shall sit on a case in which he, or his employer, or a member working for the same employer is involved. In a similar number a board member loses his post if absent from a specified number of consecutive meetings.

Most constitutions state the specific dollar amounts or the method of determining the salaries of full-time and part-time officers. The exact salary is prescribed in some of the local union constitutions. In a smaller number no specific amount is mentioned but authority is given to the local union to decide. In one case salaries are set by the executive board with the approval of the local union. In two instances salaries are determined by a formula in relation to the basic wage of a journeyman. One-fourth of the constitutions make no reference at all to salaries of officers.

Part-time officers are paid in a variety of methods. Where a specific amount is mentioned the highest appears to be $172 per month with a substantial cluster around the figure of $25–$50 per month. Where only the method of determining remuneration is stated those recurring frequently are (a) payment on a lost-time basis, (b) reimbursement of dues or reimbursement of dues plus a nominal amount like $5 per month. One secretary-treasurer is paid on the basis of the number of entries in the books of account.

Most local union constitutions do not mention expenses as such for officers. Those that do mention expenses or other perquisites generally state either a formula or a specific amount. In one case the recipient was explicitly not required to account for his expenses. A few constitutions provide for upkeep of the officer's automobile and for a mileage allowance.

Almost all constitutions provide a method for disciplining local union officers. The method is generally that prescribed for members. When this method is not prescribed some of the constitutions provide for the intervention of the national union in the disciplining of local union officers.

BARGAINING

Local union constitutions do not typically treat the collective bargaining function in detail. When mentioned at all a substantial minority of constitutions deal with collective bargaining briefly and perfunctorily. Of the local unions that describe the composition of the bargaining committee there is an equal division between (1) those that constitute the bargaining agency in the form of a committee—usually the executive board—plus additional members, and (2) those that simply specify either one or two of the top officers. All of the locals that do mention collective bargaining in their constitutions also provide for reporting to and approval of the general membership, either at a meeting or by referendum. A sizable minority requires a two-thirds vote; a similar number requires a simple majority and a small number have a three-fourths majority requirement. An equally small number do not provide any information on this point. Every local union constitution makes obligatory the approval of the general executive board or the international president, or the authorized international representative before strike action is taken by a local union.

The base from which the majority is obtained is invariably unclear with no distinction as to whether the base is those attending the strike-vote meeting, those engaged in the strike, or the total membership of the local union. A few constitutions restrict the number of members eligible to vote on a strike issue. In such cases the general requirement seems to be a minimum of six months' membership in the local union. Although some constitutions specify that a special meeting, with due notice to all members be called for the strike vote, a majority of the constitutions do not indicate it. Most of the constitutions require a vote by secret ballot.

A small number of constitutions do not make reference to the method for calling off a strike. Of those that do, some require a majority vote by secret ballot of the affected members; in a small number of cases the strike may also be called off by the parent international organization.

FINANCES

In contrast to the collective bargaining function, the financial organization of the local is dealt with in considerable detail. Almost all unions specify the payment of an initiation fee. A majority of the unions set the initiation fee at $25 and under. A substantial minority cluster around $5 and $10, mostly the industrial or the factory unions. A substantial minority of the unions—mostly the craft unions—are above $25 with a small cluster in the $100 category. A substantial minority of unions also specify the initiation fee in terms of a range, a minimum, or a sliding scale, generally varying with the wage category of the member. A small number of the locals exempt service men from the payment of initiation fees.

Just about a majority of local unions specify monthly dues in the $3 to $4 range with a moderate number at $5 and a very few, higher than $5, the highest amount indicated being $11 per month. Almost half of the locals set their dues on a sliding scale with dues typically varying with earnings. Dues sometimes vary with participation in beneficiary features of the union or with full-time or part-time work. A small number of constitutions provide preferential dues treatment for retired and unemployed members, and an equally small number specify penalty treatment for members delinquent in their dues.

The largest majority of constitutions provide for a reinstatement fee which ranges from $1 to $200. In the upper range the reinstatement fee is mentioned as being equivalent to the initiation fee which, in effect, means that the reinstated member is being treated as a new member. There is a small cluster of reinstatement fees in and around $25, but no other signs of general tendency. Almost all local union constitutions provide for a withdrawal card for a fairly low fee. And similarly, almost all locals provide for a transfer card authorizing members to transfer from one local to another at a small, or no, fee.

All locals authorize the levying of assessments. A majority of local union constitutions prescribe in whole or in part the purposes for which assessments may be levied for example, when local or international funds fall below a specified level. Financing of strikes is another recurring example of purposes for which assessments may be levied. A very small number of locals put a dollar ceiling on the amount of assessment. A large majority of the union specify membership approval of assessment and in many instances approval by an extraordinary majority. Internal evidence suggests, however, that this is limited to local assessments although referenda appear to be required in a small minority of cases for assessments by the international union.

Dues and other fees as reported by local unions under LMRDA as of June 1960[3] (available to me after the present sample survey was completed), are in general—but not exact—accord with the data derived from the sample.

1. Over three-fifths of the LMRDA reporting locals had a prevailing initiation fee of $10 or less, with the two most substantial clusters at the $5 and $10 figures respectively.

2. Of LMRDA reporting unions indicating a specific amount "more than half had a rate of less than $4 per month." Among the range-of-dues group over half set their maximum dues at $3 per month.

3. Only a small proportion of the LMRDA reporting unions collect transfer fees. Of those reporting transfer fees "more than half set them at $3 and 37 per cent at less than $1.

The majority of constitutions provide for fines which are generally related to specific offenses. The constitutions of the craft unions characteristically fine for offenses such as members working with nonmembers, working below the scale, failure to show union card (common), and failure to report violation of working rules; a few constitutions specify indecorous personal behavior such as using profane language, coming to a meeting while drunk, and slander. One constitution prescribes a fine for discussing union business outside of the union hall. The amount of the fine varies widely among union constitutions and within union constitutions. The interunion range of fines is 25 cents to $250 and within the same local constitution fines range from $2 to $250. The $250 fine was specified in one case for a member who has caused a strike or lockout, the implication being an illegal strike or lockout. One local limits the fine to no more than $25.

Local union constitutions commonly regulate a variety of disbursements. The per capita to the international union is uniformly included. A minority of unions set forth their per capita contributions to intermediate bodies within the international union and to the city and state central bodies of the AFL–CIO. A substantial minority set up benefit funds for death benefits, floral tributes, and unemployment. A small number of local union constitutions provide for strike or defense funds. Almost all of the constitutions

[3] U.S. Department of Labor, Bureau of Labor-Management Reports (BLMR), *Report, Fiscal Year 1960* (Washington, D.C.), p. 25 ff.

provide for the depositing of union monies in a bank of "reliable reputation."

A substantial minority of unions put stated limitations on the disbursement of funds. A small group permits no disbursements except with the express approval of the membership. In one union constitution it is provided that "the funds of the union shall not be invested or loaned to any business enterprise; provided however that publicly traded securities of widely held corporations may be purchased, so long as no individual holding is substantial enough to affect or influence the course of any employer's decision." This is apparently the application of an AFL–CIO ethical practices code provision.

All constitutions provide for an auditing and reporting procedure with respect to finances. By far the most common method of getting the books of the local union audited is through an elected committee which is either the trustees or a finance committee. In a small number of cases the auditing committee is appointed. A majority of the locals provide for the auditing of books by a certified public accountant or equivalent, either as an alternative to the committee or as a supplement. In a very small number, the local union auditing instrumentality is the executive board of the local. Close to a majority of local union constitutions provide that the books of account must be made available for auditing by representatives of the international union. The common frequency is quarterly for internal union auditing and annually for auditing by the CPA. A substantial minority of locals provide for more frequent auditing either on a monthly or bimonthly basis. It is almost universal for the locals to submit a monthly financial report and a quarterly audit report to the international union. The same situation prevails with respect to reports to the membership.

THEORY AND PRACTICE

The preceding analysis of local union constitutions is likely to fall short of reflecting actual local union practice because of: (1) violation and evasion; (2) custom and tradition lacking constitutional sanction; and (3) because the present sample on which the analysis is based does not encompass the full range of constitutional variations.

It is not possible to measure with finality the precise extent to which this analysis suffers from these defects. From other evidence it *is* possible, however, to remedy some of these defects, at least partially.

The disparity between theory and practice of local union government is visible in a variety of circumstances:

1. The circumstance in which membership involvement is indispensable to the effectiveness of policies and actions, as in strikes and collective bargaining. Here the effect of the disparity between theory and practice is to achieve *greater* membership participation than is constitutionally required. For example, in the case of strikes:

> The most conclusive finding is that the procedures of local unions for calling strikes are considerably more democratic than reference to their international constitutions would suggest. In many cases where the international constitution contains no provision for strike votes, they are nevertheless required by the constitution or by-laws of the local union. In other cases, the local union constitution requires *secret* strike ballots where the international constitution calls for strike authorization by the rank and file without prescribing the manner of voting. In still other cases, secret strike ballots are firmly entrenched in the practice of the local union despite the absence of any constitutional requirement. As a result, while less than half of the unions in the sample are required by their international constitutions to obtain approval by a majority of the voters in a secret ballot before calling a strike, over three-fourths do so in practice.[4]

2. The characteristic circumstance that local union officers are working people and, unlike public officials, are not temperamentally oriented to strict adherence to laws as part of their jobs.

> Many locals have elaborate rituals designed to guarantee free elections. Nominations must be taken by an official not connected with the local (sometimes not even belonging to the same international) and no motion may be made to close nominations until this outside official asks three times, "Are there any more nominations?" Only then can nominations be closed. Yet, al-

[4] Herbert S. Parnes, *Union Strike Votes*, Princeton University, Department of Economics and Sociology, Industrial Relations Section, 1956, p. 67. See also George Strauss and Don Willner, *Government Regulation of Local Union Democracy*, Cornell University, New York State School of Industrial and Labor Relations, Reprint Series, no. 18, from *Labor Law Journal*, August 1953.

though members say "this is required by our union" neither the local nor international constitution mentions it.[5]

3. The circumstance in which the ins—or for that matter not infrequently the outs—seek an expedient advantage from evasion or violation. Here typically the object is to win. When deviations occur it may be a casual act or part of a pattern of behavior in which disregard for constitutional government is endemic.

The casual acts in violation of the constitution are likely to be on the order of insufficient quorum, parliamentary defects in the conduct of the meeting, "hanky-panky" in allocating expenditures among the established accounting categories. It is the kind of minor short-circuiting of prescribed procedures that goes on in every organization.

Endemic indifference to local union law where it exists, is likely to be found most frequently in the election of officers and in financial administration. Cases in point are the union types celebrated by the McClellan investigation. The elections of Local 107 of the Teamsters were characterized by stacked meetings, arbitrary closing of nominations, violation of ballot secrecy, illegal removal of elected officers, and illegal appointments to offices requiring elections.[6] The pattern of conduct revealed in certain locals of the Operating Engineers has been in the same mold:[7] trumped-up charges against rivals by the dominant clique, rigging of elections, falsification of books of record and accounts, unvouchered large-scale expenditures.

4. The circumstance that the local union seeks to restrict membership on economic, ethnic, kinship, or standards of skill grounds. The admission policies of some unions fall within this grouping; specifically, (a) the closing (intermittently) of membership rolls, (b) the restriction of membership to relatives of members, and (c) discrimination against Negroes. And once members are admitted some locals limit full participation in union rights and benefits for certain classes of members.

All of these practices are in general characteristic of hiring hall unions—that is, where unions perform a hiring function for employers whom they bargain with; and where, in effect, union membership is a *prior* condition of employment. Where the latter

[5] Strauss and Willner, *op. cit.*, p. 523
[6] McClellan investigation, part 27, pp. 10385 ff.
[7] *Ibid., First Interim Report*, p. 458–459.

40

situation exists it is a violation of the Taft-Hartley law but the practice has been proof against such enforcement as has been given to this portion of the law.

MEMBERSHIP RESTRICTION

Some local unions close their membership rolls in the hiring hall situations when they believe the labor supply is overextended in relation to demand. Other local unions, notably in the East Coast longshore industry, almost never closed their rolls even in the face of a chronic glut of manpower. These ILA locals were more concerned with the dues and kick-back perquisites of membership admission than they were with achieving some balance between supply and demand enabling those in the industry to earn a decent wage. The beginnings of decasualization of the New York waterfront had to wait on the establishment of the Waterfront Commission.[8] Confronted with an oversupply of labor, Local 10 of the West Coast longshoremen closed down its rolls after World War II and reopened them in the spring of 1958.

> For the first time in twelve years, Local 10 is due for a spurt in membership. To avoid spreading the available work too thinly, the rolls were closed after a postwar influx. Last spring, in response to the clamor for admission and to employers' pleas for a bigger labor pool, the local invited membership applications from qualified men between 21 and 40. It was swamped with some 9,000 applications.
>
> In a preliminary screening for physical fitness and experience, the field was narrowed to 900.
>
> Last week, a joint committee of employers and union representatives began interviews with the 900 for further tests of their capability. The men also face rigid comprehensive physical examinations in the next couple of weeks. Survivors probably will be eligible for dispatch after May 1.
>
> Men on the "B" list will enjoy limited registration privileges in the hiring hall. By paying a prorata share of the hiring hall costs, but not union dues, they'll be entitled to job assignments after the dispatchers have exhausted the supply of fully registered men. As attrition creates vacancies in the union, new members will be drawn from the "B" list, and they will commence to pay dues.

[8] Waterfront Commission of New York Harbor, *Annual Report* (New York: 1960), p. 20 ff.

Right now, all but two of the men dispatched from the hiring hall are members of Local 10. These two were expelled from the union after trial, but they retain and use their registration privileges.[9]

By way of further example the membership rolls were kept artificially low in the Seattle local of the Asbestos Workers. Where there was more work than there were full members employment was given to "'travellers,' that is, members of another local union in the international who have been granted a temporary permit by the Seattle local to work in its jurisdiction; 'work permit' men from other unions such as the Plasterers, or nonmembers who had made application for membership in the local." The Asbestos local in Portland, in contrast, maintained a substantially higher ratio between employment opportunities and members by making apprenticeship status more accessible.[10]

Information on the closing of membership rolls is generally hard to come by, and the chances are that the practice is relatively rare,[11] mostly because of the high level employment prevailing in most of the hiring hall industries in the post-World War II years and the relative decline of apprenticeship as a route to journeyman status. Bromwich asserts categorically that apprenticeship "rules are fixed with an eye to the maximum security of the journeyman rather than to the skill requirements of a particular trade.[12] In the large majority of building trades locals of one city where information was available the entrance rate of new members has actually been higher over a period of years than in two selected large industrial plants.[13]

The effect of membership limitation is achieved through arbi-

[9] *Business Week*, March 14, 1959, p. 121.

[10] Kenneth M. McCaffree, "Union Membership Policies and Labor Productivity among Asbestos Workers," *Industrial and Labor Relations Review,* January 1961, p. 233.

[11] Benjamin Aaron and Michael I. Komaroff, "Statutory Regulations of Internal Union Affairs. II," *Illinois Law Review,* 44 (1949), 425–466. See also Sumner H. Slichter, James J. Healy, and E. Robert Livernash, *The Impact of Collective Bargaining on Management* (Washington, D.C.: Brookings Institution, 1960), pp. 41–42.

[12] Leo Bromwich, *Union Constitutions,* A Report to the Fund for the Republic (New York, 1959), p. 5 (he cites no specific cases). See also Jack Barbash, *The Practice of Unionism* (New York: Harper, 1956), p. 172.

[13] Donald E. Brocher, *Wages, Fringes, and Income in the Building Trades,* unpublished M.S. thesis, Industrial Relations, University of Wisconsin, 1960, p. 44.

trarily high initiation fees (illegal under Taft-Hartley section 8(b)(5) where the purpose is restriction rather than revenue, as the NLRB found in the case of the Screen Cartoonist Guild. This Taft-Hartley provision has, however, yielded few cases.[14]

Some locals limit membership to relatives of present members. Here again there is no reliable evidence as to the extent. The New York City local of Newspaper and Mail Deliverers has been characterized as

> a closed and tightly-knit unit. Its membership originally was limited to sons and close male relatives of members, but outsiders have found a way in through the payoff. . . . You'll hear stories of as much as $5,000 being paid for a union card; the more usual price is in the neighborhood of $500.[15]

This situation is closely tied to racketeering influences which have existed in this local.[16]

The problem of Negro discrimination in admission policies— treated only briefly here—clusters around the building trades unions even though the constitutions of the building trades internationals no longer contain color bars. Denial of admission takes the form either of direct refusal to admit Negro workers into the union or refusal to admit them to apprenticeship status which can have the same effect. The NAACP (National Association for the Advancement of Colored People) asserts that:

> In virtually every large urban center Negro workers are today denied employment in major industrial and residential construction projects because they are barred from membership in the building trades craft unions.[17]

There is no material disagreement as to the locus of discrimination. There has been sharp disagreement as to (a) whether progress is being made by the labor movement in eliminating discrimination, and (b) the complicity of building trades contractors. Those who believe progress has been made point to the positive role which the AFL–CIO has taken in pressuring the constituent internationals in dropping discriminatory provisions so that only one international—the recently affiliated Brotherhood of Locomo-

[14] *The New York Times,* October 12, 1958.
[15] Fred J. Cook, "The Truth About New York Newspaper Strike," *The Nation,* January 3, 1959.
[16] McClellan investigation, *Final Report,* Part I (1960).
[17] Herbert Hill, letter, *The New Leader,* June 20, 1960.

tive Firemen and Enginemen—still has such a constitutional provision. The problem now is to get the locals to abide by these principles and here too progress is seen as even building trades locals under AFL–CIO pressure and the pressure of local and state fair employment practice bodies recede from discrimination.

The NAACP attack is regarded as consistently failing "to recognize that membership composition of unions is determined by the hiring policy of the employer and that the major attack on discrimination must be against employers' discriminatory practices."[18]

The Negro worker is also the major victim of segregation within the local union after he gets in. Biracial locals have increased considerably. But in the South, especially, where the union attitudes respond to the prevailing winds of Negro segregration, the plant barriers to upgrading of colored workers limits the Negro workers to the lower grade custodial jobs—a situation characterized by one union officer as "segregation within the framework of integration."[19]

Yet the industrial unions of CIO origin have frequently jeopardized their local situations by forcing their local unions to abandon discriminatory status for Negroes within Southern locals. Most recently the Secretary of Labor upheld (in effect) the right of the UAW to continue a trusteeship over the Memphis local which has refused to conform to UAW law in respect to eliminating segregation.[20]

Differential status within the union is occasionally maintained on other than ethnic grounds, most commonly on the basis of differences in professional achievement or craft status. The Screen Actors Guild provides for a "Junior Membership for those who have not acted in at least two motion pictures in parts receiving screen credits."[21] Until recently the Airline Pilots gave copilots

[18] Harry Fleischman, letter, *The New Leader*, August 15–22, 1960, pp. 30–31. See also "Negro Pressure on Unions," *Business Week*, April 30, 1960, pp. 139–140; Will Chasan, "American Labor Attacks Its Own Segregation," *The Reporter*, May 1, 1958; Harry Fleischman, "Labor and Civil Rights," *The New Leader*, April 18, 1960; Herbert Hill, "Labor Unions and the Negro," *Commentary*, December 1959; National Association for the Advancement of Colored People, *Racism Within Organized Labor: A Report of Five Years of the AFL–CIO, 1955–60*, 1961 (mimeo).

[19] Chasan, *loc. cit.*

[20] BLMR, *op. cit.*, p. 34.

[21] William M. Leiserson, *American Trade Union Democracy* (New York: Columbia University Press, 1959), p. 114.

44

one-half of the vote for purposes of convention representation. Some craft unions have established A and B membership classes as between craftsmen and production workers. The B nonbeneficiary members pay lower dues but they accordingly do not share in the internal insurance program established by the union. The A member in the IBEW locals has five times the national convention representation of the B member. A similar arrangement prevails as between craft and noncraft members in the Flint Glass Workers and in the Wall Paper Craftsmen.[22] The Long Island local of the Operating Engineers disenfranchised the largest part of its membership to permit more closely knit control.[23]

PUBLIC LAW

The constitutional framework of local union government has in effect been augmented by two types of public intervention into the internal affairs of unions: (1) the Labor-Management Reporting and Disclosure Act, and (2) the courts under common law.

This is probably not the place or the time, considering the brief experience with LMRDA as this is being written, to spell out in detail the impact of this law on local union constitutional government. Following the scheme set out on page 26, the following generalizations suggest the scope of statutory intervention:

1. The law does not appear to apply to the admission of new members.[24]

2. LMRDA appears to outlaw unreasonably discriminatory membership classifications, for example, where the effect is to disenfranchise members beyond a reasonable period of probation. (101(a)(1).)

3. Title I, the "Bill of Rights" creates a scheme in respect to the grounds for disciplinary action and in respect to disciplinary procedures. Although approved grounds are not set forth affirmatively it is evident that disciplinary action against members for criticizing union policies and union officers, which does not put the union in "clear and present danger" (to borrow a judicial principle from another context of law) as an institution will en-

[22] *Ibid.*, p. 115.
[23] McClellan investigation, *Interim Report* (1958), p. 438.
[24] American Bar Association, Section on the Development of the Law of Union Administration and Procedure, *Report* (1960), (mimeo.), p. 29.

counter difficulties in the courts if such actions are challenged. (101(a)(2).) Disciplinary action for recourse to court action by union members is also regulated so that the union's law may require the member to exhaust "reasonable hearing procedures" within the union only if such procedures do not take more than four months. (101(a)(4).)

4. Procedurally, the law requires (except in cases involving nonpayment of dues) the serving of written specific charges, reasonable time for preparation of defense, and "a full and fair hearing" in union disciplinary actions. None of these procedural standards is further defined in the law. Depending on how far the courts go in interpreting the reach of these standards, particularly "full and fair hearing," the law can conceivably make major transformations in the unions' laws. (101(a)(4).)

5. LMRDA imposes notice requirements for local union meetings dealing with increases in financial obligations of members (101(a)(3)), and with the elections of officers (401(e)). The law also undertakes to safeguard the right to free participation in meetings by the membership, subject to reasonable rules. (101(a)(1) and (2).)

6. The early cases interpreting the meaning of the law as to the rights of officers as such suggest a more limited application than to the rights of members. The emphasis is on officers' responsibilities, not on rights.[25] Possible "conflict of interest" transactions (my characterization, not the law's) by officers and union employees require public disclosure. (202(a).) The manner in which nominations, campaigns and elections for union office are regulated to the purpose that the "ins" shall not use union money and resources in advancing their standing. Officers may not serve within five years of their conviction for stated offenses or within five years of membership in the Communist party. This in effect writes into every union constitution an antifelon and anti-Communist qualification provision for holding office. The law also writes in bonding requirements and removal requirements for officers.

7. The law places union officers in "positions of trust" and imposes a "fiduciary responsibility." It sets forth broad fiduciary standards of conduct for union officers in relation to accountability and the handling of union funds and property primarily to elimi-

[25] *Ibid.*, p. 28.

46

nate conflict-of-interest transactions between officers and the union. It makes these standards enforceable in federal and state courts. (501.)

8. The reporting provision relating to the union as an organization imposes a detailed scheme for financial reporting of assets and liabilities, income and expenditures, with specific information required as to—among others—officer salaries, expense accounts, allowances, and loans. (201(b).)

Informed judgment is that most of the rights created by LMRDA existed at common law but the "codification [of these rights] in highly publicized legislation will bring them to the attention of union members and their lawyers and, for a time at least, will both facilitate the litigation and reduce the fear of reprisals."[26]

[26] Archibald Cox, *Law and the National Labor Policy*, University of California, Los Angeles, Institute of Industrial Relations, 1960, p. 106. See also Archibald Cox, "The Role of Law in Preserving Union Democracy," in *Labor in a Free Society* (Berkeley: University of California Press, 1959); New York State Department of Labor, *Union Democracy* (Albany, 1960). The literature on judicial regulation of internal union affairs is sizable: see anthology and bibliography in U.S. Senate, Committee on Labor and Public Welfare, *Government Regulation of Internal Union Affairs Affecting the Rights of Members*, 85th Cong., 2d Sess., 1958.

THE UNION MEETING

The union meeting, as has been said, is constitutionally the supreme instrumentality of government within the local union. The union meeting can be distinguished as to the concrete objective which it serves and as to the degree of influence exercised by the leadership in relation to the meeting participants.

The objective of a union meeting is to carry on the union's routine business: this is the classic meeting. From time to time the objective is to deal with a critical issue in the life of the local.

REGULAR MEETINGS

The regular business meeting is commonly held monthly or semimonthly. For most local unions the regular meeting is constitutionally indispensable for the carrying on of its routine activities. It is likely to be much like this routine meeting of a factory local union in the Midwest.

"If it weren't for the door prize they wouldn't come at all," confided the president of the local. The doorkeeper stood with his bowl of dimes, religiously unlocking and relocking the door as each member presented himself for admittance, reaching at the same time into his trousers pocket for his 10¢ contribution to the evening's sweepstake.

Outside the temperature was 10 degrees below freezing; inside, the gas heater on the ceiling buzzed noisily. One by one, the members flopped into the vacant chairs, unzipped their padded jackets, and smoked and chewed and chatted happily. The room was pleasantly warm, the chairs uncomfortably hard, and the walls had the timeless dinginess of dark green paint.

On the dais at one end, between the narrow trestle table covered with files, dues books, and loose papers sat the four officers of the local. To one side, leaning precariously in a wobbly standard holder, was the Flag.

From the wall behind the dais, past presidents of the international and the state federation of labor looked down on the meeting. Between them was the charter of the local; around the other walls, in varying degrees of ornateness, were the framed charters of different locals in the town which also used the Labor Temple. A painted piano in one corner, a refrigerator and a row of coat hangers completed the furnishings.

Smiling broadly, the president rose and banged his gavel on the table gently. The hubbub subsided rapidly as he began reading the historic formula for opening the meeting.

. . . There were about 40 members present. The president being ill, the vice-president conducted the meeting, which started at 7:45 P.M. After the minutes had been read, a detailed and patient report on recent grievances was given by the chairman of the grievance committee.

Questions and complaints from members followed thick and fast. There was a prolonged argument as to whether job cards were grouped or not by management. This led into a further discussion about "down time" which the chairman of the grievance committee urged members to claim whenever they were entitled to it and assured them that if it were refused the union would take up the matter as a grievance.

There was some argument, from contrary experiences, against the practicability of this procedure. One member then asserted that the contract was useless, as the workers could not even secure the rights laid down in it. He alleged that the grievance committee had not yet settled a grievance on overtime raised in the summer; and went on to complain that management in the past had taken work from the blacksmiths to give to the welders who were short of work, but that now the welders had plenty of overtime while the blacksmiths had only 40 hours of work per week.

The chairman answered this by explaining that their union was not a craft but an industrial union, and that therefore the local union could not claim jurisdiction over jobs which was the preserve of management.

At this point the business agent stood up to correct (or, as he put it, "come to the rescue of") the chairman of the grievance committee. He said theirs was not a craft union, but had both craft and industrial workers in it, and reminisced at some length about his own experiences as a skilled worker and the nature of craft grievances.

After this the nominations for officers were read out. No new names were added, and it was announced that the night men would make their nominations at their meeting on the following Tuesday.

A report on the retired members banquet which had been held since the last meeting, was read, and it was decided to hold another one next year. There was some discussion about a dance for members and their wives, to be held in the new year as part of the twenty-first anniversary celebrations of the local. The treasurer's statement was read as usual, and permission sought and obtained to buy candies and masks for the children's Christmas party. At 9:10 the meeting was closed.[1]

Less typical, but not rare, are the kinds of regular meetings seen in giant-sized Local 3 of the IBEW in New York. The union meetings are held at Manhattan Center,

. . . one of the larger meeting halls in New York, which is usually jammed to the rafters for them. There is a 50¢ fine for non-attendance. When I asked whether this was not democracy by compulsion, Van Arsdale [the business manager of Local 3] replied, "Any labor leader who wants undemocratic control over his union prefers to have small, tight meetings— only the administrative gang present, all resolutions passed, everything moving like clockwork. Not me. You've been to our meetings, you ought to know."

I had been and I do know. They are unbelievable meetings. There are long debates from the floor, with every man who has something to say getting his chance, items in the treasurer's report being challenged: "$600 for postage, that's a lot of money, Brother Chairman, why can't we send postcards?" It seemed to me democracy carried almost to the point of tedium.[2]

---

[1] J. F. C. Harrison, "For the Good of the Association, American Trade Unionism at the Grass Roots," *British Association for American Studies Bulletin,* no. 9, November 1959 (mimeo.), p. 7.

[2] Charles Yale Harrison, "Van Arsdale's Tight Little Island," *The Reporter,* April 11, 1950, p. 13. See also Scott Greer, *Last Man In* Glencoe: Free Press, 1959), p. 41 ff.; William M. Leiserson, *American Trade Union Democracy* (New York: Columbia University Press, 1959), pp. 282–286.

Here is still another report of a routine meeting in "Steeltown" local:

Meeting called to order by president, 7:30; recording secretary reads incoming correspondence, appeals for money. President announces that union loses NLRB election as a new company recently moved into town, international representative makes fiery speech attacking Chamber of Commerce as being anti-union and favoring sweatshops. Next order of business—new contract.

A member asked, "I'd like to find out just how you interpret my job classification. How come it says I am supposed to direct men, doesn't that make me a boss and part of management?" An officer explained, "Here is how that came about. . . . When we made your classification in the wage inequities program we went through everything we could think of for your duties so that we could get you the highest classification possible. So don't go complaining about it. You're not really supervisory. You can't report any man or discipline anybody or make out records. As a group leader you just tell them what work has to be done. It's not up to you to enforce it. So forget about it. We got you a wage boost. If you want the clause taken away you may lose money." The member was quite obviously satisfied and said no more.

President calls on international representative who asks for a counterpropaganda campaign to combat anti-unionism of NAM and Chamber of Commerce. Motion approved to have chairman appoint a three-man committee and to use 10 per cent of per capita refunds for this purpose.

Discussion on high cost of living. Delegate to the Pennsylvania State CIO convention reports on convention. International representative reports on meeting of union delegation to Washington to influence War Department to keep the mill in Elwood City as essential to national defense. Meeting adjourned at 10:30.[3]

Routine business meetings are attended by a small proportion of the membership rarely exceeding 5 per cent, unless a fine or dues rebate system is in effect. The meetings are attended by the officers, by a small number of rank and file members as an act of civic duty, and by lonely members who have no place else

[3] Charles R. Walker, *Steeltown: An Industrial Case History of the Conflict between Progress and Security* (New York: Harper, 1950), pp. 39–41.

to go.[4] The exception to low attendance at routine meetings is when a power struggle exists with a shifting majority. Attendance in these situations is likely to be higher as we shall see.

The objections to local union meetings voiced by a group of Chicago packinghouse workers are typical. (This is a local with a large Negro membership.)

> Arguing and squabbling too much—I'm tired at night. . . . Anyway there's too much argument in the union. . . . [Woman member] No time to go to union meetings, after work I go shopping or I go and clean house and I like to watch television at night. . . . I used to go to meetings but I got no time to go now, it's just talk. . . . [White member] There are just 4 or 5 white and 200 colored. . . . If you go to meetings at 7:30 they don't start until 9. . . . It's inconvenient. . . . When I get home I take my shoes off and put my slippers on, I got no time to go to meetings. . . . I don't like to go—type of girl I am, I don't like to go alone, I don't talk much though I like to listen. . . . Go to meetings maybe once or twice a year, usually I am tired and I go home, besides it's just business and normal routine. . . . I go to several meetings a year, I don't like to argue in the debates but I like the dances. . . . I go to union meetings once a month but we don't have the old fellows there like we should [steward], the fellows who could really help are fed up. . . .[5]

The situation with respect to regular union meeting attendance may be summed up as follows:

1. The average member is bored with and indifferent to the routine of the union meeting.

2. He comes if he has a personal problem. He is not interested in hearing about other members' personal problems.

3. He is also repelled by "too much talk" and by what he generally characterizes as "bickering" and "politics" in the local meeting.

4. The failure to attend meetings is not due to conflicting

[4] Leonard R. Sayles and George Strauss, *The Local Union: Its Place in the Industrial Plant* (New York: Harper, 1953), chap. 12. See also Leiserson, *op. cit.*, p. 282; Dalton E. McFarland, *Leadership in a Local Labor Union Undergoing Organizational Stress,* unpublished Ph.D. dissertation, New York State School of Industrial and Labor Relations, 1952, p. 35.

[5] Theodore V. Purcell, *The Worker Speaks His Mind on Company and Union* (Cambridge: Harvard University Press, 1953), p. 200 ff.

organizational obligations but, when reasons are given, to personal and recreational interests.

5. The union member appreciates the role of the union meeting in the democratic government of the union even if he doesn't attend regularly.

6. Low union meeting attendance cannot be taken as an indication of low union morale since all unions suffer from this condition.

7. All gimmicks—fines, door prizes, free beer, "educational" speakers, movies—to improve attendance invariably fail.[6]

In general, craftsmen's locals seem to have a higher proportion of attendance than industrial locals. For one thing this is due to the fact that craft locals tend to have a smaller membership and the percentage of attendance at union meetings seems to vary inversely with the size of membership. Meeting attendance is likely to be better because the meeting serves important communications purposes in a craft, nonfactory situation which otherwise provides few opportunities for workers to see one another except in small clusters on the job. The meeting is therefore the occasion for finding out about the economic situation in the trade, about new jobs, and new materials. The union meeting is also the

[6] See Industrial Relations Center, University of Chicago, *Summary Report of Membership Attitudes toward the Union,* January 1954 (mimeo.), p. 6; Donald W. Hill, *Labor-Management Relations between the Rochester Transit Corporation and the Amalgamated Association of Street, Electric Railway and Motor Coach Employees of America, Division 282, AFL,* unpublished M.S. thesis, New York State School of Industrial and Labor Relations, 1955; Purcell, *The Worker Speaks His Mind,* p. 199; Glenn W. Miller and James E. Young, "Member Participation in the Trade Union Local," *American Journal of Economics and Sociology,* vol. 15 (1955), p. 40 ff.; Hjalmar Rosen and R. A. H. Rosen, *The Union Member Speaks* (New York: Prentice-Hall, 1955), p. 31; Fred H. Blum, *Toward a Democratic Work Process,* The Hormel-Packinghouse Workers' Experiment (New York: Harper, 1953), p. 40; James Phillip Dee, *An Analysis of the Formal Channels of Communication in an Industrial Union Local,* unpublished Ph.D. dissertation, Ohio State University, 1957, p. 56; Milton Derber, "Case Study 1, Grain Processing," in *Labor-Management Relations in Illini City,* University of Illinois, Institute of Labor and Industrial Relations, 1953, p. 272; Edward W. Murphy, *A Study of a Building Trades Local Union,* unpublished M.B.A. thesis, Northeastern University, 1956, p. 18. And the following unpublished case studies of local unions by University of Wisconsin graduate students: Raymond J. Barrett, *The Structure of a Local Union* (1959); Ronald Coyte, *A Teamsters Local* (1960); Dwight Scarborough, *The Federal Labor Union: A Case Study* (1959).

best place to get hold of the business agent. The union meeting serves a social purpose because common craft identification is a basis for off-the-job social relationships, not nearly as common in factory employment.[7]

There are some locals that hold no routine business meetings, limiting themselves to special meetings as the occasion arises. In one case—a 450-member retail clerks local—the randomness of meetings was part of a pattern of casual constitutional government: the business agent simply improvised a policy to suit each situation.[8] In a 600-member textile local regular membership meetings were abandoned because of poor attendance and replaced by three or four meetings a year to deal with major issues.[9] And of course many racket locals of the "paper" variety run no meetings at all.

"CRISIS" MEETINGS

The "crisis" meeting deals with such issues as the formulation of union contract demands, the approval of a proposed contract, a dues increase, or an increase in per capita contribution to the national union. As one local labor leader put it, "When the chips are down the boys will come out."[10] Attendance at the crisis meetings is relatively high clustering between 30–60 per cent.[11] Special election meetings tend to bring out a higher proportion of the membership.[12]

Here is a description of a crisis meeting on whether to strike in an apparel plant that had not yet recognized the union;[13] 125

[7] Joel Seidman, Jack London, Bernard Karsh, and Daisy L. Tagliacozzo, *The Worker Views His Union* (Chicago: University of Chicago Press, 1958), p. 189. See also Miller and Young, *op. cit.*, p. 36; Sayles and Strauss, *op. cit.*, p. 173; and Greer, *op. cit.*, p. 47.

[8] Wayne Lawrence Inks, *Unionism in the Retail Food Industry: A Local Case Study of Structure and Function*, unpublished M.A. thesis, University of Illinois, Institute of Labor and Industrial Relations, 1959, p. 100.

[9] Richard A. Lester and Edward A. Robie, *Constructive Labor Relations*, Princeton University, Industrial Relations Section, 1948, p. 26.

[10] Greer, *op. cit.*, p. 51.

[11] Sayles and Strauss, *op. cit.*, pp. 174–175; see also Seymour Martin Lipset, Martin Trow, and James Coleman, *Union Democracy: The Inside Politics of the International Typographical Union* (Glencoe: Free Press, 1956), p. 65.

[12] Greer, *op. cit.*, p. 51.

[13] Bernard Karsh, *Diary of a Strike* (Urbana: University of Illinois Press, 1958), pp. 66–67.

millworkers out of 200 in the work force attended the meeting. The meeting had to be convened in a hurry and,

> . . . since there was no time to distribute leaflets each committee member was given a block of names and telephone numbers of union members and instructed to notify them of the special meeting that evening at the local Trades and Labor hall.

Approximately 125 mill workers were present when Phil dispassionately reported on the conduct of negotiation and the final company offer. The union's attorney spoke in detail on the company's position and how the union interpreted it. Phil again took the floor to announce that the international union was recommending a strike. He listed what he considered to be the alternatives: accept the company's final offer which probably would result in the disappearance of the union, abandon the entire effort, or force the issue through a strike. The union had been very patient, he said; it had not taken this step until all legal procedures had been exhausted. It had given the firm every opportunity to come to a fair agreement with the union. But he insisted that any agreement had to include a union security clause, because unless the union had this protection, the company would never cease trying to destroy it. Further, any agreement had to include a "decent" wage increase. Since the company was unwilling to concede these issues through discussion, a strike was the only alternative. He promised that the strike would be fully supported by the resources of an international union with more than 400,000 members. The local union president made a short speech in support of Phil's strike motion. He was convinced, he said, that only a strike could show Tom Miller that the union members were absolutely determined to get a "decent" contract. He told the meeting that the bargaining committee stood "100 per cent" behind Phil and the strike move and that, although they had all hoped this action might be avoided, they were unanimous in the belief that there was now no other recourse.

A short discussion period followed. Someone asked if any strike benefits would be paid. Phil replied that it was the policy of the international to pay benefits to strikers and to make sure that no one suffered "undue hardship." He again emphasized the resources of the union, trying to assure those present that the union "would take care of them." Someone else asked if they would have to picket and Phil replied that all strikers would be asked to picket but those who felt that they could not would be given other tasks to do such as running the strike head-quarters and the kitchen which would be set up. The discussion continued for about thirty minutes after which the motion to strike was put to a standing vote. About 115 of the 125 present stood for the organizer's motion. The strike was on.

In another crisis meeting the issue is which international union, if any, a federal local shall affiliate with. The meeting is scheduled on a Sunday noon and held at a large auditorium. Outside organizers for the various international union interests are distributing leaflets promoting their respective organizations (identified here as U1, U2, U3, U4, and U5).[14]

The meeting is opened promptly by the chairman of the affiliation committee of the local. The crowd is small at first but by the time the vote is taken it mounts to about 1,000 out of a total membership of 5,600. The U2 partisans are out in force judging by the conspicuous T-shirts marked "Vote U2."

The chairman announces that he is going to run the meeting strictly according to the rules. He reports that he received an anonymous phone call warning him that he had better watch his step "or else." The rules are that each international union spokesman will get thirty minutes for his presentation and fifteen minutes to answer questions.

The chairman recognizes a local union officer, who moves that speakers be heard and that the final membership election to decide which of the international unions shall go on the ballot together with the present federal labor union be held ten days later on voting machines. There are shouts of "no" from the audience. A member says the motion is out of order because the announcement calling the meeting stated that the vote will be held now. The chairman finds the motion is in order. His decision is appealed and a standing vote upholds the appeal by 243 to 127.

A motion by a leader of one of the union caucuses most confident of winning moves that a general discussion from the floor be held following the statements of the spokesmen from the internationals. The motion is passed by voice vote.

The U1 partisans are represented by its international president, also an important figure in the larger labor movement. The applause is light. As advantages for affiliating with his union, he

[14] Reported to me by an observer.

gives the democratic character of the union, the overwhelming industrial character of the union, the large membership, the substantial size of the treasury, the resources of the union in field staff, and headquarters technical personnel available to service the union. More specifically he offers to waive initiation fees, make all members in good standing eligible for strike benefits, pay one-half of the salary of three full-time representatives, local determination of affiliation to district organization, representation at international convention two months hence, and retention of its treasury.

A question period follows:

Q. Do we have to affiliate with an international?
A. No.
Q. Can any international come in and split us up?
A. No.
Q. Do all members receive the same amount of benefits for the duration of a strike?
A. Yes, with two qualifications. They must have been members for six months to receive any benefits and there must be $500,000 in the strike fund. When the strike fund is depleted below $500,000 the executive board pays out strike benefits from the general fund in a lesser amount.
Q. I have heard that in your union it's the crafts first and the industrial workers second.
A. That is not true and I say that without any reservation at all.
Q. Couldn't the AFL–CIO executive council dissolve the federal labor unions and split their membership between various international unions?
A. I suppose the AFL–CIO executive council could if it wanted to, but it never will. The AFL–CIO constitution says that no union will be dissolved.
Q. I was a member of your international once. My local followed a policy of secrecy. It wouldn't give non-members the by-laws or tell them what the dues were.
A. That is not our policy. We have no reservation at all about disclosure.
(Good applause)

A spokesman of the U2 is introduced and represented by a vice-president. This is another very large international union. (Good applause.) He cites the reasons for affiliating with U2: the large membership, U2 already represents competitors of the company now represented by the federal labor union, democracy

57

in U2, the servicing facilities of the union, the apportionment of dues between local and international, the size of the strike fund, local autonomy generally and specifically in the calling of strikes subject to international union authorization. He defends the strike record of the international and emphasizes U2's support of civil rights programs. He justifies the increased per capita which the local union will have to pay as a U2 affiliate in terms of services rendered.

Q. Can't your executive board raise the dues by $5 for the strike fund?

A. Before our last convention, the executive board could increase the dues by $5 a month. The regular contribution was 25 cents. The executive board could act in emergencies. At the convention, the delegates said they would rather have it uniform, so it was set at $1.25 and the executive board cannot change that.

Q. Must contracts be ratified by the executive board of the international?

A. Contracts must be submitted to the international. But whether it approves them or not, if the local signs, the contract is effective.

Q. I have a brother who works at "A" Co. The dues there are $7.50 a month. What about that?

A. If they are, it is because the members of the local voted to put them there. I think they just bought a new building. They may be trying to pay for it fast. But, any dues over $5 a month are set by the local. We don't have anything to do with that.

Q. The guys at "B" company were on strike for a long time and they didn't get anything more than what they were offered to begin with. You've been on strike at "C" for a long time. You didn't do so well at "D."

A. The "B" workers did get a lot more than they were offered to begin with. And they voted to strike and voted to accept the settlement. At "D" the workers voted to strike and we have not run away from them. We have given them ten million dollars plus a lot more in services. At "C," as long as our members take that position, we will continue to support them.

Q. Must we join an international?

A. I guess the AFL–CIO would have authority to revoke your charter, but I've never heard of any talk of anything like that. At this point, I would say that no one could revoke your charter. I guess they possibly could cut you loose, give an international union jurisdiction over you, then you could decide whether you wanted to join it.

Q. What will the initiation fee be if we come in?

A. Nothing for present members. For future members it will be a minimum of $5 and a maximum of $15, with $1 of that to the international.

Q. (By a woman) If the "B" workers are so happy, why can't you organize the office there?

A. "B" is pretty paternalistic insofar as its office workers are concerned. They are pretty well under the company's thumb. There is a difference between the shop and office.

Q. (By same woman) That's what I mean. You say the office is different. There are a lot of office workers in our local and you say you can't do anything for us.

A. I didn't say we couldn't do anything for you. I'm not saying you won't get representation. I'm saying the problems are different in the office and the shop. We have offices organized at [he mentions three other companies].

The spokesman for U3 is introduced, this time from a small international. He stresses the smallness of his union as an asset protecting the local from being "a little spoke in a big wheel" and holds out hope of getting representation on the U3 executive board. He cites the small per capita as another inducement.

The chairman breaks in to call people back from the bar.

The U3 spokesman continues. He promises a written guarantee that the local will hold on to its funds and to its building. He points to U3's no assessment policy and scope of industrial representation. He denies that U3 is a craft organization. The chairman interrupts again and complains about some organization giving free beer to take the audience away from other speakers.

Q. What are your assets and membership?

A. We have about _____ members. Our assets are _____ million, four hundred and some thousand dollars.

Chairman interrupts saying that If that party isn't broken up, I'll adjourn this meeting. Motion made that the bar be closed. Motion is passed by a roar of ayes, no noes.

Q. Is there any pressure to force federal unions into internationals?

A. It appears that there is a policy or a trend to eliminate

59

federal charters. The fact is that no federal charters are being granted; that the federal unions are disappearing. That the per capita has been raised for federals indicates a trend in that direction.

There are more exchanges between the chairman and members from the floor about the beer drinking situation in back of the hall. The speaker for U4 is introduced. He is an international representative from a large international union. He emphasizes the economies of his international per capita in contrast to the local's present per capita and in contrast to the per capitas of the other internationals. He cites the size of the international union treasury, the assignment of a headquarters pension expert in a local bargaining situation, the absence of strikes. He explains in some detail two types of membership, depending on welfare benefits.

Q. Do you have a strike fund?
A. We have never found it necessary because we have conducted our business responsibly. We feel that it is better for the locals to contribute into their own strike fund if they want one than to have the big brass squandering their money somewhere else without the members of the other locals having any say. At "E," only members on the picket line got $35 and the others had to sign their strike benefit checks and they went back to the strike fund.

The chairman is about to introduce the regional director of U5 when he is interrogated from the floor as to U5's receiving preferred treatment allegedly in private meetings with the officers. The U5 spokesman expresses support for the principle of industrial unionism and describes U5's history. He describes allocation of per capita and the headquarters services, particularly the legal services, available to the local. He calls attention to the absence of previous pressure to affiliate and U5's good record in getting contracts from stubborn employers. He promises that if after a year the local is dissatisfied with affiliation the local will be permitted to disaffiliate regardless of other constitutional provisions.

Q. Why didn't you settle the "E" strike?
A. The toolroom recently called off a strike at "E." They belonged to another international union.

Q. Even if we can disaffiliate from U5 after a year, where are we going to go if they aren't issuing any federal union charters?

A. You may affiliate with any union you wish to without any objection from us.

Q. Will you also guarantee that the AFL–CIO will reissue our charter?

A. I can't do that because I'm not the AFL–CIO.

Q. (Reads excerpt from U5 constitution that says upon disaffiliation, a local's property, assets, books, records, etc., revert to the international union.) How can you supersede the constitution?

A. The executive board interprets the constitution. If you seceded against our wishes, all of your funds would revert to the international. That's why we gave you our agreement that we would not object if you disaffiliated.

Q. What is your membership and assets?

A. About ——— members and $——— in assets.

A member speaks up from the floor to put U2 on the ballot. A motion is made to poll the affiliation committee on its choice. All except two vote for U5.

From the floor: I'm proud to stand on this floor for U2. The union did not, as inferred, try to raid this plant. This is the dawn of a bright new day. . . . We are about to get into the mainstream of the labor movement, and that's where most of the water is. The union is the strongest free union in the world today.

Member of affiliation committee: I'm disappointed at the small turnout here today because here we are talking about a situation where the dues could be raised by as much as $2 and how many are here? I'm also disappointed that the vote to delay the vote didn't carry so we could have it on our voting machines.

Member: If the people that aren't here thought anything of their union, they'd be sitting right here.

Member of affiliation committee: I'm only telling you that I'm disappointed that we don't have full representation. I like to think of it as buying a good suit of clothes (carries on analogy between union and suit at some length: does it fit, is price right, etc.). We're going to be wearing it for a long time. I wish we could get this on the voting machines and get the true sentiment of the members.

From the floor: Our federal labor union has $250,000 in assets and a building worth a quarter of a million. I can't understand why U5 doesn't have more. U2 is aggressive, I know, but strikes are okay if they benefit a fellow. . . . I recommend we ride along with FLU.

Member of affiliation committee: I like the U5 because it was the first union to give us a promise we would keep our assets. It also was the only one who has guts enough to say we could get out in a year if we didn't like it. I like a parachute.

Officer: They are all good internationals. My choice is U3. If we join U2, when we get into negotiations, especially in the frame division, we will be involved in country-wide bargaining and we'd have a heck of a time getting more because we're 50 cents ahead of them right now.

From the floor: I recommend the U3. We could stay at $3 dues. If we affiliate with U2, immediately your dues will go up to $5. If we go on strike, you'll be getting nothing from the U2. Don't let them kid you. We are at least 50 cents above "F" company; we have a better pension plan than "F" company. What can U2 give us that we haven't already got? We haven't had any difficulties with our company to compare with the U2. Our company could say to U2, go back to "G" company and get what we've got and then come back and see us.

From the floor: I'm for U2.

Officer: (Refers back to the U5 meeting with the stewards and committeemen which had been hanging in the air.) The reason that the meeting was called for the stewards—when we got through with the June 12 meeting, we certainly got everything but approval (the affiliation committee recommended the U5 and the membership in effect rejected that and said let's hear from the five unions) and thought we ought to take stock. We called U5 in to ask questions. Our FLU is our favorite organization and if it wasn't for the danger of being forced into some international, we'd stay with it. If we get into too deep water some of us can't swim so well and we may be damn sorry we're there. Only our obligation to study the question for six months and tell you how we feel.

(At this point, there is a line-up at both mikes about eight deep. The chairman is recognizing guys alternately at mikes and also members of affiliation committee behind him. It's around 5:30 P.M. and local has to vacate hall by 6 P.M. U2 worried, fear a filibuster to prevent vote.)

Member: I make a motion to cut off general discussion.

Officer: I make a motion to adjourn.

Chairman: I can't accept a motion to adjourn because there's a motion on the floor.

(Some discussion about this. Chairman finally puts motion to cut off discussion. Ayes have it. Vote is held. U2 wins—therefore rejecting recommendation for U5.)

It is not unusual for the membership majority at the "crisis" meeting to override the recommendations of the local leaders. It is obviously impossible to say how often this happens but without any particular effort I have been able to collect the following instances, in addition to the case immediately above:

1. A teamsters local of 5,000 overrides contract recommendations of officers.[15]

2. An 8,000-member local of aircraft workers overrode recommendation of national union leadership to approve contract.[16]

3. A large brewery local rejected recommendation of executive board with respect to recording secretary who is, in this case, equivalent to the business agent.[17]

4. A Boston plumbers local—it is "not uncommon for the members to refuse to accept the opinion [of the business agent] and set their own [bargaining] recommendation."[18]

5. A San Francisco teamsters local of 6,500 members rejected a three-year contract negotiated by officers.[19]

6. A local of the UAW in Racine, Wisconsin, twice rejected the request of officers for strike authorization. The local approved the third time.

7. The Newspaper and Mail Deliverers local, New York, "is said to be noted for the frequency with which the membership overrides the policies of its officers."[20]

8. A Textile local meeting in New England rejects settlement worked out by international representative to give relief to marginal employer.[21]

[15] *The New York Times,* September 1, 1959.
[16] *The Milwaukee Journal,* May 11, 1958.
[17] *Ibid.,* September 19, 1960.
[18] Murphy, *op. cit.,* p. 18.
[19] *The New York Times,* August 15, 1959.
[20] McClellan investigation, *Final Report,* part 1, p. 96.
[21] Irwin L. Herrnstadt, "The Reaction of Three Local Unions to Economic Adversity," *Journal of Political Economy,* October 1954, p. 429.

The explanation is probably simple, too, as to why the crisis meeting not infrequently results in the overriding of leadership recommendations. The crisis meeting deals with issues that the membership feels strongly about. Moreover, it is not unlikely either that factional division develops over the crisis issues and that this transitory factionalism results in getting the vote out.

In respect to the degree of leadership control—not necessarily always majority leadership—one may distinguish: (a) the guided meeting, (b) the managed meeting, and (c) the rigged meeting.

GUIDED MEETINGS
The guided meeting is one in which the state is set by the local-wide officers but genuine opportunity—exercised frequently —exists for the meeting to override the officers and determine its own course. This is probably the typical union meeting.

MANAGED MEETINGS
In the managed meeting the scenario of the meeting is pre-arranged by the top leaders so as to yield a particular outcome, but only a determined effort can effect a change. Port meetings of the Marine Cooks and Stewards in the 1950s have been reported as follows:

> Every week in every port the union holds meetings for those members who are ashore at the time. Of these meetings three out of every six are compulsory, attendance being checked through the medium of shipping cards. At these regular meetings the administration has an increased advantage of influencing and controlling the membership because it has control of the platform for the duration of the meeting. However, it is rare that the port-agent fills the chair, this being filled from nominations from the floor. . . . In San Francisco two or three individuals are nominated and then somebody calls for the closing of nominations. Those nominated, it has been noticed are either lesser officials or rank-and-file supporters of the administration. When questioned as to whether or not they will accept nomination, the predominant practice is for all except one to decline. . . .

> The agenda is broad enough in its standard terms to make the content unknown until the meeting develops. The weekly membership meeting then provides the officials with an opportunity for regular and guaranteed contact with the rank and file.

Thus, all new environmental developments can be presented to the membership, and the policy which the administration has adopted to meet them can be placed before the meetings for immediate approval. In this manner a continuously developing policy can be approved by stages, thus weakening any attempt made at the convention to effect a change of the whole. Furthermore, presentation at these meetings makes it easier for the administration to win approval since the material to be discussed is unknown before the meeting, thus placing the administration in the position of having all the relevant facts for its case while any opposition which might be latent in the meeting is left with nothing solid with which to back its case.[22]

Another situation that seems to partake of the characteristics of a managed meeting is in a 600-member UE local in upstate New York. The "manager" seems to be "Foster," the paid representative of the local.

Rarely do participants of a meeting approve policy or take action to which Foster is opposed. Although the actual decision may take the form of a vote by members of the group, Foster's views dominate the group. Foster's lack of precision in parliamentary procedure allows him great latitude in choosing the techniques most appropriate for his own ends although he does this cautiously. On strongly debated issues he maintains strict procedure and good order. His method of getting an item passed or preventing passage is to urge complete discussion when he is against the measure. During the discussion he gradually gets his real views across to the participants. Toward the close of the discussion he makes a forceful statement of his position. The officers and active members who have a high regard for Foster's opinions usually wait until they discern what Foster wants and act accordingly. . . . Rarely does Foster silence a speaker by the sheer force of his gavel except when an individual is actually not entitled to the floor. Scheduling of items on the agenda is important to Foster's conduct of meetings. First routine matters, then matters requiring long discussion. There is a lack of predictability in the order of business. . . . Frequently Foster fails to see that voted decisions are carried out as agreed upon and he seldom reports back to the membership in such instances. There is also a lack of con-

[22] John Ingram, *The National Union of Marine Cooks and Stewards, CIO: A Case Study of Democracy and Bureaucracy in American Trade Unions*, unpublished M.A. thesis, University of California, 1951, pp. 194–195.

tinuity in carrying the decisions from the board to the membership and Foster follows no clearcut procedures in this matter.[23]

RIGGED MEETING

The rigged meeting—the word "stacked" might do just as well—
differs from the managed meeting in that the control is overt and
frequently accompanied by a show of force and intimidation.
Only a resolute effort can override the leadership in control of
the meeting. Here is a newspaper reporter's account of the meeting of the Mail Deliverers Union in New York City to vote on
a contract.

> Practically the entire union membership of more than 2,000
> men turned out for the meeting to decide whether they should
> take a formal vote the next day on the contract. But it was
> evident almost from the start that decision rested not with the
> overwhelming mass of the rank and file, but with a hard and
> organized core that had come prepared to wrest power from
> the hands of Feldman and Schwartz [the incumbent leader and
> his lawyer respectively].
>
> They came early in a phalanx, they pre-empted all the front
> seats in the meeting hall, forming a solid block of strength,
> prepared placards ready to wave on signal. Leaders of the
> group held whispered conferences, couriers scurried out with
> messages circulated in the rear of the hall, came back for fur-
> ther instructions. When Feldman tried to speak on the proposal,
> so much noise was made that hardly anyone could hear him.
> When an expression of sentiment was finally asked, it was over-
> whelming—about 80 per cent shouting and stamping their deci-
> sion not to reconsider the contract.[24]

The rigged meeting, accompanied by systematic violence is
revealed by the McClellan committee report on the Operating
Engineers Long Island local controlled by the William DeKonings, junior and senior. (The John DeKoning in the story is a
dissident cousin of the ruling family openly identified with the
opposition group.)

> Peter Batalias gave a vivid story of what happens to a member
> of Local 138 who persists in objecting to acts of officers of the
> union. In May of 1954 a motion had been made to return all the
> officers to their positions in the local with the exception of

[23] McFarland, *Leadership in a Local Labor Union*, p. 48 ff.
[24] Fred J. Cook, "The Truth About New York Newspaper Strike,"
The Nation, January 3, 1959, p. 7.

William DeKoning, Jr. who had to stay out of union affairs for a year because of his probation.

When the meeting was held in June actually to hold the election Batalias said that the name of John DeKoning who was a business agent had been deleted from the list. The recording secretary explained to the members that a business agent was an appointive job and that no one could be elected to that office. The members then passed a resolution making the business agent's job an elective one and proceeded to vote John DeKoning into office. The only dissenting vote was cast by Verner Sofield, the union's recording secretary.

The next meeting took place in September of 1954. When the minutes of the June meeting were read all the actions of the membership relative to the making of the business agent's position elective and the election of John DeKoning had been deleted. William DeKoning, Jr., in direct violation of his probationary status, was at the meeting and spoke for almost three hours. A battle ensued which lasted until 1 o'clock in the morning, when the membership present forced a secret ballot on the question of whether or not the minutes of the June meeting were incorrect. The vote sustained the position that they were incorrect.

The members then attempted to declare the office of business manager elective. This resulted in further turmoil, which lasted until 5 o'clock in the morning. Present at the meeting was Richard Knowland, the eastern district representative of the IUOE, who told the members they could not elect a business manager until General President William E. Maloney ruled on the subject.

Batalias said that this was the first time in the history of Local 138 that they'd ever had a secret ballot. The union leadership quickly retaliated against the membership. John DeKoning was fired, and at the next meeting, which Batalias said was "stacked" a motion was quickly forced through approving the actions of the executive board. Knowland was permitted to find out just what the executive board had done which the membership was being asked to approve. What the members had actually done was to pass the authority for the running of the union from the members to the executive board. . . . Following this meeting Batalias was visited on a project where he was working by business agent Jack Dunning and Paul Konya, a union tough, and told that he had better change his attitude, that "if I didn't change my attitude they would find me in the gutter." He also received a number of threatening phone calls and was followed wherever he went.

Just before the general meeting Batalias received a phone call telling him to stay away. Batalias did not heed the warning and went to the meeting anyway. At the meeting Batalias objected to some of the actions and was ordered thrown out of the hall by Verner Sofield. Four men then attacked him, two hitting him in the stomach and two giving him bruises on the back of his neck.[25]

The most scientific practitioners of the rigged meeting are the Communists. Joe Curran talks from his experience with the Communist control group of the National Maritime Union.

[The communists] come to the meetings well organized, having met before the meeting at outside meeting places. All of their members are fully instructed and have their resolutions in their pockets. Their speakers are chosen. They are trained and disciplined, and above all are prepared to stay all night at a meeting in order to tire out the non-communist members, make them disgusted and leave the meeting, then they have full control of the meeting and are able to pass any resolutions and actions they want.

If the communists cannot outlast the rest of the members at a meeting, they do everything possible to disrupt the meeting raising points of order . . . and whenever votes are taken they make sure their people count the votes and if necessary make a short count on the vote if it is against them.[26]

An anti-Communist in the Marine Cooks and Stewards, Dan Rotan, who for a time was friendly with the communist forces in power, has testified as to the instructions that were given to him by MCS officer Eddie Tangen on how to deal with criticism at a union meeting.

I was to convert any statements of opposition to my leadership as ship's delegate into opposition of the union and the union's

[25] McClellan investigation, *Interim Report,* Report No. 1417, 85th Cong., 2d Sess.; see also part 19, p. 7765; report of meeting of local, part 29, p. 11498 ff. For other "rigged" meetings see Robert W. Ozanne, *The Effects of Communist Leadership on American Trade Unions, UAW Local 248,* unpublished Ph.D. dissertation, University of Wisconsin, 1954, p. 297; McClellan investigation on the Teamsters meetings, part 27, p. 10409, and on the San Francisco Operating Engineers, *Interim Report,* p. 439.

[26] National Maritime Union, "Report to the Membership," *The Pilot,* July 5, 1946.

program. . . . [Tangen] told me that where I noticed a member of the steward's group was repeatedly raising his voice to me I was to prepare an individual to speak in opposition to that person, and an additional individual for each additional person who spoke against me, such that the final appearance at a meeting would be that each person speaking in opposition to me was in turn being opposed by a specific individual who would appear to be speaking as a regular member of the rank and file who disagreed with the opposition. The final and total appearance of this opposition was to the membership the equivalent of leaving the union official completely in the clear and from all appearances, one who had substantial support from the rank and file. This sort of prepared opposition also contributed to the creation of an atmosphere and pattern which assisted in keeping down those who might have otherwise voiced themselves against the union leadership.[27]

DELEGATE ASSEMBLY

Thus far we have seen that the local unions' affairs are, according to union law, run under a system of direct membership government, with the union meeting as the supreme authority within the local. Very large locals, however, frequently resort to forms of representative government. In these situations direct membership government stops at some sublocal unit and the latter elects delegates to a representative local-wide body. In many instances the meetings of the sublocal units are in addition to the general membership meeting. These sublocal units are variously called units, chapters, chapels, departments, branches, etc.

The need for this sort of structural adaptation arises where substantial numbers of members of one local union are to be found among (a) several employers, (b) several locations of the same employer, and (c) several departments in a plant of one large (measured by work force) employer.

Local 3 of the American Newspaper Guild in the New York area has 8,400 members in fifty employer units, including newspapers, news services, magazines, radios, and periodicals throughout the five boroughs of the city and metropolitan Connecticut and New Jersey. This local uses the employer unit as a sublocal instrumentality of government. Members in each of these units

[27] U.S. Senate, Committee on Labor and Public Welfare, Subcommittee on Labor and Labor-Management Relations, *Marine Cooks and Stewards,* Staff Report, 82d Cong., 2d Sess., 1953, p. 142.

elect unit officers and approve or reject contracts for each unit. Each unit is entitled to one delegate and one alternate for each twenty-five members in the unit to the representative assembly. The voting strength of the unit corresponds to its membership in good standing.

The New York representative assembly of the Guild has three hundred delegates; it meets once a month, although the executive board of the local may call special meetings and any six members of the assembly may also ask for a meeting. The assembly has its own officers, a chairman or a vice-chairman; the members of the executive board have no vote ex officio, but may vote as representatives from their own units. Attendance at assembly meetings is under one-half. The meeting has the authority to alter the decisions of the executive board, but this power is not frequently exercised. When the guild was divided internally between the communists and the anti-communist forces, the conflict between the assembly and the executive board was frequent and intense.[28]

The local with membership in several locations of one employer is likely to set up sublocal units for each of the various locations and/or departments, as for example Local 100 of the Transport Workers Union in New York which covers all of the employees of the municipally owned transit system. The local is divided into seventy-eight sections. Each section is governed by a chairman, recording secretary, vice-chairman, and stewards. The local-wide body is the joint executive committee made up of the chairman and recording secretary of each section.[29] Ford UAW Local 600 in Detroit and the IUE local of the General Electric in Schenectady provide additional instances of sublocal governments of this sort.[30] Local 420 of the American Federation of State, County and Municipal Employees is made up of employees in four hundred city hospitals. The primary unit is the chapter. The lower-paid employees (attendants, etc.) are in an individual hos-

[28] Benjamin D. Segal, "Some Efforts at Democratic Union Participation," *Papers and Proceedings,* American Economic Association, 1957, p. 55.
[29] Arthur J. Goldberg, *et al., Appropriate Collective Bargaining Units For Employees of the New York City Transit Authority,* briefs submitted by Transport Workers Union of America, AFL–CIO, 1957, pp. 42–45.
[30] William M. Leiserson, *American Trade Union Democracy* (New York: Columbia University Press, 1959), p. 295.

pital chapter. The higher-paid professionals are in a city-wide "craft" chapter.

The Chicago Teachers Union (American Federation of Teachers) covering the teachers in the Chicago public school system, is governed by a "house of representatives" and an executive board subject to it. The House of Representatives meets monthly with each delegate speaking for fifty members in a particular functional group—elementary schools, high schools, principals, etc. This system functions side by side with a school delegate—a sort of shop steward—system in which the school is the primary unit, but the latter has no legislative authority; it is rather more a system of communication.[31]

Invariably, then, a member in a local of any substantial size, can find an intermediate point between himself and the local union meeting in the form of a shop unit, section, department, or chapel. The shop meetings are invariably better attended; the discussion is more diffused and better informed, although narrower in scope. The inhibitions that operate on the individual member at the local union meeting do not operate at the unit meeting where he talks freely and holds his unit officers closely to account.[32]

These sublocal units may on occasion act as a medium for the dispersion of power within the local union. In the ITU chapel "the chairmen of the ITU chapels have a relatively independent position vis-à-vis the local union administration. . . . The political autonomy of the chapel and the chapel chairman is one of the important structural supports of the democratic political life of the union."[33]

"SHOP SOCIETY"

An important source of membership involvement in the life of the union is the informal society of the worksite. The binding effect of the worksite as a form of social organization is likely to

[31] Charles Paul Skibbens, *The Chicago Teachers Union: A Study of Its Program, Problems and Possibilities,* unpublished M.S. and I.R. thesis. Loyola University, June 1956. See also Emma Schweppe, *The Firemen's and Patrolmen's Unions in the City of New York* (New York: King's Crown Press, Columbia University, 1948), p. 202.

[32] Joseph Kovner and Herbert J. Lahne, "Shop Society and the Union," *Industrial and Labor Relations Review,* vol. 7, no. 1, October 1953; Seidman, London, Karsh, and Tagliacozzo, *op. cit.,* p. 191 ff.; Lipset, Trow, and Coleman, *op. cit.,* p. 144 ff.

[33] Lipset, Trow, and Coleman, *op. cit.,* p. 145.

be greater in the factory than in the nonfactory situation because the former provides a more continuing and a more stable basis for association. In any case, however, the formal organization of the union is effectively complemented by the opportunities provided for association through the shop society. This process was found to be at work in a study of members in several factory locals.

> It's always talked around all over, it's talked around the shop and down at the meeting. . . .

> There are a couple of stewards, that I can depend on pretty well (they speak for me) very often. That's what they're stewards for. . . .

> Usually if I'm not at a meeting and I know that some points should be brought up, I usually tell a committee woman to bring it up. . . .

> Sometimes we get together and talk it over before. We elect someone to speak for us, we can't all do it. . . .[34]

A UAW local union officer in Buffalo observed:

> Why, it takes me more than an hour to get from one part of the plant to the other when I have to make such a trip. Do you know why? Because all along the way I am stopped by guys in every department wanting to know what the Union has done about this problem and that problem, what the Union plans to do about something that isn't coming up perhaps for a month or so, and so on.[35]

Among legitimate-theatre actors the same shop society was found, only more intense and articulate.

> The actor's relation with his fellow workers . . . is quite different from workers in other occupations. A carpenter for example breaks off relations with his co-workers at the end of the work day. There can be little doubt that the actor's relationships are much more binding both in time and psychologically. The major topic of conversation during the course of this tremendous amount of interaction is the theatre. However, not an unfrequent topic is Equity itself, there being sometimes heated debates over the current issues in which the union is involved. Ob-

[34] Arnold S. Tannenbaum and Robert L. Kahn, *Participation in Union Locals* (Evanston: Row, Peterson, 1958), p. 168.

[35] Joseph Shister and William Hamovitch, *Conflict and Stability in Labor Relations: A Case Study*, University of Buffalo, 1952, p. 56.

viously this extended interaction makes for high-level interest and participation in union activities and is certainly an important variable in understanding the relatively democratic nature of the union.[36]

Kovner and Lahne were probably the first to sharpen the idea of shop society in the government of the local union and other researchers have borne this out fully.[37]

The shop is not only a place of employment; it is also a social meeting place—a place of talk. Union affairs are one of the more frequent topics of conversation, ranking high with sex, sports, political affairs, and personal gossip. Members who do not attend meetings hear in the shop about what happened at the meeting from those who were there. In one instance, when a shop chairman reported to a unit meeting on the new contract demands, his report was received without comment from the attendants. He scolded them, saying that he knew there would be no lack of discussion in the factory washrooms. A staff representative of the Steelworkers said, "If we could do away with the bath-house meetings we could get more members out to the regular meeting." (One does not have to know parliamentary law to discuss a subject in a bath-house!) A telephone workers local found that only 30% of its 2,500 members voted in an important referendum on its relation with the strengthened federation. But the subject was thoroughly discussed by nearly every employee. The operators and office help talked about it in the restrooms and at lunch, and in snatches between working moments. The repair and installation crews work in twos and threes, and they discussed it as they worked and traveled from one working spot to another. The decision on the proposal was formulated in these talks among the employees at work, and the referendum merely registered a developed sentiment. Many members did not take the trouble to vote because they knew what the result was going to be. In discussing whether or not the Rubber Workers would vote to strike in 1947, a shop chairman of one local said, "There were some people in the National Office who thought that the vote would be against the strike, or that it would be close; but I said it

[36] Leonard I. Pearlin and Henry E. Richards, "Equity: A Study of Union Democracy," in Walter Galenson and Seymour Martin Lipset, ed., *Labor and Trade Unionism, An Interdisciplinary Reader* (New York: John Wiley, 1960), p. 277.
[37] Seidman, London, Karsh, and Tagliacozzo, *op. cit.*, pp. 195–196. See also Arnold Tannenbaum, "Mechanisms of Control in Local Trade Unions," *The British Journal of Sociology* (London), December 1956.

would be 10–1 for the strike. I knew because I was in the plant, I knew what the workers were talking [about] in the plant and it came out 12–1 for the strike."[38]

The effect of a vital shop society is to inject another diffusing effect in the structure of power and authority in the local union, particularly the larger local union. Seidman and his associates concluded on the basis of their case investigations:

> In a large factory, with a wide variety of departments separated both spatially and in terms of function, and perhaps with different shifts as well, there tends to exist not one but several informal shop societies with somewhat different and sometimes conflicting interests. Each such grouping may then function as a pressure group within the union, sometimes "packing" the meeting to exert maximum influence on the officers or on the issue under consideration. Whether present or not, unified groups of this sort, particularly if they are large or of strategic importance in production, cannot be ignored by officers who want to have an effective union and who also want to be re-elected.[39]

LAW

The LMRDA, specifically in the "Bill of Rights" and election titles, shapes the course of the local union meeting in three important respects: first it establishes the indispensability of the meeting (or referendum) in the enactment of specified categories of local union legislation; second, it sets up procedural standards; and third, it seeks to protect certain rights of the individual union member at the union meeting.

The following local union enactments must be approved by the local union membership either at a union meeting or via a referendum: (a) increases in the "rate" of local union dues and initiation fees; (b) the levying of assessments; and (c) the election of officers.

Procedurally all of these enactments must be voted on by secret ballot. In the case of (a) and (b) above "reasonable notice" must be given by the local of the intention to put these issues to a vote at a membership meeting. The notice of an election meeting must be mailed fifteen days in advance to each member in good standing. The elections must be held according to the relevant consti-

[38] Kovner and Lahne, *op. cit.*, p. 4.
[39] Seidman, London, Karsh, and Tagliacozzo, *op. cit.*, p. 195–196.

tution and by-laws where these are not in conflict with LMRDA. When read with other provisions of the election title, the law almost seems to require a nomination meeting before the election meeting.

The law undertakes to safeguard individual membership rights at the union meeting. There is, first of all, a general "equal rights" provision for the membership, which among other things applies (a) to voting in elections, and (b) to attendance and participation "in the deliberations and voting upon the business of such meetings, subject to reasonable rules and regulations in [for the purposes of this discussion, the local] organization's constitution and by-laws." In addition the law protects freedom of speech at union meetings, again subject to reasonable rules.

5

THE BUSINESS AGENT

Union leadership in the local union derives its fundamental character from the base on which it operates. The base of leadership is either the local union office, the typical situation for the multiplant nonfactory local; or the plant, the typical situation for the factory local. The critical difference between these types of leadership turns on whether they are full-time leaders paid by the union or part-time leaders who earn their livelihood working in the plant.[1]

The union office-based leadership is in general the business agent or his equivalent. (Factory local leadership is examined in the next chapter.) The business agent is most often a full-time union official, characteristically operating in nonfactory types of employment as in the construction trades, retail trade, and the teamsters. It is not rare, however, to find the business agent operating in factory locals, particularly where the origins of a particular factory union local may reside in a nonfactory situation—as, for example, the Machinists and the International Brotherhood of Electrical Workers in mass-production locals. In these situations there is a tendency for the business agent structure to be grafted on the factory situation, if for no other reason than this has been the customary way of administering the union's affairs.

FUNCTIONS

The business agent in the construction trades is the prototype and his functions are characteristic of business agents generally. These functions are:

[1] I am indebted to Van Dusen Kennedy's highly suggestive monograph, *Non-Factory Unionism and Labor Relations,* University of California, Berkeley, Institute of Industrial Relations, 1955, for many helpful insights.

1. To represent the union in bargaining for an agreement with employers and groups of employers.

2. To act as an employment agency in referring members to jobs on request of contracting employers.

3. To protect the local union's jurisdiction as against the claims of other unions.

4. To police the various worksites under his control to see that union standards are adhered to.

5. To participate in the activities of various local labor movement bodies—notably the building trades council, the central labor body, and the local and state councils of his own union—in order to represent the interests of his local union and its members.

A union's formulation of the business agent's responsibilities is seen in the way the IBEW has set forth the requirements of the job.

> He is the contact man between the members and the employers. He keeps a vigilant eye on all shops and jobs to see that no violations of working agreements occur, and when disputes arise, settles them as quickly as possible. He has full supervision over handling of jobs for unemployed members and sees that the work is distributed fairly. In company with business representatives of local unions of other crafts, through the Central Labor and Buildings Trades Councils he is active in promoting the general union activity of his community. He is held responsible by the International Office for the protection of the jurisdiction of the electrical workers in his territory. An important part of his duties is the handling of the union office, and maintaining accurate statistical information relative to hours and wages of the members.[2]

In "Illini City" the construction business agents acted:

1. To negotiate or to lead a negotiation with the contractors over the term of the annual contracts. Most of the locals had bargaining committees, including the business agent; some of the business agents functioned as lone wolves in negotiations and then reported back to the membership.

2. To see that the terms of the contract and the work rules of the union were being adhered to on the job. While all union

[2] *Your Trade Union—the IBEW*, International Brotherhood of Electrical Workers (n.d.) p. 15.

jobs had stewards, the business agent still bore a responsibility to keep a general eye on the situation.

3. To see that union contractors did not perform work with nonunion men.

4. To see that outside contractors were registered with the Building Trades Council, employed union labor, and followed union work rules.

5. To settle grievances which the stewards were unable to settle on the job.

6. To protect the jurisdiction of the union and to straighten out disputes with other business agents.

7. To see that membership remained in good standing.

8. To meet the requests of contractors for union help and to assign workers to specific jobs. This was rarely a strict rotation process and the agent had to exercise considerable discretion.

9. To act as adviser to individual members on personal and family matters and to help out in critical situations.

10. To represent the union in dealings with the outside world— the community at large, government agencies, politicians, charity organizations, etc.[3]

The business agent normally functions from a position of strength, both in relation to the employers and to his membership. In relation to individual employers, the balance of power is weighted in favor of the business agent; first, because the business agent is likely to be the major source of manpower, and second, because the typical employer dealing with a business agent is a relatively small-scale employer without great resources for resistance. To some extent—considerable in recent years— this favorable position of the business agent is offset by the extent to which employers organize in associations locally and regionally.

But this power of the business agent involves responsibilities as well, the chief of which is that the business agent sees clearly that his policies have a good deal to do with whether his employer can stay in business or not; the business agent is highly sensitive to the immediate employment consequences of his poli-

[3] *Labor-Management Relations in Illini City*, vol. 1, University of Illinois, Institute of Labor and Industrial Relations, 1953, vol. 1, p. 691.

cies—in favor of his members, to be sure, but in a very real sense in favor of his employers. It is from this character of the relationship between the business agent and his employer that the business agent tends to develop what will shortly be described as a "man-in-the-middle" perception of his role.

In relation to his members, the business agent is also in a relatively strong position because they are dispersed over many work sites, because they are also obligated to him for jobs, and because, finally, as a local-wide officer he knows more about job conditions than any individual member is likely to know. The union member is in the nature of the situation weaker in dealing with his employer than is his business agent, and so he must rely on his business agent to protect his interests.

MAN-IN-THE-MIDDLE

The business agent characteristically regards himself as the man "in the middle between the contractor and the union."[4] As a middleman he sees himself as seeking a common ground between the exaggerated demands (the business agent believes) of his members and what it takes to get along with and keep his employers in business.

The Laborers business agent on Illini City tries to keep a "difficult bunch" in line.[5] The Teamsters business agent in Illini City sees his job as "selling my men on the best deal."[6] A business agent in an Eastern city observed, "We've got a lot of hotheads we have to hold down. They're ready to strike at the drop of a button. We don't like that."[7] And from another business agent in the same area, "If we didn't have effective opposition [from the employer], the membership would drive me to the wall with unreasonable demands."[8] A Retail Clerks business agent in a large Midwestern city sees the union "as a buffer between management and the clerks. Each has their complaints about something the other is doing. Neither the workers nor management are always right, but through the union they can work out their differences." The function of the union as he sees it is to give

[4] George Strauss, "The Business Agent in the Building Trades," *Industrial and Labor Relations Review*, January 1957, p. 237.

[5] *Illini City*, vol. 1, p. 682.

[6] *Ibid.*, p. 571.

[7] Herbert S. Parnes, *Union Strike Votes*, Princeton University, Department of Economics and Sociology, Industrial Relations Section, 1956, p. 62.

[8] *Ibid.*, p. 63.

management "a fair shake."[9] The business agent, in a factory situation as it happens, sees his middleman's role in the same terms as other business agents.

A union business agent can't be a business agent if he has a one-sided view—the union isn't always right!

You have to realize that each side [management and labor] has reasons for what it does. You can't belittle. You must realize that management has reasons too. . . . The poor agent tries to force his will through—he doesn't try to understand why management acts as it does. . . .

You've got to get all there is for the people but treat them [management] with respect; realize their problems; be fair, don't take advantage because you have the upper hand. You have to build good labor-management relations for the future.[10]

The business agent thus perceives his role as something much more than a submissive register of the wills of his constituents. He sees himself as a leader who must literally lead: "The business agent recognizes that he must be sensitive to the demands of the membership, but he has faith in his power to shape many of these demands along appropriate lines."[11]

The Illini City Laborers business agent said:

. . . that he wasn't one for letting one of his boys question his authority. It was either he or the steward (talking about a jurisdictional problem) and if he called the decision, the steward had better live up to it. . . . "It's the case of him or me—one of us goes down the road. If I'm right, as long as I'm business agent, that's that. If I happen to be wrong, then I have to let somebody else take my job."[12]

The drift of attitudes among a group of factory local business agents went along this line:

[9] Wayne Lawrence Inks, *Unionism in the Retail Food Industry: A Local Case Study of Structure and Function,* unpublished M.A. thesis, University of Illinois, Institute of Labor and Industrial Relations, 1959, p. 110.
[10] Hjalmar Rosen and R. A. H. Rosen, "The Union Business Agent Looks at Collective Bargaining," *Personnel Magazine,* May 1957.
[11] *Ibid.*
[12] *Illini City,* vol. 1, p. 682–683. See also Arnold Robert Weber, *Union Decision-Making in Collective Bargaining: A Case Study on the Local Level,* 1951 M.A., University of Illinois, Labor and Industrial Relations.

"You have to explain and teach (and often select) the stewards and committeemen so they will keep you informed and support you with the rank and file."

Conspicuous by its absence [observe the investigators] however is any mention of the stewards' or committeemen's *active* part in negotiations per se. Actually in most cases the bargaining committee plays only a supporting role.

If the committee attempts to dominate the situation, pursuing its own interests or the specific demands of the membership, its action meets strong disapproval from the business agents. Moreover, the business agents made quite a point of "control of committee and stewards" in evaluating the competence of their fellow agents. The poor agent, in their eyes, is one who "lets the committee get out of hand—loses control."[13]

The business agent is the product of a complex of forces that tends to produce aggressive personalities. There is, nevertheless, wide leeway for unique styles of leadership to assert themselves.

CHARISMATIC LEADER

The "charismatic" leader literally leads in a creative, imaginative way. By temperament he seeks the new because it is new and minimizes the old because it is old. He thinks in broad scope and magnitude. He is public-relations minded, and he thinks in terms of plan and program.

We have undoubtedly an authentic charismatic leader in the business manager of Local 3 of the IBEW, Harry Van Arsdale. "The most important single force within the administrative life of the union is the personality, human sympathy, historical perception, philosophy and energy" of the business manager of Local 3.[14] "There are gaps in the man in the human sense, but he is still basically a rank-and-filer. He thinks like his men and reacts like them, but with greater acuteness. He has the dedication of a crackpot, but he is enormously sane."[15] Van Arsdale "administers efficiently and often in a consciously ingenuous manner. His methods are controlled and tight. He surrounds these devices, however, with a democratic spirit of friendliness, open-

[13] Rosen and Rosen, "The Union Business Agent," *op. cit.*
[14] Maurice Neufeld, *Day In and Out with Local 3, IBEW* (Ithaca: Cornell University Press, 1951), p. 4.
[15] Charles Yale Harrison, "Van Arsdale's Tight Little Island," *The Reporter,* April 11, 1950, p. 13.

ness, and genuine interest in individuals. The breath of freedom within the administration of Local 3 is therefore partly illusory and partly real."[16]

The core of the local's interest is, to be sure, the classic job control of the craft union, but with the difference in Local 3 that job control has been given new dimensions. Van Arsdale has created the "welfare union" which is breath-taking even in a simple listing: death benefits, pensions, disability pensions, supplemental pensions, hospitalization and surgery, serious injury benefit, tool and workclothes replacement benefit, convalescent home benefit, scholarship benefit, dental benefit, diagnostic and preventive services, a loan fund, housing projects, and vacation expenses. "Yet," *Fortune* Magazine comments, "the industry seems to manage the burden." Contractors themselves have been the beneficiaries of the welfare union. A surplus in the administrative fund of the welfare plan was spent for a $10,000 life insurance policy for two principals of each of the 600-member firms and for assessments for the New York State Disability Fund, which are usually borne by the employers.[17]

Van Arsdale wears a belt buckle which bears the initials "N B" which stand for Naftel Bedsole, a deceased business agent of Local 3. Van Arsdale says he got from Bedsole his guiding slogan, "Give me hills to climb and strength to climb them." According to a *New York Times* profile of Van Arsdale:

> When he [Van Arsdale] became president of the city's merged labor council . . . it took him six hours of rapid-fire talking to outline his "priority projects" for union and community betterment. "If I seem impatient, it's because I am impatient," Harry Van Arsdale, Jr. told his somewhat dazed associates in the council's executive board. That was after he had listed an activity catalogue that ranged from Brooklyn to Bangkok.[18]

Another highly creative local union leader has been Harold Gibbons, director of the St. Louis Joint Council of Teamsters and currently executive vice-president under James Hoffa. Gibbons' base comprises the several locals of Retail, Wholesale, and Warehouse Workers in St. Louis. His Labor Health Institute has been

[16] Neufeld, *op. cit.*
[17] Quoted in *ibid.*, p. 61.
[18] *The New York Times*, "Dynamic Union Scholar, Harry Van Arsdale, Jr.," April 3, 1959.

regarded as a pioneer and model of superior health care financed by a negotiated health and welfare plan.

In December 1945 Gibbons received the CIO award for carrying out a no-discrimination policy. Among the activities for which the union received this award: (1) engaging in inter-racial sports in St. Louis's largest public park, thereby establishing a precedent which led to general use of the park's sports facilities by Negroes; (2) holding inter-racial banquets and balls in some St. Louis hotels, leading to a no-discrimination policy in at least one of them; (3) employing Negro office girls; (4) putting no-discrimination clauses into contracts with employers; (5) standing firm against wildcat strikes called to protest the upgrading of Negroes.[19]

When a sample of the membership was asked who they thought decides policies in the union, 20 per cent said the union director—that is, Gibbons—39 per cent said the stewards' council, 30 per cent said the rank-and-file members, and 10 per cent answered they didn't know.[20] Under Gibbons' leadership the union has developed ambitious programs in education, in small group organization, and in community and political participation. The consensus is that Gibbons is the most powerful labor leader in the City of St. Louis.

It is reported that Gibbons earns $15,000 a year as secretary-treasurer of his home local, including the expense account. There has been criticism of Gibbons' "high living." His critics think Gibbons is "power-mad" and Gibbons himself says, "Sure, I like authority—because it lets me get things done."[21]

Gibbons has been a specific subject of the McClellan committee investigation, and the committee found,

Harold J. Gibbons, international vice-president of the Teamsters and head of the St. Louis Joint Council No. 13 has been consistent in his denial of democratic rights to his critics and to the critics of the policies of James R. Hoffa. Mr. Gibbons has long proclaimed his devotion to the cause of democracy and civil rights. He apparently wants these rights for himself, but not for others within the framework of the Teamsters Union.

[19] Arnold Rose, *Union Solidarity* (Minneapolis: University of Minnesota Press, 1952), p. 26; p. 55, fn. 20.
[20] *Ibid.*, p. 55.
[21] "Harold Gibbons—Hoffa's Left Hand," *The New Republic,* September 9, 1957.

His manipulation of votes in the election in Joint Council 13 was a crude but completely undemocratic attempt to insure his own election as president of Joint Council 13. In this instance, Gibbons viewed the Teamsters' constitution with the widest possible latitude, giving himself every possible break in interpretation.

But when it became his turn to rule in cases involving opponents of the Hoffa-Gibbons regime in Joplin and Springfield, Mo. his interpretations fell into the narrowest possible category, and were designed to eliminate any and all honest rank-and-file opposition within those unions.

In Springfield an incompetent officer was thrown out by the international. His successor conducted an honest and capable administration, but the local was thrown into trusteeship by Hoffa and Gibbons appointed as trustee. He thereupon appointed the same officer who had previously been thrown out for incompetence to run the affairs of the local, and appointed as business agent Branch Wainwright, who had a long criminal record and had only recently emerged from the Missouri State Penitentiary. Members of the local who opposed the officers placed in there by Gibbons found themselves unable to secure employment in the city of Springfield.[22]

IDEOLOGICAL LEADER

There is the kind of local union business agent or his equivalent whom I have designated as ideological. The ideology need not be, and is increasingly not, cast in the traditional Marxist mold. It is ideological in the sense that the leader has a commitment to some reflective view of society, of labor-management relations, or of the role of the union.

The ideological leader has much in common with the charismatic leader in his disposition to move out ahead of the membership. But the ideological leader differs from the charismatic leader in that his reference for action is likely to be some orderly rationale. Where the charismatic leader moves on the basis of intuition, the ideological leader moves on the basis of the larger view of the situation. Like the charismatic leader, he believes that it is the function of the leader to lead, and to lead vigorously. There has, for example, always been a strong ideological tinge to Gibbons but the combination of Hoffa and health makes Gib-

[22] McClellan investigation, *Second Interim Report*, Report No. 621, 86th Cong., 1st Sess. 1959, p. 112.

bons rather more eclectic in his choice of goals than is consistent with the ideological model.

Abraham Chatman, the manager of the Rochester Joint Board of the Amalgamated Clothing Workers is probably an authentic example of the ideological leader. Sidney Hillman's philosophy of union-management cooperation has provided the foundation stone of Chatman's approach to the problems of the Rochester men's clothing market. The Amalgamated organization in Rochester is strong and Chatman's position as joint manager is "unchallenged."[23]

In the opinion of the workers, company executives, and union officers, Chatman

> has retained his position through genuine popularity. While many of the workers are aware that the leadership of their organization appears to be self-perpetuating, almost all vehemently asserted that this was the democratic expression of the membership and that no one, not even Abraham Chatman, could hold his office without rank-and-file approval.

The ingredients of the ideology as it operates here can be characterized by what has come to be known as the Amalgamated's industry-wide perspective. Union decisions nationally and locally are based on the health of the whole industry "rather than on temporary or local opportunities to gain a concession." The decisions may at times run counter to the sentiments of the rank and file

> such as moderation in wage demands when costs are soaring or strict adherence to a contract, when in the opinion of the workers, a strike or slowdown has been justified. And again the question must be raised: could a truly democratic organization maintain such a logical and reasoned course and still retain its effective unity? The answer here seems to be "yes" and the reason is this: over the years the philosophy that only what is good for the industry can, in the long run, be good for the workers, has become thoroughly accepted by the membership.

Chatman's characteristic method of operation is illustrated by excerpts from the minutes of the union joint board. For example:

[23] Donald B. Straus, *Causes of Industrial Peace under Collective Bargaining, Hickey-Freeman Co. and ACWA, Case Study No. 4,* National Planning Association; (January 1949), p. 60 *passim.*

> Last week a group of pressers from Hickey-Freeman requested the office to secure an increase in wages for them. The manager informed them that such a move at the present time is impossible; however, when the time comes that it will be possible to secure increases in wages, it will be done for all members in general, and not for any individual group.

Or at another meeting:

> Brother Chatman stated that because time and one-half for overtime [this was in 1936] cannot be enforced in other union markets at the present time, due to uncontrollable causes, he proposed that we follow the procedure in other markets. He urged the Joint Board to be on guard and under these circumstances, not place this market at a disadvantage with other clothing centers because in the long run our membership pays the price for it. The Joint Board adopted the recommendation.

HIGH-POWERED LEADER

The "high-powered" leader is like that charismatic and ideological leader, but he is not as inventive as the former nor as philosophical as the latter. Public employment situations, particularly in local government, have tended to produce high-powered leaders. The power of this sort of leadership tends to show itself in respect to the tactics directed against the employers. Lacking the ordinary channels of collective bargaining and grievance handling characteristic of private employment, the high-powered leader of public employee unionism feels that he is forced to call attention to the needs of his constituents in some dramatic fashion.

Locals of the AFSCME are likely to go in for what a representative described as the "tactic of the calculated squeeze. 'We hit the politician where it hurts, in his public prestige.' Recognizing that 'the politician treasures good will as a businessman treasures a favorable balance on the black side of the ledger' AFSCME has found that 'an embarrassing picket line, or a demonstration, at City Hall at the right moment, can work wonders.' "[24] Prominent practitioners in what has been called here the tactic of the calculated squeeze among others have been Jerry Wurf in New York and John Zinos in Milwaukee.

The pre-eminent practitioner of high-powered tactics in relation to the employer is, of course, Michael Quill of the Transport

[24] *Business Week*, March 21, 1959, p. 117.

Workers Union. Although Quill is president of the Transport Workers Union, his major eminence derives from his functioning as a local union leader in a local bargaining relationship with the now publicly owned transit system of the City of New York. Quill has been extraordinarily adept in using psychological warfare and direct action. The psychological warfare takes the form of threatening strike at peak periods, demonstrations, mass meetings. In direct action Quill has used slowdown and sick leave. One labor reporter characterized Quill's formula as "humor, audacity, and blarney."[25]

High-powered leadership among public employees shapes up in another form in a local of teachers. The president is the only full-time official. The president appoints committees and is the chief lobbyist of the union. His "virtual unlimited tenure, his presiding over all general, executive, and house [of representatives] meetings, his vast appointive powers, and his ex-officio membership of all committees and delegations makes him a most important figure with almost unlimited powers. . . . His influence and leadership undoubtedly shape the policy and program, the direction of the Chicago Teachers Union."[26] High-powered leadership is, of course, not limited to local unions of public employees, but this sort of leadership thrives in the climate of public employment.

Without being a union man himself, John J. Collins has made a professional career of organizing unions of the independent kind in the petroleum refinery industry. Collins is an "adviser to a dozen unaffiliated unions in tanker fleets of the Esso, Socony, Cities Service, and Tidewater Oil companies. When Collins was the sole representative of the Esso Tanker Men's Union with 1,300 members the union had no hiring hall and no formal right to represent men who were fired."[27]

There is a high-powered business agent in a Retail Clerks local in downstate Illinois who runs the union without even token obeisance to constitutional due process or rules because apparently nobody cares. The local union has no constitution or by-laws

[25] Jack Barbash, *Practice of Unionism* (New York: Harper, 1956), p. 384 ff.

[26] Charles Paul Skibbens, *The Teachers Union: A Study of Its Program, Problems and Possibilities,* unpublished M.S. and I.R. thesis, Loyola University, June 1956.

[27] *The New York Times,* September 10, 1959. See also "Jersey vs. the Internationals," *Fortune Magazine,* October 1950, p. 221.

of its own, although there was apparently some minimal attention paid to the international constitution. There are other officers in the local union—a president, two vice-presidents, a secretary-treasurer, a reporter, a recorder, a guard, a guide, financial committee and three trustees, in addition to a steward system. None of these mechanisms of local union government functioned.[28]

The business agent was also the secretary-treasurer. Vacancies were filled by the business agent's appointment rather than by elections. The incumbent business agent got his job when a vacancy occurred in the office and the international union appointed the incumbent as secretary-treasurer and business agent.

The president didn't preside over meetings in the rare times when they were held because he worked nights. Nor did he attend meetings. In the words of the president, the business agent took care of all of the business. "All I ever do is to sign a few papers now and then. I have to sign all the checks and the contracts. Outside of that I don't do much."[29] The president knew very little about union affairs. He didn't know who the rest of the officers were and he wasn't sure what his term of office was or when it expired. The same situation prevailed with respect to the other officers. The second vice-president was a woman—a checker almost seventy years old, who was in semi-retirement working fifteen hours a week.

The few meetings that were held were presided over by the business agent. He collected the dues—there was no check-off—handled the grievances, negotiated the contracts, and signed up new members. He presided over the meetings and took his own minutes of the meetings. The trustees did hardly anything more than sign their names to the monthly report to the international which was prepared by the business agent. "Regardless of how important the executive board is in theory, in actual practice the local functions without the services of the executive board."[30]

The business agent conducted negotiations by preparing a rough draft of proposals and reporting on them to a special meeting. These pre-negotiation meetings were the only meetings. At these meetings about 75 per cent of the membership attended

[28] Wayne Lawrence Inks, *Unionism in the Retail Food Industry: A Local Case Study of Structure and Function,* unpublished M.A. thesis, University of Illinois, Institute of Labor and Industrial Relations, 1959.
[29] *Ibid.,* p. 70.
[30] *Ibid.,* p. 74.

and then the members got an opportunity to make changes. According to a member:

> Tom [that is, the business agent] brings the contract to us and we go over it and make any changes we want to. Then we vote on it. All the members get an opportunity to express their opinions and then as a group decide what is to be included in the union's demands at the bargaining table.[31]

The business agent sends a copy of the proposed contract to the international for its approval. Green has not arrogated power to himself to accept any company offers without first receiving approval from the membership. Green's concept of the job is that "the union has to act as a buffer between management and the clerks. Each has their complaints about something the other is doing."[32] The business agent almost singlehandedly enforced the contract, but he was not very popular because sometimes even the stewards kept information from the business agent as, for example, when new employees were hired.

The grievance procedure was informal. When a clerk had a grievance he called the business agent. No one whom the investigator talked to, except the business agent, had any notion as to how the dues money was being spent. The investigator concluded:

> It is possible for one man to carry successfully the majority of the union's functions in retail food stores in this particular situation. Successful retail food store unionism, successful from the standpoint of satisfying membership demands, does not necessitate active participation, regular meetings, or committees by either the majority of the members or the officers. . . .
>
> The majority of the unionized clerks perceive their relationship to the union as being only temporary and are therefore not much interested in building a strong or lasting organization. . . . The heterogeneous nature of the membership, particularly in the presence of women and young part-time workers, results in a less aggressive union than might be the case if the membership was comprised of only full-time male clerks.[33]

The "high-powered" business agent may go outside of the arena provided by the union hall or the collective bargaining relationship to express his individuality. Harold Beck is the business

[31] Ibid., p. 100.
[32] Ibid., p. 110.
[33] Ibid., pp. 129–130.

representative of Local 9 of the Office Employees in Milwaukee. He is a member of the school board, a member of the Metropolitan Study Commission where he is vice-chairman of the Land Use and Zoning Committee, and chairman of the Public Information and Education Committee. He has been a member of the Citizens' Urban Renewal Committee, of a committee appointed by the mayor to study the high cost of living, and on another occasion to study the needs and financial problems of the city.[34]

Another Milwaukee business agent, Rex Fransway of Local 494 of the IBEW "is not content just to keep dues rolling in. He works hard at the bread-and-butter chores of Local 494 and somehow finds time to serve on the City Park Commission, the Greater Milwaukee Committee, and the local Boy Scout Commission." Fransway also directs an active political action program. Fransway is concerned with the "public relations" position of the building trades unions. Fransway says, "The old type business agent confined himself strictly to the activities of his organization." And he sees his civic duties as a way of counteracting the image of the old type business agent who is interested only in protecting a narrow craft interest.[35]

ERRAND BOY

The business agent as errand boy, who is so overwhelmed by the complexities of the job and by his need to deal with all demands put upon him that he has lost the capacity to lead, is found in a New York State situation involving a local union—the Amalgamated Association of Street Car, Electric Railway Employees—composed of the employees of the Rochester transit system. "As soon as he steps on the property, he is besieged with many complaints and grievances from the membership. Because his time is spent to a large extent in handling grievances proper planning and record keeping cannot be achieved."[36]

This business agent, who is also the president, handles most grievances from the initial step in the procedure to the final step. A few stewards in the car barns attempt to handle grievances as

[34] *The Milwaukee Journal*, October 5, 1960.
[35] Frank Wallick, "Midwest Charcoal-Grayer Keeps IBEW Local on Toes," *Labor's Daily*, December 7, 1955, p. 3.
[36] Donald W. Hill, *Labor-Management Relations Between the Rochester Transit Corporation and the Amalgamated Association of Street Electric Railway and Motor Coach Employees of America, Division 282, AFL,* unpublished M.S. thesis, New York State School of Industrial and Labor Relations, 1955, p. 101.

they arise, but the majority of them call on the business agent. He runs from office to office presenting grievances to management.

The business agent in this situation feels that the demands that the job makes upon him are so overwhelming that he has to call on the international representative for help frequently. The business agent handles 90 per cent of the grievances at the first level of procedure and 100 per cent at the higher levels.

The union attorney is elected by the membership. Any member can nominate a lawyer from the floor. Apparently the lawyer is voted upon on the basis of ethnic affiliation. The problem in this local union centers about the lack of positive leadership on the part of the business agent and there is a "serious question whether the majority's rights are being protected adequately from the vocal minority."[37]

COLLECTIVE LEADERSHIP

Although the accent in the nonfactory local is on individual leadership, the individual leader does not function in a power vacuum independent of other forces. Only the tightest authoritarian local functions on the basis of the power of one individual. More frequently, the individual leader is the dominant leader, but not the only leader. In the case of Local 3 of the IBEW and Harry Van Arsdale, we find that Van Arsdale's power is based on a key group of electrical construction journeymen in the local.

> All of the less-skilled crafts and trades within Local 3 owe their organization, economic and social welfare, continued existence, and consequently, their administrative life to the power and good will of the electrical construction workers who have repeatedly voted special assessments upon themselves to aid their weaker brothers. These top craftsmen, in turn, give their undivided allegiance to their business manager when the votes are cast.[38]

In an Illini City electricians local (200 members):

> The active membership . . . had a strong voice in the organization. Committees were appointed by the president rather than by the business agent. Bargaining and grievance sessions of a

[37] *Ibid.*, p. 102.
[38] Neufeld, *op. cit.*, pp. 4–5.

general nature were conducted by committees rather than by a single individual. . . .[39]

The business agent as part of a leadership coalition is found in a plumbers local in Boston.[40] The business manager, as he is called, in this local union has been in office for about nine years but has been opposed consistently in elections. In the last election he won by a vote of 478–224. Generally, the business manager's position is hotly contested in bad times; in better times not quite as much.

The business manager is required to report at each meeting concerning meetings attended, including regular meetings of the building trades business agents, job decisions and policies, job disputes, jobs about to begin, construction contracts let, and the general feel of the job situation.[41] A finance board supervises all funds of the local union. The executive board is composed of five members, who are not officers and who are elected for staggered terms of office.

There is a diffusion of power in the local union among the business manager, the finance board, and the executive board. "Since the offices on the executive board are strongly contested, it is not likely that a clean sweep of all offices by one faction could be made at any time."[42]

The characteristic centralization of power in the local union business agent inheres in the economic and technological organization of nonfactory employment. There are, to be sure, business agent systems in factory employment situations but these latter partake of some of the characteristics which exist in sharper focus in the nonfactory local; namely, multiplant jurisdiction, small numbers of workers at each work site and the absence of a "stratified management hierarchy"[43] at the individual work site. Occasionally the factory local approximates a limited business agent function in the person of an international or district representative. This representative performs many of the functions of the business agent but he is not on the direct payroll of the local nor is his constituency limited to the local.

[39] *Illini City*, vol. 1, p. 686.
[40] Edward W. Murphy, *A Study of a Building Trades Local Union,* unpublished M.B.A. thesis, Northeastern University, 1956, p. 25 ff.
[41] *Ibid.*, p. 27.
[42] *Ibid.*, p. 30.
[43] Kennedy, *Non-Factory Unionism*, p. 19.

MEMBERSHIP CONTROL

The considerable authority of the business agent, however, is not necessarily incompatible with membership control. The business agents in the building trades of a moderate-sized city in upstate New York felt most secure when they campaigned twelve months a year. None of these business agents had so solidified his control of the union that he had "little fear of being kicked out." They found "defeat looming" if they were not responsive to the desires of their members. "Membership participation and interest was higher than is common in industrial unions of the same size."[44]

Substantial membership control was found in a large city plumbers local with a membership of about four thousand journeymen and four hundred apprentices. Characteristic comment from rank-and-file members of this local:

> We have a good organization now, we have democracy. You can get up and speak without fear of reprisal and that's always done. I've known steamfitters who had to leave the city because they became marked men who spoke against the leadership. This couldn't happen in our union. He [the business manager] is a different kind of fellow compared to what we had in the old days. . . . He believes in running the union with brains not brawn. . . . He cleaned up the union a long way from what it used to be. . . . We all got a voice now; we can say what we like. It's not like the old days. If a guy tried to argue back with the leaders in those days he'd get conked on the head with a spittoon. We didn't know how the money was spent and when you'd ask you'd more than likely get a beating in the alley behind the hall. Now it's not like that; we have our arguments and disagreements, but we discuss it and after it's decided we're all friends again.[45]

RACKETEERING

It would be wrong to associate the business agent inherently with the exercise of arbitrary power; it would also be wrong not to recognize that the same economic and technological organization out of which the business agent system arises is the same system that creates a propensity for racketeering, collusion, and

[44] George Strauss, "Control by the Membership in Building Trades Unions," *American Journal of Sociology*, May 1956, p. 533 ff.

[45] Joel Seidman, Jack London, Bernard Karsh, and Daisy L. Tagliacozzo, *The Worker Views His Union* (Chicago: University of Chicago Press, 1958), p. 56.

what would appear—from the McClellan Committee and other sources—to be the inevitably accompanying breakdown of constitutional government in the local union.

In general, the pattern of economic organization which creates a propensity toward racketeering and collusion has these characteristics: intense competition among relatively small units, non-factory employment, labor cost as a high proportion of total cost of production—and a high time-and-place utility of manpower; in these racket-prone industries, labor is so strategically situated in the productive process that the employer cannot normally withstand even a temporary delay in the application of labor power.

To the extent that the source material on racketeering and collusion also contain material relating to the quality of local union government, the conclusion seems inescapable that racketeering and collusion go hand-in-hand with the breakdown of constitutional government in the local union: it may be an arguable point as to whether there is a causal relationship.

In the New York "paper local" situation involving the (then) United Automobile Workers—AFL, and the International Brotherhood of Teamsters in New York, the McClellan committee found:

> Some of the most shocking testimony heard by this committee during its first year of operations revolved around the collusive agreements signed by these UAW–AFL leaders with a number of small business operators in New York City, which had the virtual effect of legitimatizing the misery of thousands of Negro and Puerto Rican workers. Contracts were signed calling for the bare national minimum wage—$1 an hour—or slightly more. Out of these munificent sums of $40 or $42 a week, the workers were obliged to pay $25 initiation fees and $3.50 a month dues. There were no welfare funds, no provisions for seniority, and according to the vivid testimony of one of the workers, Bertha Nunez, a 27-year old woman born in Honduras, the factory is unheated in the winter and so hot in the summer that the workers could not work. They were "top-down" contracts signed directly between the union and the employers, with the workers having no right to indicate any choice in the matter.

> The evidence clearly indicated that when the workers did have a choice, the racket-controlled unions were summarily thrown out. A number of employers paraded before the committee and justified the signing of the substandard contracts. . . . Such

deals in the committee's mind were profitable to the employer and in many cases profitable to the union business agent. The ones who suffered were the working men and women who had to live on the wages and under the conditions set for them by these racketeer-controlled unions and unscrupulous gangsters.[46]

In the collusive arrangement between the Chicago Restaurant Association and certain "mobster-dominated locals of the Hotel and Restaurant Employees' Union in the Chicago area" the unions "served only the purpose of giving a cloak of legitimacy to what was nothing more than a pure extortion racket."

> The committee finds that these labor racketeers preyed upon restaurant owners and employees alike, with the latter cast in the unhappy role of hopeless captives from the moment their membership became an accomplished fact, if they ever knew at all that they were in the union. There is testimony that many never did learn that they had been put into the union, and there were still others who were aware of their affiliation but never did find out to which local they belonged.

> There is irrefutable testimony that the employees were never contacted by the union representative about their wages or working conditions and were never told what benefits, if any, they derived from union membership. In a great many of the cases reviewed the committee found that the forced induction of the employees into the union were never accompanied by the formality of a contract. In those cases where a contract did exist, the terms of it were never brought to the attention of the membership. . . .

> The committee finds as an undisputed fact that restaurant operators who dealt with the union representatives in the manner heretofore described profited from the arrangement to the extent of thousands of dollars annually because the union representatives interested only in the sustained flow of dues payment into their hands, never made the lightest effort to enforce the prevailing minimum wage scale specified by the standard contract for the Chicago area.[47]

Collusion between local leaders of the Operating Engineers and employing contractors was endemic. According to John De-Koning, dissident cousin of the reigning family of Local 138:

[46] McClellan investigation, *Interim Report* (1958), pp. 218–219.
[47] McClellan investigation, *Second Interim Report,* part 1 (1959), p. 673.

The union [i.e., Local 138] through its jurisdiction has the authority to adjudicate how many men should be on a job and the conditions of the job. The union in collusion with the contractors of the Nassau-Suffolk area, the favorite ones, they would interpret the contract in a soft light.

In other words, the best way to describe it, is if there is a million dollar job, and if a firm like Hendrickson was figuring the job, they could write their own ticket. They could do the job with no particular problem, with maybe 50% less required help than an outside contractor would.[48]

The trustees of Local 542 of the Operating Engineers [Hunter P. Wharton and Harry W. Lavery], previously under the domination of Joseph S. Fay,

. . . participated in a questionable contract signed with the Standard Dithulithic Company which called for lower wages than those other contractors in the same area were forced to pay. The testimony of Wharton and Lavery on this point was tortuous and contradictory. It left the record with the admissions that the Standard Dithulithic contract was inferior to other contracts, and that members of Local 542, forced to work under this contract were denied the opportunity of looking at it or finding out what its provisions were.[49]

The Operating Engineers conformed in some measure to the appearances of union constitutional government. That is, there were business agents who visited jobs, there were constitutions and local union meetings, officers were elected, and collective bargaining was carried on. Members generally knew they were members. If there was some shadow, there was no substance, to constitutional government in many locals of the Operating Engineers. In its detailed investigations of Operating Engineers local unions in suburban New York, Philadelphia, and San Francisco, the McClellan committee found:

1. The systematic disenfranchisement of members by denial of voting rights and the indiscriminate imposition of receiverships.

Only 46% of the union's 280,000 members are even allowed to vote for their own officers. . . .

As in the case with other IUOE locals, Local 138 was split into various divisions—i.e., Local 138, Local 138a, and Local 138b—

[48] McClellan investigation, part 19 (1958), pp. 7791–7792.
[49] McClellan investigation, *Interim Report* (1958), p. 440.

and only members of Local 138 were permitted to vote for officers. The committee testimony showed that there was no regular manner in which an operating engineer on Long Island could gain admission into parent Local 138, but that such advancement was based on the whim and caprice of Mr. William DeKoning and his friends rather than on a standard of ability as an operating engineer.[50]

2. The integrity of Local 138's governing processes were impaired by permitting employers and their representatives to function as voting members in the local. Between 160 and 170 of the 500-member Local 138 (the branch of the local that could vote for its own officers) were employers.[51]

3. The dimensions of geographical jurisdiction had the effect of disenfranchising large numbers of local union members. The local based in San Francisco covered northern California, northern Nevada, Utah, and the Hawaiian Islands.[52] Local 542 based in Philadelphia covered thirty-four counties in Pennsylvania and the entire state of Delaware.[53] None of these locals appeared to have procedures for sublocal units to compensate for the broad geographic coverage.

4. Systematic suppression of opposition and criticism by the local officers in power. In Local 138 the committee found "that all opposition to the DeKonings was remorselessly suppressed, often in a violent manner."[54] In Local 542 in Philadelphia, T. C. McCarty "was beaten by union goons after protesting the management of Local 542. The evidence shows that Wharton ordered the use of union funds to defend the men who participated in the assault on McCarty and to pay their fines after they were convicted."[55]

Collusion of a more cautious kind characterized the relationship between certain Meat Cutter locals in New York headed by the Block brothers, and the A & P stores. On this point the McClellan committee found:

> . . . that the A & P and high-ranking officials of the Meat Cutters Union participated in an elaborate conspiracy to force the more than 10,000 unorganized eastern division store em-

[50] *Ibid.*, pp. 437–438.
[51] McClellan investigation, part 19 (1958), p. 7756.
[52] *Ibid.*, p. 7514.
[53] *Ibid.*, p. 7924.
[54] McClellan investigation, *Interim Report* (1958), p. 438.
[55] *Ibid.*, p. 440.

ployees into the union in ruthless and calculated disregard of their rights to be represented by a collective bargaining agent of their own choice.

The quid-pro-quo for this highly improper and collusive arrangement was the secret guarantee by regional and national officers of the Meat Cutters Union that the A & P would retain the then existing 45-hour work week until 1957, an extremely attractive and profitable incentive for the A & P measurable according to the company's own records in millions of dollars.[56]

The Blocks in the Amalgamated Meat Cutters New York City Locals 342 and 640 went through the motions of conforming to constitutional procedure but the McClellan committee nevertheless found

. . . that the 1952 election of officers, where no notice was given to the membership of the proposed balloting and where those in attendance cast token ballots based upon continuing the incumbent administration in office for another four years. . . . When opposition did crystallize in 1956, the Block administration forces improperly used funds from the union treasury for propaganda purposes and spent $3,300 for poll watchers from the dues money of the members.[57]

Racketeering among the East Coast Longshoremen (ILA) was accompanied by a pattern of antidemocratic practices.

1. The failure, in a large number of cases, to maintain democratic standards and procedures in conducting the affairs of the local.

2. The failure to hold periodic elections in many local unions. Certain locals have failed to hold elections of officers for a period of 10 years or more.

3. The failure of some locals to have bank accounts. . . .

4. The failure for long periods of time to hold regular meetings or special meetings.

5. The failure properly to elect delegates to the wage-scale conference. Although the locals are required to elect delegates to the Wage Scale Conference, which is the collective bargaining agency for the union, the board found that in many of the

[56] McClellan investigation, *Second Interim Report,* part 1 (1959), p 303.
[57] *Ibid.,* p. 373.

locals the officers designate themselves as delegates without holding an election or consulting the membership.

6. The failure to keep adequate records, including those dealing with finances. Some locals have no financial records.

7. The failure to bond officers handling funds of locals in accordance with the requirements of the International Longshoremen's Association constitution.

8. The failure in many cases periodically to audit the financial affairs of each local by a certified public accountant.[58]

The considerable power and authority of the business agent system arise out of economic and social necessities, most frequently found in the nonfactory local but found to some degree in certain kinds of factory locals. Characteristically the business agent uses the individual power and authority inherent in the situation. Not infrequently business agents either do not choose to, or are inhibited from otherwise utilizing the full potential of authority. In these cases, either because of temperament or because of particular political circumstances, the accent is on collective leadership with the business agent functioning only as part of the collective leadership group.

The substantial individual power exercised by the business agent, however, proves not to be incompatible with substantial membership control. At the same time this power of the business agent will from time to time burst out of the boundaries of constitutional government and, when it does, it is not infrequently part of a racketeering-collusion context.

By the same token the room which the business agent has for free action also contributes to a boldness, imagination, and inventiveness in the local's activities that contribute mightily to the beneficial effect of the local on the union's members, on the industry, and in the community.

[58] New York State Board of Inquiry on Longshore Industry Work Stoppage, October–November 1951, Port of New York, *Final Report to the Industrial Commissioner*, State of New York, January 22, 1952 (mimeo.), pp. 23–24.

6

LEADERSHIP IN THE FACTORY LOCAL

There are three significant levels of leadership in the factory local union: (1) the full-time paid officer in larger locals, who is frequently called a business manager; equally as often he may be designated as the president or secretary-treasurer of the local union; (2) the unpaid local-wide leader: president, secretary-treasurer, and chairman of the bargaining committee, as well as members of the bargaining committee are typically the most important local-wide officers in addition to such housekeeping local-wide officers as trustees, sergeants-at-arms, and members of the executive board; and (3) shop leadership—that is, the steward.

Most factory local unions, even the larger ones, do not have full-time paid officers. The only full-time paid work, where it exists at all, is performed by a clerical employee in the office of the local union. Invariably the officers of the local union continue to work at their jobs in the factory and receive some nominal monthly fee for their services, which may take the form of a remission of dues and of lost-time perquisites.

COLLECTIVE LEADERSHIP

The salient fact about the leadership of the factory local union is that the locus of power is more likely to be in a collective leadership group rather than in one dominant leader. Just as the setting in which the nonfactory union functions creates a proneness toward individual leadership, the setting of the factory union creates a proneness toward collective leadership.

Collective leadership in the factory union can be attributed to these characteristics of the factory situation:

1. The relative permanency of the employer-employee relationship at one work site creates the underlying conditions for the development of a shop society. This is by way of contrast with

the *union hall* society of the nonfactory union. The existence of the more integrated shop society in the factory employment[1] situation exposes the officers at all levels to a more sustained exposure to their constituency. The opportunities for face-to-face encounter between the leadership and the membership are multiplied in the factory situation.

2. The leadership of the factory union local plays a more limited role and necessarily exercises less power vis-à-vis management and vis-à-vis the individual union member. The hiring hall in factory employment is either rare or nonexistent. The employer does the hiring; this fact diminishes or completely eliminates the kind of employment function which the business agent in the nonfactory union situation exercises. The scope of the bargaining unit in the factory situation is likely to be occupationally broader, thus minimizing the power which derives from policing jurisdiction. The presence of larger numbers of workers at one work site in the factory, in contrast to the relatively small number of workers in the nonfactory situation at the work site, gives the individual member the courage of numbers in confronting leadership.

3. The probabilities are that factory management, company for company, is in a stronger bargaining position in relation to its union leadership than is the nonfactory management. The factory management is characteristically better organized internally to carry out its personnel and collective bargaining function, its financial staying-power is greater, and it is not quite as dependent on human labor as is the nonfactory management. Factories are capital-intensive in contrast to the labor-intensive quality of the nonfactory situation. This latter fact also makes it less attractive for factory management to seek differential treatment through the back door in its labor costs—the entering wedge for racketeering and collusion in the nonfactory situation.

The net effect of these contrasting settings, quite aside from individual personality variations, is to accent personal power in the case of the nonfactory situation and to inhibit personal power in the factory situation. Thus, the styles of leadership of business agents—that is, charismatic, ideological, etc.—exist in the factory situation, as we shall shortly see, but with nothing like the free-

[1] Van Dusen Kennedy, *Non-Factory Unionism and Labor Relations,* University of California, Berkeley, Institute of Industrial Relations, 1955.

wheeling quality of a Van Arsdale or a Gibbons in nonfactory locals. Instead the leadership operates through coalitions. The typical leader, then, in the factory local situation is the unpaid leader rather than the paid leader, and power tends to rest in a collective leadership rather than in an individual leader

PERQUISITES

The job of the factory union leader is not without its perquisites. The most significant appears to be the opportunity to be away from the production job on company-paid time or lost-time paid by the union. Payment by management for the handling of grievances by union personnel is widespread and in many larger factories the handling of grievances, particularly for the chairman of the grievance committee, becomes almost a full-time job. One local union officer analyzed the situation this way:

> The top [shop] committee doesn't even work. The chairman of the top committee is supposed to have seven hours a day for bargaining; the rest of the members five hours. But you can't use a man for one hour or three hours in lots of jobs in the shop; so it means that they don't work at all, lots of times, and the foreman just assumes that he has to get along without the top committeeman doing any work—unless the company decides to tie them up for a while and keep them at work as much as they can.[2]

The unpaid local leader gets a feeling of power and authority out of his union position which comes from being able to deal with management on an equal basis. "You know, I didn't even know what the general manager looked like before I joined the union, and now I sit right across from him two or three times a week and when I talk he has to listen."[3] When a group of local UAW leaders were asked what keeps leaders active in local union affairs 52 per cent said, in effect, that they liked being able to prevent the boss "from pushing us around."[4]

[2] Eli Chinoy, "Local Union Leadership," in Alvin Gouldner, *Studies in Leadership* (New York: Harper, 1950), p. 164. See also U.S. Department of Labor, Bureau of Labor Statistics, *Collective Bargaining Clauses: Company Pay for Time Spent on Union Business,* Bulletin #1266, 1959: Leonard R. Sayles and George Strauss, *The Local Union: Its Place in the Industrial Plant* (New York: Harper, 1953), p. 117.

[3] Sayles and Strauss, *op. cit.,* p. 118.

[4] Constance S. Tonat, *A Case Study of a Local Union: Participation, Loyalty and Attitudes of Local Union Members,* unpublished M.A. thesis, Wayne State University, 1956, p. 101.

Superseniority provisions in many agreements permit union officers to have preferred treatment in layoff on the theory that the union officer who is also a plant employee will be unwilling to stick his neck out for his constituents unless he has some assurance that management will not discriminate against him for his aggressiveness.[5] Nor does the local union officer resist the opportunities to be involved in union affairs away from the shop— membership in the central labor body or in union conferences away from his home city. All these perquisites add up to relief from the tedium of factory routine and the chance to cut a wider swath than is possible in the workaday life of the factory.

There is also what Father Purcell calls "game-mindedness." In his investigation of Packinghouse Workers local union leadership in the Swift plant in Chicago, he found that "some men simply enjoy the politics of union leadership as a sheer engrossing game like a boxing match, or a ball game or a horse race. There is a thrill in competition and in strategy."[6]

The lower levels of leadership are frequently not attractive at all. Consequently, rank-and-file members have to be coopted into the job of steward, to use the most common example.

BONDS OF LEADERSHIP

Within the framework of constitutional authority and processes the kinds of ties that hold collective leadership together vary widely from one situation to another. The bonds of leadership most frequently observed have been derived from (1) strategic position in the government of the union; (2) high wage and skill status; (3) ideology; (4) ethnic ties; (5) long service; and (6) chance.

It is likely that the most pervasive bond for the exercise of collective leadership is the location of the group in the government of the union. For most factory unions, the most important function is collective bargaining, and the group that directs collective bargaining is more often than not likely to be the group exercising the greatest influence in the local union. This ordinarily means the bargaining committee or its equivalent. Power in a Chicago UAW local was located in the shop committee rather than in the executive board because the shop committee "negotiates the

[5] Bureau of National Affairs, *Collective Bargaining Negotiations and Contracts*, 75:3.

[6] Theodore V. Purcell, *The Worker Speaks His Mind, on Company and Union* (Cambridge: Harvard University Press, 1953), p. 210.

collective bargaining agreement and processes the grievances that arise under it; this body consists of seven committeemen, each of whom is selected from a 'zone,' a major department or a cluster of nearby departments."[7] In a Buffalo UAW local the shop committee and the president were found to be the major power force.[8] In four industrial locals in Michigan, the bargaining committee was found "to exercise a considerable degree of influence on other matters in the local" because of its "critical role" in the negotiation process.[9] In the Illini City UAW–AFL local in the grain-processing industry:

> The most important committee of the union was the bargaining committee. . . . The chairman of the bargaining committee was the only full-time official of the local. His salary was paid by the company at the rate of his old job, in which he retained his seniority, and he was supplied an office in the plant of the company. He was the key union representative of the grievance procedure. . . . Apart from the main officers and the members of the bargaining committee the most important local union figures were the stewards.[10]

The centralization of the leadership function in a packinghouse local of the Amalgamated Meat Cutters was located in the executive board comprising the two full-time officers plus six additional members.

> The six male members of this board constitute the negotiating committee for the local. In addition, these board members occupy prominent positions in all union functions: they are chairmen of all important committees and sometimes constitute the entire membership of a committee; they represent the local on various labor and civic bodies at city and state levels; and they are the local's delegates to the union's regional meetings and international conventions.[11]

[7] Joel Seidman, Jack London, Bernard Karsh, Daisy L. Tagliacozzo, *The Worker Views His Union* (Chicago: University of Chicago Press, 1958), p. 96.

[8] Joseph Shister and William Hamovitch, *Conflict and Stability in Labor Relations: A Case Study,* University of Buffalo, 1952, p. 14.

[9] Arnold S. Tannenbaum and Robert L. Kahn, *Participation in Union Locals* (Evanston: Row, Peterson, 1958), p. 23.

[10] *Labor-Management Relations in Illini City,* University of Illinois, Institute of Labor and Industrial Relations, 1953, vol. 1, p. 166.

[11] William H. Keown, "Some Dimensions of Company-Union Downward Communication," *Wisconsin Commerce Reports,* University of Wisconsin, vol. 4, chap. 3, June 1955, p. 82.

In a West Coast UAW local "the most influential men in the local" were the president, the chairman of the bargaining committee, and the recording secretary. The president and the recording secretary were ex officio members of the bargaining committee.[12]

Collective leadership typically comes out of a high-skill group in the factory not so much as a result of a will to leadership as from the natural dynamics of the local union situation which tends to push high skill groups to the fore. Sayles and Strauss concluded from their investigation into local unions that there is a "general tendency for union leaders to be selected from higher-paid and more skilled workers. Unionwide officers often hold the highest paid jobs under the jurisdiction of the local; stewards frequently are the highest paid in their department."[13]

Ideology, particularly communist ideology, represents a disciplined bond as the basis for the exercise of collective leadership. Union policy is controlled by a "party fraction" which gets its instructions from the appropriate Communist party functionary. The power of the fraction is in its ironbound discipline and in its unity of purpose. It enables the fraction to put loyal followers on the key committees and in the key offices of the union, and to exert vastly more authority than would be justified by the weight of sheer numbers alone.[14] In the Chicago local of the United Packinghouse Workers at the Swift Company:

> Less than 1% of the local membership, around thirty men and women, largely run the union affairs of five thousand workers in the Swift-UPWA community. These thirty people are the very active core of local union life. It is they who organize the local political caucuses, plan the election campaigns, raise funds, run for office or electioneer, comprise the local executive board, run the local committees such as grievance, bargaining, entertainment, edit The Flash [the local union newspaper] and faithfully attend local membership meetings. . . .
>
> Clearly the power and influence of this inner core is great. We have already seen the apathy and lack of participation of the rank and file in the plant community. . . . Hence it is not sur-

[12] James L. Stern, "The Role of the Local Union: Case Study of Local 844, UAW–CIO," unpublished Ph.D. dissertation, University of California, August 1954, p. 31.

[13] Op. cit., p. 144.

[14] Jack Barbash, The Practice of Unionism (New York: Harper, 1956), p. 344 ff.

prising that a small number of disciplined and convinced communists, well-trained in parliamentary law, electioneering, and propaganda techniques could come in and seize control of a large local union like Local 28. It is not numbers, but political ability and determined work which secure control over Local 28 government.[15]

ETHNIC

Ethnic kinship provides a highly cohesive bond for collective leadership. The most detailed investigation of the role of ethnic groups in the union has been made among Negro and Mexican groups in the Los Angeles area.[16] Access of the ethnic groups to leadership in the union has been analyzed in terms of a three-stage process: first, the entry into the labor force; second, entry into the union "not only as card carriers and dues payers, but as active participants in organizational meetings"; and third, entry into the leadership of the local.

Representation in the steward body is made easier for the ethnics if there is a substantial portion of skilled workers among the ethnic groups. The rung from the lowest level of leadership, the steward body, to executive board membership is more "shaky." In a previously white-dominated local, the ethnics need to have a large proportion of the membership before they become executive board members, and frequently the proportion of executive board membership is less than would be warranted by the general distribution of ethnics among the membership, although this varies from local to local.

Where leadership does not come from a dominant ethnic group, it may continue in power only so long as it maintains a balance of support among important ethnic groups. "In two situations observed, rival ethnic groups were of equal strength. . . . The local president was elected from the small minority of Anglo-Saxons. In each case the president's most difficult task was to avoid charges of favoritism by one group or another."[17] Or we find the ethnic and ideological bonds intertwined as in Local 28 of the Packinghouse Workers in Chicago, where the local leader-

[15] Purcell, *The Worker Speaks His Mind*, p. 209.

[16] Scott Greer, *Last Man In* (Glencoe: Free Press, 1959), chap. 3.

[17] Leonard R. Sayles and George Strauss, *The Local Union: Its Place in the Industrial Plant* (New York: Harper, 1953), p. 217. See also Seidman, London, Karsh, and Tagliacozzo, *The Worker Views His Union*, p. 70.

ship has been characterized as "dominated by left-wing mostly Negro."[18]

Leadership in the factory local apparently can be co-extensive with the membership itself, at least as represented through a membership meeting. In the Textile Workers Union local in the American Velvet Company "the membership is entirely responsible for actions of the union." There is constant turnover in the leadership not so much because of dissatisfaction but because "it is time to give someone else a chance." There have been eight presidents of the local in thirteen years. Membership meetings are well-attended and lively, even after the "achievement of good employment conditions." The leadership is "intelligently questioned" and management proposals are subject to detailed debate.[19]

The seven locals functioning in the Nashua Gummed and Coated Paper Company provide another instance of where the "real locus of power . . . is in the membership." The membership exercises influence at various stages in the bargaining process: in drafting proposals, in instructing the bargaining committee, and in the final approval of the contract. During protracted negotiations there are likely to be additional meetings. Officers and grievance committeemen are changed frequently, in one local by deliberate rotation. Membership attendance at meetings is average, "yet on issues which affect the members more directly, such as approval of a proposed new contract, the membership attendance is greater 'than 50%.'" Membership participation in these locals is "important and . . . it did not have the 'rubber stamp' quality found in some other groups." On several occasions the membership rejected tentative settlements and the negotiators were directed to "go back for more."[20] In a 700-member industrial local in Michigan "the membership as a whole had a significantly greater amount of control than either the bargaining committee, the executive board, or the president."[21]

[18] Theodore V. Purcell, *Blue Collar Man* (Cambridge: Harvard University Press, 1960), p. 27.
[19] George S. Paul, *Causes of Industrial Peace Under Collective Bargaining, American Velvet Company and Textile Workers Union of America*, Case Study No. 11 (Washington: NPA, 1953), p. 18 ff.
[20] Charles A. Myers and George P. Shultz, *Causes of Industrial Peace Under Collective Bargaining, Nashua Gummed and Coated Paper Company and Seven AFL Unions*, Case Study No. 7 (Washington: NPA, 1950), pp. 30–31.
[21] Tannenbaum and Kahn, *op. cit.*, p. 16.

INDIVIDUAL LEADERSHIP

The environment in which the factory functions, to be sure, favors collective leadership, but this does not always preclude the emergence of individual leadership types who, however, are likely to operate within a narrower scope than is true of the leadership in the nonfactory local.

The "charismatic" leader in the factory local is seen in the Michigan "Sergeant" local with 850 members. (The characterization is that of the authors.) At one of the regular union meetings of the local,

> . . . Strong sentiment had been mobilized for strike action in order to obtain desired concessions from management. The proponents of this view had spoken vigorously, and the attending members expressed agreement with their ideas. There was an obvious majority in favor of strike preparations. Opposition was relatively weak and came mostly from some of the local officers, who cautioned the members against rash action. Their appeal, however, was ineffectual. Finally the president arose. He expounded in simple, eloquent and forceful terms the need for the members to stand behind the bargaining committee. The bargaining committee, he felt, could get exactly what they wanted *without* striking. Furthermore, the strike action advocated by some of the members would ensnare the union in some of the technicalities of the Taft-Hartley law. A 10-minute speech—listened to with great attention by the members—turned the tide and a voice vote completely supported the president's view.[22]

"Tom Coburn" is a case in point of an ideologically oriented factory local leader. Coburn is a semiskilled worker in the Acme Brass Mill in a small New England town and also an officer of a 300-member local of the International Union of Mine, Mill and Smelter Workers. The union is generally regarded as being under Communist control, and Tom "is in full sympathy with this leadership." He achieved leadership because he had a sense of assurance in dealing with management and enjoyed the affection of the men in the plant. "Though he insists that as a leader he merely does what the union members instruct him to do, Tom actually leads by deliberate attempts to bring the men around to his point of view on political as well as local union matters."

Coburn is respected by the management who regard him as a tough but fair bargainer. He does not seem to be personally

[22] *Ibid.,* p. 28.

ambitious for office in the local union or in the international union but looks forward ultimately to a life of full-time farming. He "sincerely believes in the fellow-traveling politics of the union hierarchy, and is therefore a willing carrier of its message to the Acme workers." His capacity to act as a transmission belt for the international union's ideological message is provided by his capacity to provide the bread-and-butter goals of the rank-and-file union member who would reject the international union's politics if Tom urged it.

The ultimate test of how far Tom could carry the membership with him ideologically was made when he supported Henry Wallace for President in 1948 and ran for Congress on the Progressive ticket. He got 125 Acme workers to sign his petition, but in the final vote he won only 74 out of 5,140 votes in the districts where most of the Acme workers live. As Alexander and Berger observed, "Business unionism is the vessel on which the ideology of the leadership is carried to the rank and file, but the cargo doesn't always get there with the vessel itself."[23]

Harold Christoffel represented Communist ideological leadership in a factory local during the late thirties and forties, but Christoffel's leadership, in contrast to "Coburn" was less permissive.

The administration of local 248 is rife with examples of minority control. At times violence was used to express opposition to Christoffel. These charges have been made by many different sources.

At the Buffalo convention of the United Auto Workers in 1941, Mr. R. J. Thomas, president of the UAW, verified this lack of democracy in Local 248 in the following words: "When Brother Christoffel talks about democracy he ought to remember that I was on the platform of the Allis-Chalmers local and saw that he refused the floor to members who were not on his side. I told him then that if I used such tactics at an international convention he would be the first to protest."

The 1941 convention refused to seat the Local 248 delegates because of election irregularities. The convention report of the credentials committee claimed that in the Local 248 elections of July 13, 1941, the polls were open only thirty minutes and that the highest vote cast for any delegate was 221 out of a claimed membership of four thousand. The credentials committee con-

[23] John W. Alexander and Morroe Berger, "Grass Roots Labor Leader," in Alvin Gouldner, *Studies in Leadership* (New York: Harper, 1950), pp. 175–183 *passim*.

tinued, "We charge this procedure as just a resume of the procedure by which this group has dominated this local for years until the membership has lost interest in the functioning of the local to the extent that the last meeting of the local was attended by only sixty-one members."

. . . To the incumbent machine any opposition to the Christoffel administration by those either within or without the union was considered akin to treason. In 1938–1939 those few union members who had sided with the Homer Martin faction were driven out of the union and out of the plant. Extreme measures were used to drive such "disrupters" from the plant. In 1939 and 1940 some fifteen work stoppages were carried out to force management to fire Christoffel opponents. In the 1937, 1938, and 1940 local union elections no one appeared to run against Harold Christoffel.[24]

Individual leadership control can function in the local factory union made up of white collar workers, as was found in a Steelworkers local of 175–200 members. The president of this local exercises "almost complete authority over its internal affairs. The twelve-man executive board is seldom convened and the few members who attend meetings almost automatically approve any recommendation; therefore the president's authority to act officially for the local seems almost complete."[25]

"High-powered" leadership manifests itself in the factory local although I would judge less frequently than in the nonfactory local. More often than not the high-powered leader in the factory local is likely to be the paid official, that is, paid by the local. For example, in a large federal factory local:

The president is the key figure in the local union structure. A former chipper in the foundry division, the president is a skilled and able negotiator, who occupies a full-time paid position. He has presided over the local continuously for sixteen years except for a defeat suffered in the 1955 elections. However, he was called back to office and was, once again, unopposed in the last election. Caucus developments in the union reflect a "pro or anti president" position rather than liberal and conservative divisions on union issues. Yet, on the whole, the president has

[24] Robert W. Ozanne, *The Effects of Communist Leadership on American Trade Unions, UAW Local 248,* unpublished Ph.D. dissertation, University of Wisconsin, 1954, pp. 288–291.

[25] Robert Dean Garton, "Job Classification in the Steel Industry; the Experience of Two Local Unions," *IL Research,* vol. 5, Fall 1959, New York State School of Industrial and Labor Relations, p. 9.

been typically supported by the more outspoken, militant unionists.

The members have come to depend on the president, because of his great knowledge of the contract. Thus, great authority is vested in his position. The union power structure is a classic demonstration of Michel's thesis on "oligarchic tendencies." The most important questions of the local union are simply referred to and handled by its most informed member, the president, who is the full-time union functionary. But, his power is neither dictatorial nor arbitrary. Democratic procedure in the union organization is scrupulously regarded and sporadic opposition elements are able to legitimately flourish.[26]

"MIDDLEMAN"

The factory local union leader has fewer of the middleman perceptions of the business agent in the nonfactory local. Part of the business agent's middleman psychology stems in the first instance from a position of strength in relation to the employer and a sense of responsibility in using that strength. In contrast the part-time factory union local leader does not typically see himself as bargaining from a position of security in his relationship to management. The tougher management is, the less secure he feels. And the less sure he is of himself in relation to management, the less he sees himself as a middleman and the more he sees himself as a defense attorney in behalf of his member.

The feeling of insecurity in the factory local is pervasive even in the strongest local. The local union activist, in assessing the effectiveness of the plant grievance procedure, generally finds that the chief obstacle is the underlying fear and timidity that the average worker experiences in filing grievances because he may incur the displeasure of management. In the nonfactory relationship it is the business agent who represents the symbol of greater power to the union member. In the factory setting the situation is reversed: it is the management that stands for overriding power in the job relationship.[27]

[26] Sidney M. Peck, *The Rank and File Leader*, Ph.D. dissertation, University of Wisconsin, 1959, p. 120.
[27] As a way of getting at the pressing problems of the local in the plant in connection with steward-training classes, I circulate a questionnaire to the participants. In the dozen or so locals in which I have used this procedure, the results universally show that fear of management is the most frequently cited defect in the grievance procedure. This holds true—although in varying degrees—irrespective of the size of the local and the quality of the union-management relationship.

7

THE STEWARD

MODEL

The classic conception of the steward is set forth in a Teamster publication:

> Within the policing and enforcement apparatus, the shop steward serves as the policeman on the "beat." With this important assignment, he is the key person in the maintenance and enforcement of the collective bargaining agreement. The shop steward is the top sergeant of U.S. unionism. The strength and vitality of American trade unionism flows from this vast army of policemen on the beat in a countless number of shops, plants, and factories throughout the country. Without the shop steward, the entire superstructure of contract enforcement would fall with thunderous economic repercussions.

> As the functional base unit of union leadership, the shop steward can make or break the collective bargaining agreement. With weak enforcement at the shop level, the most adequate contract provision can become a nightmare of confusion and cause for the great dissension within the ranks [sic]. Conversely with vigorous and intelligent contract enforcement the weakest provision can become a tower of security for the working membership.[1]

The steward is the first rung of union leadership. He is rather more a part of the in-plant phase of the local union's government rather than the in-union phase of its government. But it is not unusual for the steward to function in both aspects of government, particularly if the influence of the steward is reinforced through

[1] Ernest Calloway, *The Nature and Structure of the Collective Bargaining Agreement*, 1956, International Brotherhood of Teamsters, Joint Council of Teamsters Number 13, St. Louis, Research Department (mimeo.), p. 27.

a steward's council, or if the steward body also functions as a local executive board.

In the idealized state the steward, who also is frequently called committeeman, or chairlady in the case of the garment workers, is the key figure in the handling of grievances in unionized industry.[2] He is the day-to-day line of communication between the workers in the shop and the front line management, and between the workers in the shop and the top union leaders.

The steward, as has been said, is the first point of union contact in the administration of the grievance procedure under the contract. A typical method of handling grievances in factory employment and in nonfactory large employee units is through a graduated procedure of one sort or another. The individual worker takes his grievance to his steward; the steward attempts to settle it with the foreman. If no settlement is reached, then perhaps the chief steward of the plant will take it to the general superintendent. If this fails, it may go to the bargaining committee or its equivalent, which will discuss it with the director of industrial relations. If this step fails to yield a settlement, it may then be submitted either to an impartial umpire or to a bipartisan board or a combination of a bipartisan board with an impartial third person to settle deadlocks. The variations are in the number of steps that exhaust the grievance remedies, the presence or absence of a provision for an impartial umpire, and the kind of dispute between the union and the management that are allowable grievances.

In the smaller nonfactory situation a systematic grievance procedure is relatively rare. If a steward system exists, as it does for example in the construction trades or in the teamsters, the role of the steward is that of a watchdog or a referral agency for the business agent. It is unusual for the steward in nonfactory employment to have much power.

The expectations of the steward's role as distilled from the many steward training manuals—perhaps the most popular type of factory union publication—run something like this: The steward must know the contract, his department, the men in it, and the step-by-step procedure involved in the handling of grievances.

---

[2] The quotes are from the steward training manual of the CIO Paperworkers and it is a fair sample of perhaps one hundred other steward training manuals. This section is adapted from Jack Barbash, *The Practice of Unionism* (New York: Harper, 1956), pp. 197–199.

When the steward is confronted by a worker's complaint, he must be able to distinguish between a gripe and a grievance. It's a gripe if it can't be related to a contract provision. If the worker has no case, the steward should tell him so and show him why the contract does not cover his particular complaint.

If the complaining worker has a case, the steward should get the facts and get all the facts. When he thinks he has all the facts, he should put them in writing and get the written grievance signed by the worker. The steward should keep a record of all the grievances handled.

The steward must be prudent in his relationship with the foreman, who usually represents the management's first stage in the procedure. "Avoid building up personal rivalry between yourself and the foreman. Don't get into a position where you habitually work against each other." The steward should be able to settle the grievances at the first level if this is possible. If the grievances are settled in the first stage the later stages in the machinery will not get clogged up, which means that the later stages can handle the really major issues.

The steward will be able to settle his grievances in the first stage if he makes a "sincere effort to see the other side of the story without losing sight of [his] own position. He should avoid horse-trading on cases. Either there is a grievance to be settled legitimately or there is no grievance at all. . . . Give the other fellow a chance to save face. You may need to save yours some day. . . . Never go over the head of the foreman—or any other supervisor —without telling him. If the [steward] intends to appeal from his decision the foreman should be told." A positive, not a defensive, approach is best. The steward shouldn't give his opponent an advantage by losing his temper. "Shouting and pounding tables never settled anything." A capacity for listening is helpful to the steward, and when it's the steward's turn to talk, he should "stick to the point."

If it is a committee that is meeting with management, the union should keep a "united front" on its side. The steward should avoid "empty threats." Bluffing is a shortsighted and dangerous tactic for a steward.

TYPES OF GRIEVANCES

The most persistent and bothersome grievances are those dealing with (in general terms) discipline, job classification, and seniority—roughly in that order. We have no general statistics on the incidence of types of grievances at the first stage of the grievance procedure. Data relating to the content of grievances on any generalized basis are derived from the analysis of arbitration awards. We cannot be certain, therefore, that this is the rank order which would prevail in the grievances handled by the steward since most grievances are settled in the first stage and the overwhelming majority do not reach the final arbitration stage. Nonetheless, arbitrated grievances convey the general direction if not the precise magnitude.

The Federal Conciliation and Mediation Service, a public agency, and the American Arbitration Association, a nongovernment agency, are the main clearing houses for the referral of arbitrators. It is these two sources that therefore provide the most reliable indication of the general incidence of grievances in industry at large.

ISSUES MOST FREQUENTLY ADJUDICATED BY ARBITRATORS

From FMCS-provided Panels, Fiscal 1959

Issues	Frequency
Total	2,240
Disciplinary	606
Job classification and work assignment	303
Seniority in demotion	245
Management rights	227
Overtime and hours	192
Seniority in promotion	192
Pay for time not worked	168
Incentive rates—standards	143
Miscellaneous	97
Union security	67

Source: U.S. Federal Mediation and Conciliation Service, *12th Annual Report, Fiscal year 1959*, p. 35.

The flavor of the kinds of grievances handled directly by the steward in a functioning steward situation is indicated by the stewards' experiences in a West Coast automobile plant:[3]

Bill Stich had a question on overtime which I settled with the foreman.

[3] James Stern, "The Role of the Local Union: Case Study of Local 844, UAW–CIO," unpublished Ph.D. dissertation, University of California, August 1954.

Type of Issue	Fre-quency	Type of Issue	Fre-quency
Discipline and Discharge		*Others*	
Inefficiency, negligence, and damage to company property	111	Job evaluation issues	223
		Incentive plans	107
		Overtime	82
Absenteeism	59	Vacation	61
Dishonesty	32	Holidays	50
Insubordination	29	Wages	46
Leaving job without permission	24	Welfare provisions	42
		Arbitrability as the sole issue	41
Refusal to perform job assignment	24	Foremen and supervisors	31
		Hours of work	29
Assault and fighting	20	Guaranteed employment	26
Strike activity	19	Transfer	26
Intoxication	14	Union security issues	22
Abusive language	12	Observance of grievance procedure	19
Slowdown	12		
Union activity	12	Pay for time not worked	18
Refusal to work overtime	11	Apprentice and probationary period	14
Sleeping on the job	10		
Lateness	9	Call-in and reporting pay	13
Physical disability	9	Premium pay (other than overtime)	13
Security risk	1		
Miscellaneous	48	Progression and merit increases	13
Total	(456)	Subcontracting	10
Seniority		Auxiliary pay practices	9
		Leave of absence	8
Layoff and bumping	125	Pensions	8
Promotion and bidding rights	66	Severance pay	7
Transfer, including demotion	26	Union elections	5
Work out of bargaining unit and seniority upon return	20	Safety	4
		Bonus (other than incentive)	2
Recall from layoff	19	Security risk (other than discharge)	1
Superseniority for union officials	19		
		Miscellaneous	41
Distribution of overtime	18		
Computation of seniority	6	Total	(971)
Miscellaneous	2		
Total	(301)	Grand Total	1,728

Source: American Arbitration Association, *Procedural and Substantive Aspects of Grievance Arbitration,* n.d. (probably 1957–1958).

Martin Lash, the high seniority man, was overlooked when a promotion was made. I got it straightened out with the help of a committeeman and general foreman.

Jake Hanover wasn't paid double time for work done on Sunday. Checked with foreman and got agreement to pay Jake.

Borden had a dispute about his pay which I settled to his satisfaction with the foreman.

Ken Grant thought he was misclassified. I arranged for a reexamination of his job to see if it could be reclassified.

Pete Short didn't get relief. Saw foreman and he was relieved immediately. Then Bill Piper yelled he hadn't been relieved so it was arranged he would be taken care of next.

Conway, Book, Kelly, and Corley had pay shortages which I fixed.

Carl Joseph had an extra operation added. Saw foreman.

Tony said that the foreman was working while men were going to be laid off. I questioned the men and found out that the foreman was only instructing Tony and Al who were new on their operation.

John said that the line was going too fast. Checked and found that it was. Saw general foreman and told him about it. Did not get satisfactory answer. Called committeeman and referred it to him. He said he would take it up with the superintendent. The line was slowed down to normal after dinner.

Brower complained about working conditions. Said too many Dodge bodies being run in a row, causing overwork. Saw foreman and got him help.

Got foreman to tear up reprimands on Jones, Black, Harmon, and Towner for poor work.

Checked on overspray in paint booth for Wells and Green.

Speed-up. The company tried to make up too many cars and six guys kicked. We got it straightened out.

Bins and Carter said poor materials were giving them trouble. I told the foreman.

Hart said the foreman was playing favorites.

Rice asked me to prevent his transfer out of the division. I did.

Paterson said he can't get the quota the way the material is coming.

Dusty said foreman was intimidating him. Spoke to foreman.

Allen driving jitney but not getting driver's pay.

Jackson had to jump across pit. Settled with foreman as was safety hazard.

Cliff, change of operation.

James, rate of production.

Titus, speed of line. Settled with foreman.

Mott, too much production. After quite a hassle, settled by median plant superintendent.

Speed-up, 14 complaints. Much big hassle. Settled with general foreman.

Formal grievances are not all. The steward is subject to a wide variety of informal questions by individual workers.

Howard Small called me to ask whether we were going to be able to get his discharge removed.

Jack Peters asked how many cars are scheduled today and whether we will work eight hours.

Billings asked about the transfer procedure.

Bell asked me how he can get a ride to and from work.

Rollins wanted to know how to get a leave-of-absence.

Decker wanted information about negotiated paid holidays.

Orson wanted information as to whether and how to apply for U.S. savings bonds deductions.

Parks wanted to know about double-time pay.

Farmer wanted to know why he hadn't received a check-off card.

Morgan wanted information about the Permanente health plan.

Crabtree lost his income statement and wants another one.

Ash wanted to know how to join the union.

Reed requested information regarding the cost-of-living increase or decrease.

Calkins asked when does he rank seniority after a transfer from another department.

Bandol wanted the lawyer's phone number.

Levy wanted to see the seniority list.

Carter wanted information about the blood bank.

Miller asked me to pay his hospital dues.

Romano wanted to get a receipt for his insurance.

Brinker wanted to know his classification.

Pete Harden came in to ask about collecting unemployment compensation from out-of-state.

Al Sontag laid off. Called saying he did not get 24 hours' notice when laid off. He was informed that since he was sick and at home on date of lay-off that company was not obliged to give him 24 hours' notice. Umpire's decisions were cited.

Bob Knight, officer of the credit union, asked for cooperation of the local.

Now every steward system will not be as busy as this, but it is fair to say that every steward will, in varying degrees, deal with the order of grievances and problems indicated in these listings.

STEWARD SYSTEMS

The structure of steward systems can be seen in the table below based on an informal analysis of steward systems (probably typical) in twelve local unions of a large international.

The characteristics which emerge are:

1. The ratio of stewards to workers is typically under 1 to 50. In general the ratio is likely to depend on the distribution of employees by operating unit. It is therefore not infrequent for the steward ratio to reach 1 to 100.[4]

2. The steward is usually elected by the workers in the unit which he represents. It is not rare, however, for the steward to be coopted by the local union officers.

3. Regular meetings for stewards are common.

4. Stewards are usually compensated (dues remission and/or a nominal fee) for their services but compensation is contingent on attendance at steward meetings and membership meetings.

EFFECTIVENESS

The effectiveness of the stewards varies. Following are instances derived from firsthand observation in which the steward and the steward body are functioning effectively even if not always successfully.

COAL MINING

Disputes which have not been satisfactorily adjusted by the foreman are referred by the aggrieved employee to a member or members of the mine (pit) committee . . . In practice an effort is usually made to elect committeemen representing each shift and more than one section of the local mine. The committeeman receiving the largest number of votes generally serves as chairman of the committee. Because grievance han-

[4] See also Bureau of National Affairs, *Collective Bargaining Negotiations and Contracts*, 51:161.

STEWARD SYSTEMS IN TWELVE LOCAL UNIONS, AUGUST 1959

Local Union			Stewards				Selection		Steward Meetings		Compensation			Recall	
	Approx. member-ship	No. of shops	Title	No.	Method	Term	Who votes	How often	Who conducts	Type (MM is membership meeting)	Requirements to qualify for pay	Est. cost as % of LU inc.	For non-attend. at meet.	Meetings missed to recall	By member-ship
A	2,300	42	Committeeman	33	Elect.	1 yr.	Shop	Mo.	Business Representative	1.50 per MM attended (3.00 per mo.)	Attendance	3%	No		Yes
B	3,000	18	Dept Committeeman	18	Elect.	1 yr.	Shop	Bimo.	Business Representative	Dues (4.00) +5.00 (9.00 per mo.)	Attend 2 MM per month	4%	No		Yes
C	472	10	Shop Committeeman	3	Elect.	1 yr.	Local	Irreg.		21.00 for 3 mo. (7.00 per mo.)	Attend 5 of 6 MM in 3 mo.	3%	Yes	2 of 6 MM in 3 mo.	No
D	1,600	7	Steward	32	Elect.	1 yr.	Dept.	Mo.	Business Rep. & Chmn.	4.00 per mo.	Attend all MM	5%	Yes	3 MM in a row	Yes
E	3,500	1	Steward	120	Elect.	3 yr.		Mo.	Pres. & Chmn. of Grievance Comm.	5.00 per mo.	Attend steward or 1 MM per mo.	12%	No		Yes
F	150	1	Steward	6	Elect.	1 yr.	Local	None		None		None	Yes	2 MM in a row	No
G	400	4	Steward	8	Appt. by Ex. Bd.	1 yr.		Week.	Pres. & Chmn. of Comm.	3.00 + lost time	Attend meetings		Yes	3 meetings	Yes
H	800	14	Chairman	7	Elect.	1 yr.	Shop	Mo.	Comm. Chmn.	None		None	No		No
I	4,900	700	Shop steward	300	Appt. by BR	Indef.		Mo.	Business Representative	None (Annual banquet held for stewards and wives)			Yes		No
J	900	1	Steward	24	Elect.	1 yr.	Dept.	Mo.	Pres.	3.50 per mo.	Attend steward meeting and 1 MM per mo.	6%	Yes	3 Steward meetings	No
K	3,500	2	Shop steward	130	Elect.	1 yr.	Shop	Mo.	Chmn. of Grievance Comm.	Dues (4.70)	Attend steward meeting and 1 MM per mo.	12%	Yes	3 meetings	Yes—Charge by member, voted by EB
L	200	1	Steward	9	Elect.	1 yr.	Dept.	Bimo.	Shop Chmn.	Dues (5.00)	Attend MM	15%	Yes	3 meetings	No

dling is the major function of the local mine union, the chairman's position is of prime importance and is further enhanced when, as is often the case, the chairman also serves as union president. Since grievances are handled after work hours and the local union often compensates for committee work at the base hourly wage rate, membership in the mine committee may provide a valued source of additional income. Committee work also offers opportunity for continuing contact with management and district union officials and has sometimes been a means of promotional advancement. In spite of these advantages, the committeeman's position is not always readily filled, and resignations of committeemen are common.[5]

TEXTILES

Employees expected to get most of their information concerning the labor contract from the steward, and, from past experience, consider him the most helpful source of such information. In contrast, however, it appeared that the stewards had not been effective in getting union ideas unrelated to the work situation to the membership.[6]

GRAIN PROCESSING—ILLINI CITY

Apart from the main officers and the members of the bargaining committee, the most important local union figures were the stewards. . . . In 1949 the union had 89 stewards. The main function of the steward was to take up individual or group grievances with the foreman of his department. The steward was usually one of the more active union members. Most of them worked closely with the full-time chairman of the bargaining committee who was thoroughly familiar with the interpretations of contract provisions. Apart from the satisfaction and prestige of being elected by his fellow-employees (in the department) and of settling grievances, the steward received two types of compensation for his work: he headed his departmental seniority list in time of layoff and recall from the department; and his union dues were paid for by the union provided he attended the regular monthly stewards' meeting.[7]

[5] Gerald G. Somers, *Grievance Settlement in Coal Mining*, West Virginia University Business and Economic Studies, vol. 4, chap. 4, June 1956, p. 5.
[6] Helen Baker, John W. Ballantine, and John M. True, *Transmitting Information through Management and Union Channels: Two Case Studies*, Industrial Relations Section, Princeton University, 1949, p. 53.
[7] *Labor-Management Relations in Illini City*, University of Illinois, Institute of Labor and Industrial Relations, vol. 1, 1953, pp. 166–167.

UE—UPSTATE NEW YORK

[Ray] Jones's skill as a leader was clearly evidenced in the manner in which he created a strong, effective group of stewards. Since the principal bargaining function of local X is 'the handling of grievances arising from the enforcement and interpretation of the master contract, the stewards had an opportunity to perform an outstanding service for the membership. Jones had a high regard for the stewards and constantly praised them and reminded the membership of their importance. He met with the stewards' council twice a month, helped them with their problems and, perhaps most important, allowed them a great deal of latitude in settling grievances at the first step, and then backed them up in their decisions. There was no indication that he attempted to obtain the election as steward of men who agreed with his own political leanings [which are "far to the left" of that of his followers in local X]. Largely as a result of his efforts, there was a group of able stewards that took pride in their office and were respected by the workers. Thus a majority of the officers and active members of local X felt that the most important function of the local, grievance handling, was being carried out very effectively.[8]

PRINTING TRADES—NEW YORK (ITU)

In the larger plants the chapel chairman rather than the foreman is the most powerful man in the composing room. He can make life difficult for a non-cooperative foreman by insisting on the rigid application of the numerous union and chapel rules. . . . Both management and union administration have little control over the men in the shops or their elected leaders, the chapel chairmen. Management's power is limited by the power of the union, which is made explicit in rules which bar non-members of the union from the floor of the print shop during working hours. The union officialdom's control over the members or chapel chairmen is minimized by the existence of strongly-held union norms which inhibit efforts by union leaders to punish men for their opinions or to influence the election of chapel (shop) officers. . . . The larger chapels, by generating and supporting a body of union activists who have gained political and administrative skills and a personal following independent of the union administration, thus perform perhaps a major function for the union's political system—providing sources of power and

[8] Dalton E. McFarland, "Left-Wing Domination of Labor Unions: A Case Study of Local Union Leadership," *IL Research,* New York State School of Industrial and Labor Relations, vol. 1, June 1955, p. 3.

leadership outside and independent of the union administration. . . . The many separately owned print shops of different types require the chapel chairman, in all but the smaller shops, to function like a kind of labor lawyer, applying the general provisions of a local-wide union contract to the special circumstances which obtain in his shop. Some measure of autonomy on the part of the chapel chairman is almost demanded by the difficulty of administering the contract in detail from local headquarters. . . . This independence of the body of first-line union officers has many consequences for the operation of the union's political system. . . . But among other things it means that they cannot be counted on to "sell" union administration decisions and policies to the members, or to uncritically transmit information slanted in favor of the administration. On the contrary, the independence of the chapel chairman and the discipline of an administration machine means that administrative acts may be subject to as much criticism as support in the process of being transmitted to the members.[9]

FOUR INDUSTRIAL LOCALS—VARYING SIZES

The results of the present study suggest that high membership control appears to exist where stewards and other leaders are aware of and responsive to members' needs and problems. Stewards in locals where membership control is high appear to have taken on added responsibility and to give serious weight to their supervisory role in the union. They are stewards not only in the formal sense of the word, but they take on some of the functions of consultants, communicators, and mentors. They interact with their men over and beyond the formal requirements of their role. They let their men know what is going on and in turn obtain the opinions of the men on union matters. They appear to value their men as individuals. It seems likely that these skills and behaviors are among the causes of member participation and that they facilitate a member-controlled local.[10]

SHOE INDUSTRY—THE BROTHERHOOD OF SHOE AND ALLIED CRAFTSMEN

Experience with this steward system varies from group to group, even within the same factory: in some plants, according to the

[9] Seymour Martin, Martin Trow, and James Coleman, *Union Democracy: The Inside Politics of the International Typographical Union* (Glencoe: Free Press, 1956), pp. 25, 149–150, 182.

[10] Arnold S. Tannenbaum and Robert L. Kahn, *Participation in Union Locals* (Evanston: Row, Peterson, 1958), p. 226.

management, "They keep the pot boiling all the time," but in others, "Nobody wants the headaches." In general, though, the steward organization has taken effective responsibility for grievances centering around shop problems. But further, though the original intention may not have been for the stewards to "run the room" this is in effect what has happened. For example, craft representatives may supervise the division of work in departments where "hard" and "easy" jobs are frequent, and the chief steward must grant permission before overtime or Saturday work may be performed. Thus as a result of the steward system, union representatives exercise positive control over several important phases of factory operation.[11]

INDUSTRIAL LOCAL—COLUMBUS, OHIO

The offices of Local X reported few instances of members bypassing committeemen in attempting to settle grievances. There was considerable competition in elections of committeemen, and resignations were not excessive, according to those officers. The role of committeeman reportedly carried prestige and respect.[12]

TEAMSTERS—ST. LOUIS

Under Harold Gibbons, Local 688 of the International Brotherhood of Teamsters in St. Louis is reputed to have built up a steward system functioning through a stewards' council. The minutes of the stewards' council are reported in the local newspaper. The following is a summary of a council meeting selected at random:[13]

1. Financial report for the quarter.
2. Questions on organization expense, political fund deficit.
3. Nothing new to report on indictment of local union officers.
4. Discussion of fines committee.
5. Report on political activity.
6. Request for contacts in various retail stores.
7. Report on projected arbitration cases
8. Report on negotiations.
9. Community action report.
10. Good and welfare—patronizing union grocery stores.

[11] George P. Shultz, *Pressures on Wage Decisions: A Case Study in the Shoe Industry* (New York: John Wiley and Cambridge: Massachusetts Institute of Technology, 1951), p. 48.
[12] Glenn W. Miller and James E. Young, "Members' Attitudes toward the Shop Steward," *Industrial and Labor Relations Review,* July 1957, p. 517.
[13] *Midwest Labor World,* August 1960.

INEFFECTIVENESS

Here are some instances of situations in which the steward system did not function effectively:

GARMENT MANUFACTURE—ILLINI CITY

The steward handled worker grievances on the local shop level. There was a great deal of variation in the manner in which the stewards handled their jobs. According to the contract, the stewards could have been assisted in their functioning by a price committee, composed of workers representing the various operations in the factory, but in practice, these committees were rarely employed. At company A the steward had assistants in each line who collected the workers' grievance cards. When in need of assistance in processing a grievance, the steward appealed directly to the business agent. In some establishments the steward called the business agent regularly while in others the business agent was rarely summoned for consultation on grievances. The steward was compensated by the union for time lost from work while executing union duties, but most of them agreed that their earnings had suffered. For one thing they hesitated to charge the union for the actual time devoted to the job. Then, too, their piece-work earning suffered because constant interruptions hampered their ability to build up speed. Some employers seemed to allocate less desirable operations to the stewards on the grounds that they could not be depended upon for steady output. Stewards who were anxious to keep their earnings high were unpopular with the workers, for they gave poor service. Stewardships were the least popular of all local offices, and the local leaders had difficulty in persuading workers to assume these positions.[14]

TEAMSTERS—ILLINI CITY

. . . The union business agent usually made the basic interpretation of the contract. At company A there had been no steward since 1947; at company B there was a steward but his main function was largely one of reporting presumed violations to the union business agent, who made the decisions.[15]

RETAIL CLERKS—LARGE MIDWESTERN CITY

The policy of the union was to have a steward in stores of ten or more employees. His job was to collect dues and to forward grievances, not to handle them. The grievances were forwarded to the business agent. The function of the steward, who was usually the cashier or bookkeeper in each store, was to collect

[14] Derber in *Illini City*, vol. 1, pp. 407–408.
[15] *Ibid.*, pp. 616–617.

dues and report to the business agent on the hiring of new employees. The steward was appointed, not elected, and his perquisite was remission of dues.[16]

LARGE MIDWEST INDUSTRIAL LOCAL

The 1947 settlement reduced the number of stewards and restricted their movements. In the last agreement the number of authorized stewards was doubled from 35 to 60. The big problem is getting stewards to function. The chief obstacle is the fact that there are no inducements to the steward such as superseniority. In a few departments, the local has been unable to get stewards at all; specifically, in the experimental department and among the cleaners. There is a feeling of intimidation in the plant so stewards refuse to take jobs. There is no prestige and no incentive associated with the job. Departmental meetings are very uneven. There is a monthly stewards' meeting with an average attendance of 38 out of a possible 48 stewards. The turnover is very large.[17]

UPSTATE NEW YORK BUILDING TRADES

To a slight extent the business agent was assisted in the job by stewards yet stewards had a far less important role than in industrial unions. At times, they collected dues and handled minor problems. More commonly, they were instructed merely to "call the business agent whenever there is trouble."[18]

CONSTRUCTION—ILLINI CITY

The grievance procedure did not seem to play a major role in the construction bargaining relationship. Most of the grievances that appeared seemed to stem from jurisdictional disputes and the enforcement of union work-rules. The case study revealed that, to some extent, the workers at construction B feared management retaliation if they filed complaints regarding the failure to observe work-rules. One employee remarked, "If you stick too close to the union rules, it makes a difference—you won't last long." On the other hand, no such difficulties were reported by the workers at construction A. The grievances there were settled

[16] Wayne Lawrence Inks, *Unionism in the Retail Food Industry: A Local Case Study of Structure and Function,* unpublished M.A. thesis, University of Illinois, Institute of Labor and Industrial Relations, 1959, p. 80.

[17] Raymond J. Barrett, *The Structure of a Local Union,* unpublished thesis, University of Wisconsin, 1959.

[18] George Strauss, "The Business Agent in the Building Trades," *Industrial and Labor Relations Review,* January 1957, p. 239.

on an informal basis to the apparent satisfaction of both parties.[19]

SMALL MINE AND FACTORY GYPSUM LOCAL

A crucial situational factor was the ineffectiveness of the union's grievance machinery prior to the strike. . . . The formal grievance machinery had broken down under the rising tide of grievances. As Crackery stated, "The union committee found that there was a pile-up on grievances. There were a lot of grievances that the Company wasn't handling. . . . The Company wouldn't pay much attention to the grievances. They wouldn't fulfill their promises. They're supposed to write down their answers to the grievance when it's filed. They said we're thinking about it and they'd let you know one way or the other." Since Byta's clique was ambivalent toward the workers' grievances and doubtful of their legitimacy, they did not "push them." They could not represent them to management with anything like the strong affect that their followers felt. In other words, Byta's conciliatory attitude toward the grievances actually did much to prevent conciliation between management and labor.[20]

STEWARDS AND POWER

To the extent that the steward system is effective it is in the performance of a phase of the collective bargaining relationship; namely, the administration of the union's side of the grievance procedure. Stewards do not normally constitute an autonomous power center in the way that they do in some European industrial relations systems. In the American industrial relations systems the steward is characteristically a part of the main line of union leadership rather than a contender for power in opposition to the local-wide leader. The most immediate reason for this state of affairs is the principle of exclusive representation which prevails in custom and in law; namely, that there is only one representative within a given bargaining unit, and therefore the in-plant leadership is integrated with the union leadership.

The more general reason why the stewards do not constitute separate power centers stems from the nonideological character of the American labor movement, which accounts for the absence in leadership at all levels of any clearly defined ideological goals —beyond the bread-and-butter ones—that the steward might

[19] Derber, in *Illini City*, vol. 2, p. 177.
[20] Alvin W. Gouldner, *Wildcat Strike* (Yellow Springs: Antioch Press, 1954), pp. 97–98.

conceivably assert against higher leadership. Unlike his European counterpart, therefore, the steward is oriented toward union leadership rather than toward the rank-and-file member. One intensive inquiry into industrial stewards' attitudes revealed that:

> For the most part union stewards unequivocally defend the top leadership. While some may urge the compulsory retirement of aged officials and others call for the periodic return of leadership to the plant, criticism of the political aims and objectives which top leadership sets for the union movement is absent. Most union stewards tend to express official union ideology as their very own.

> What the study does reveal is the deep hostility which stewards have toward the rank and file. While top leadership is rarely subject to intense criticism, rank-and-file workers are denounced as apathetic, ungrateful, uncooperative, indifferent, etc. The class bond, which unites the rank-and-file leader to the departmental worker on a personal, intimate level in the shop, seems to be weakened by status considerations. Union stewards perceive the problems of corruption in policies as a function of rank-and-file apathy, just as top leadership does. Only on occasion do isolated stewards question whether or not the organizational policies of union leadership deliberately impede rank-and-file participation.[21]

To be sure, the stewards will frequently find themselves at odds with other segments of leadership in the local union, but this sort of political controversy is on personal grounds and has little to do with their role of stewards as a class.

In respect to the steward's functions in the grievance procedure, there is some feeling that the steward is declining in importance and that he is being bypassed by higher officers.[22] The evidence is not conclusive or even persuasive on this point in one direction or another. All it is possible to say is that there are effective steward systems and ineffective steward systems. The influential factors that seem to characterize the effective steward system are: (1) the attitude of top local union leadership to the steward;

[21] S. M. Peck, *The Rank and File Leader*, Ph.D. dissertation, University of Wisconsin, 1959, p. 626.

[22] Joel Seidman, Jack London, Bernard Karsh, and Daisy L. Tagliacozzo, *The Worker Views His Union* (Chicago: University of Chicago Press, 1958), pp. 160–165. See also Leonard R. Sayles and George Strauss, *The Local Union: Its Place in the Industrial Plant* (New York: Harper, 1953), chap. 4.

(2) the existence of a functioning grievance machinery; (3) the availability of perquisites for the steward; (4) the character of employment and of the collective bargaining relationship.

The importance which top local leadership attaches to the steward may be the single most significant element in the functioning of the steward system. The test as to whether the steward is of consequence so far as the higher leadership is concerned is whether they let him function and do not use him simply as an errand boy. A Gibbons or a "Foster," as seen in the case situations examined, come close to seeing the steward as part of a communications system extending to the rank and file. This view of the steward is almost a piece of ideology, in which it is believed that leadership must always function close to the rank-and-file member and that the steward constitutes the main channel. Many local union leaders say they believe this; the point, of course, is to act upon it. In the case of Gibbons and "Foster," we see them acting upon this conviction. One important method of enhancing the steward's prestige is the creation of a formal stewards' body meeting regularly. In some locals the stewards' body constitutes the executive board of the local union.

It takes the two parties (management and union) to create a functioning grievance machinery; and hence, whether the machinery functions or not may be out of the control of the union altogether. If, as a matter of top management policy, it wants to keep settlement of grievances centralized, the foreman is unable to come to terms with the steward; or if management is forced into the bargaining relationship in the first place, it may pursue a strategy of dragging its feet in grievance handling in order not to enhance the union's prestige. In either case the effect is to impair the standing of the steward. But if the foreman has real power to settle grievances at the first stage, this necessarily enhances the effectiveness of the steward in the settlement of grievances. And it is from his ability and capacity to settle these grievances that he derives his effectiveness.

Another characteristic of steward effectiveness is the perquisites attached to the position, and here again this is a bilateral decision. The two most important perquisites are "superseniority" and compensation. In superseniority the steward is the last man to be fired or laid off. This perquisite may also extend to preference in the allotment of overtime work. By way of compensation, the steward is characteristically paid for lost time in the handling of grievances, frequently by management, and many local unions follow the practice of remitting the steward's dues or giving him some nominal sum for each meeting of the stewards' body which he attends.

The character of employment influences the effectiveness of the steward, in the sense that the relatively large factory with a stratified administration of the management function is more likely to produce an industrial relations situation in which the steward serves a genuine need; more likely than, for example, the relatively small establishment, nonfactory in character, where the management function is largely undifferentiated. Such situations do not favor the development of a steward system. Rather they favor face-to-face dealings between management and top local officers. The larger establishment will more probably depend on a formal system of rules and procedures. This formalization of work-rules generates overt disputes and thus provides a more potent reason for the existence of the steward than does the simple, uncomplicated administration in the smaller establishment.

8

THE LOCAL
IN THE WEB OF ORGANIZATIONS

UNION LAW

The local union is part of a network of external relationships. The network design consists of three main strands: the international union, the strategic relationships to other unions outside its own international, and the labor movement in the form of city and state federations. (The meaning which I give to "international union" follows.) The international union is the most significant external force affecting the local.

The main sources that formally define the relationship between the local and the international are: (a) the international union constitution, (b) statutory law, and (c) case law. If the general character of the international-local relationship is set out at all it is in the international union constitution. Statutory law and case law deal with partial segments of the relationship and then only when the relationship is under stress.

Reference has already been made to the influence of the international on the governing documents of the local. Here we are concerned with the broader aspects of the local-international relationship—the points of operational intersection between the local and the international. This is hardly ever spelled out comprehensively in a written document.

The doctrine incorporated in most international union constitutions is that the local is a subordinate body of the international. "The locals of each union now have only such measure of home rule as the national constitutions grant them."[1] However, the net effect of public intervention in the international-local relation-

[1] William M. Leiserson, *American Trade Union Democracy* (New York: Columbia University Press, 1959), p. 280.

ship has been to dilute the control of the former over the latter—particularly where the international represents in the view of the courts a communist or racketeering interest.

PUBLIC LAW

The issue which most frequently brings an international-local relationship into the courts is the disposition of assets when that relationship is disrupted or threatened with disruption. In general, judicial doctrine has moved through three stages. In the first stage, prior to 1949, the courts tended to accept as given the international-local relationship incorporated in the international constitution; which meant in general that a seceding local was not entitled to hold on to its assets after secession. This has been characterized as the "orthodox contract" doctrine; the international union constitution has created a constructive contract between the international union and its constituent local unions through a constitution.

The second stage in the evolution of judicial doctrine was brought about by the local union secession cases in the IUE–UE controversy. In these cases the courts, for the most part, developed doctrines substantially modifying the full thrust of the "orthodox contract" theory by permitting seceding locals to retain their assets as against the claims of the UE. Three theories were asserted to achieve this result. The independent entity doctrine, in effect, reversed the role of the local union in the labor movement's constitutional law and made the local union an autonomous entity. The doctrine of "implied contract" asserted that the CIO affiliation of the international—in this case the UE—was an implied condition of the international-local contract, which was breached when the UE was expelled from the CIO on grounds of communist domination. The "clean hands" doctrine asserted that the UE's domination by communist elements, the "malevolent acts of communism," prevented the international union from coming into court with clean hands in asserting its claim to the seceding local union's assets. In the third stage, marked by the secession cases against the Bakery and Confectionery Workers—expelled from the AFL–CIO on grounds of racketeering—the "clean hands" doctrine came into its own as a counterweight to the "orthodox contract" doctrine.

The communist and corruption issues have had a similar effect on National Labor Relations Board doctrine insofar as a schism between a local and an international has raised a question of representation during the life of an existing contract. Prior to 1950 an existing contract was a bar to the raising of a question of representation unless, in the case of a local, a disaffiliation vote was taken in a manner to create a "doubt" as to the identity of the bargaining representative; or if the local union had become defunct.

Since 1950 the National Labor Relations Board has modified its schism doctrine to make the raising of a question of representation during the life of a contract easier with respect to schism movements. It has been argued that the mere act of expulsion from the AFL–CIO on grounds of corruption or communist domination in and of itself creates a presumption of instability in the union-management relationship which should be settled by resolving the question of representation.[2]

The Labor-Management Reporting and Disclosure Act of 1959, in the main, centers on the internal affairs of unions in contrast to the collective bargaining focus of Taft-Hartley. But the emphasis in LMRDA—other than in the provisions explicitly amending Taft-Hartley—is primarily on the member-union relationship rather than on the local-international relationship; regulation of trusteeships is an exception.

To sum up: Although the constitutional tradition of the labor movement makes the local union generally a subordinate part of the national union, government regulation effectively circumscribes (a) the authority of the national union at several points, and (b) the procedure through which that authority can be exercised. The courts, for the most part, provide a forum in which control over property becomes a litigable controversy; the NLRB regulates the appropriate unit for collective bargaining and the extent to which a local-international conflict raises a doubt as to the identity of the bargaining representative; the Labor Reform law regulates the reasons for and the manner in which the

[2] This account owes much to Clyde W. Summers, "Union Schism in Perspective: Flexible Doctrines, Double Standards, and Project Answers," 45 *Virginia Law Review*, 2. See also in *loc. cit.*, "Note: Disposition of Union Assets on Affiliation"; in addition see George Rose, "The Relationship of the Local Union to the International Organization," *Labor Law Journal*, vol. 4, chap. 5 (1953); Sidney E. Cohn, "The International and the Local Union," *Proceedings of New York University 11th Annual Conference on Labor* (Albany: Mathew Bender, 1958); Robert W. Gilbert, "The International Union—A New Legal Entity," *Labor Law Journal*, vol. 8, chap. 6 (1956), p. 337.

national union can set aside the self-government of the local union.

The operational facts of international-local relationship are seen more realistically in the ways the relationship actually functions—and this is the main subject of this chapter.

The international union as an operating fact is a pluralistic enterprise, which in turn is the product of a proliferation of internal governmental forms. Moreover, the international-local relationship is expressed in a variety of encounters. At different times the national union is the headquarters staff ranging from the president of the international union down to the auditor or the office manager, or the supply depot; or the international union may mean the intermediate bodies of one kind or another which derive their authority from the international union.

INTERMEDIATE BODIES

The intermediate body is the form of supralocal authority which impinges most pervasively on the life of the local union. Of 2,650 of these intermediate bodies reported under LMRDA, 2,095 were composed of locals of the same international and 555 were composed of local unions of different internationals.[3]

Intermediate bodies are fundamentally of two kinds. Closest to the international union—in a real sense a part of it—is the intermediate body which is an extension of the administrative power of the international, most frequently on some regional basis. The most common example of this is the regional director or the district director in the large mass production unions, with a responsibility for a constitutionally defined geographic area, usually, although not always, multistate in character. These regional officers are elected frequently by a caucus at the international conventions or in a separate election, held among representatives of the constituent locals. These regional officers tend to function in subordinate relationship to the international, and the regional director functions in effect as the agent or the spokesman for the international union in his region.

In contrast is the semi-autonomous, policy-making intermediate body which is sanctioned by the international union constitution

[3] BLMR, *op. cit.*, pp. 24–25; I am indebted to Mr. L. A. O'Donnell's forthcoming Ph.D. thesis on intermediate bodies for valuable detail (University of Wisconsin); Herbert Lahne, "The Intermediate Body in Collective Bargaining," *Industrial and Labor Relations Review*, January 1953, is a pioneering study in the field.

but which derives its authority and power primarily through its coordinating role among the constituent local unions. It will ordinarily function on an area-wide basis, as for example the District Council of Carpenters in a city, the Joint Council of Teamsters, and the joint boards of the Textile, Amalgamated, and Ladies' Garment Workers' Unions. It will function on an industry-wide or multiplant company basis, as for example the General Electric Conference Board of the IUE, the General Motors conference of the UAW, or the system boards of the railroad unions. More recently the large industrial unions have developed occupational intermediate bodies like the White Collar and Professional Conference Board of the IUE, or the Skilled Trades Conference of the UAW. A variant is the intermediate body composed of locals of different internationals, as for example, the New York Hotel Trades Council or the Allied Printing Trades Council. The authority of these semi-autonomous intermediate bodies will invariably derive from some continuing representative mechanism in which the participating local unions are represented. The LMRDA now requires the election of intermediate body officers by a delegate body elected in turn by membership secret ballot or directly by the members of the constituent local unions.[4]

The scope of authority of the semi-autonomous intermediate bodies will range from consultation to control in relation to their constituent locals. In general, the "control" quality of the intermediate body will be more characteristic among the nonfactory unions: teamsters, construction, and perhaps railroads. The purpose is to bring to bear authority comparable in scope to the scope of the labor market drawn on by the employer or the product market scope of the employer's operations. It is thus possible to achieve a degree of unity of action among locals with a common interest. In some situations this may be only a good reason for the intermediate body. The real reason may be nothing more complicated than the aggrandizement of union power of an individual or a group.

The Teamsters conference structure—seeded by the "Trotskyite" Dunne brothers in Minneapolis, sharpened by Dave Beck on the West Coast, and developed to a high point of proficiency by James Hoffa—is an attempt to mobilize for both area and product

[4] Title IV.

135

market. Thus, within any given conference (Northeast, Central States, etc.) product interests are organized in a series of divisions within each conference, i.e., milk, bakery, over-the-road, etc.[5]

The local union is subject to four types of functional influences from above. (1) In the directive relationship the local union is subject to initial instructions as to what it may do or what it may not do. (2) In the review relationship the local takes the initiative but such action is subject to review, inspection, or auditing by a superior body. (3) In the appellatory relationship the superior body functions as a line of appeal from disciplinary decisions made in the local union. (4) In the service relationship the superior body provides guidance, counsel and analysis, generally on the initiative of the local.

My plan at this point is to discuss the extent to which collective bargaining affecting the local union is subject to direction from above by supralocal agencies, mostly within the international, and in so doing to distinguish between negotiation and enforcement as phases of the collective bargaining process. This is followed by an examination of trusteeships as an aspect of the directive relationship.

INTERNATIONAL DIRECTIVE—BARGAINING

We have no precise measure of the extent to which the local is subject to international directive in bargaining negotiations. And if we are concerned ultimately with the effect on the local's capacity for self-determination we need to know whether representative mechanisms exist through which the local can make its views felt. We have no precise answers here either and in both cases we shall have to make do with the best judgments. As a matter of judgment, then, the involvement of supralocal units in the negotiation of agreements is substantial. This trend is not, however, well-defined; and the available evidence suggests contrasting directions depending on the unions involved.

The evidence suggests that the nonfactory unions have been moving away from local union control to control by intermediate bodies in the negotiation of agreements.

[5] Philip Taft, *The Structure and Government of Labor Unions* (Cambridge: Harvard University Press, 1954), p. 229 ff. See also Paul Jacobs, "The World of Jimmy Hoffa—I," *The Reporter*, January 24, 1957, p. 15 ff.

WEST COAST CONSTRUCTION

The outstanding feature of the collective bargaining experience in northern California since 1940 has been the extensive regional system evolved in certain of the trade. . . . The regional system of bargaining is used by all five of the basic trades: carpenters, construction laborers, operating engineers, cement masons, and construction teamsters. . . . One master contract which covers all forty-six counties of northern California is negotiated by the Associated General Contractors with each of the unions in the basic trades, excepting the carpenters.[6]

PACIFIC NORTHWEST LUMBER INDUSTRY

The policy of the Northwestern Council of Lumber and Sawmill Workers [a branch of the Brotherhood of Carpenters and Joiners] is to call wage conferences after the first of the year to establish a coordinated plan for negotiations. The results of the conference are recommendations on uniform wage increases and fringe issues. District councils and local unions have a formal right to decide whether or not they will accept the recommendations of the wage conference, and in addition, to determine those local issues which will be included in their negotiations.[7]

PACIFIC NORTHWEST CONSTRUCTION INDUSTRY

. . . The growth in the geographic coverage of single collective bargaining agreements is quite clear in the Pacific Northwest construction industry and seems to be representative of a national trend toward regional labor agreements in the industry. . . . The trend to area and regional bargaining is widespread in its effect and appears to concentrate further functions and responsibility in the international union, to diminish the importance of Building Trades Councils. . . .[8]

WEST COAST TEAMSTERS

The locus of decision-making on key issues of collective bargaining strategy or policy will tend to move upward from the local unions and the joint councils to the trade divisions of the conference. This trend will be more marked in certain industries

[6] Gordon W. Bertram and Sherman J. Maisel, *Industrial Relations in the Construction Industry, The Northern California Experience,* University of California, Berkeley, Institute of Industrial Relations, 1955, p. 15.

[7] Margaret S. Glock, *Collective Bargaining in the Pacific Northwest Lumber Industry,* University of California, Berkeley, Institute of Industrial Relations, 1955, p. 33.

[8] Kenneth M. McCaffree, "Regional Labor Agreements in the Construction Industry," *Industrial and Labor Relations Review,* July 1956, p. 609.

(e.g. milk production, baking, canning, auto freight) than in others.[9]

In most of the construction unions district councils, generally limited to a metropolitan labor market, have long had a primary role in the negotiation of the agreement; the Carpenters district councils go back to the early origins of the union. Currently there are on the order of three hundred such councils. Now regionalization of collective bargaining in the construction industry puts negatiations at an additional remove from the local union.[10]

In the mass production unions the international unions have always been importantly involved in the negotiation of the agreement, particularly industry-wide and multiplant agreements. But in recent years the tendency has been to create corporation or industry intermediate bodies. These latter are a part of the international union, to be sure, but they are more than administrative mechanisms of the international union headquarters and can exercise a good deal of independence in the negotiation of agreements. The joint board structures in the International Ladies' Garment Workers Union, the Amalgamated Clothing Workers, and the Textile Workers have always been the major force in the negotiation of agreements in the areas where these bodies existed.[11]

The intermediate body in the railroad unions has uniformly been the major agency in the negotiation of the contract and in the adjustment of grievances under the contract. These bodies are known variously as a General Committee of Adjustment, General Protective Committee, System Board of Adjustment—but they have in common that they constitute the generating force for bar-

[9] J. B. Gillingham, *The Teamsters Union on the West Coast,* University of California, Berkeley, Institute of Industrial Relations, 1956, p. 9.
[10] L. A. O'Donnell, *op. cit.* See also Robert A. Christie, *Empire in Wood: a History of the United Brotherhood of Carpenters and Joiners of America,* New York State School of Industrial Relations, Cornell University, 1956, pp. 63–64.
[11] See Richard A. Lester and Edward A. Robie, *Constructive Labor Relations,* Princeton University, Industrial Relations Section, 1948; Herbert Shepard, "Democratic Control in a Labor Union (ACWA) Toronto," *American Journal of Sociology,* 54, p. 311; Aaron Howard Myers, *Crisis Bargaining Management-Union Relations in Marginal Situations,* Northeastern University, Bureau of Business and Economic Research, 1957.

gaining activity in respect to each individual railroad.[12] The international union president of the Brotherhood of Sleeping Car Porters can displace any local chairman of a grievance committee.[13]

The wholesale involvement of the superior bodies in the adjustment of grievances is especially marked among the railroad unions, although it is not unknown in other situations. This is in large part due to the importance of the National Railroad Adjustment Board under the Railway Labor Act, which acts as a court of final adjudication of grievances. In the case of the Sleeping Car Porters, the control of the international union over the grievance procedure stems from a fear that if the grievance machinery were left solely in local hands the local committee could not properly cope with the power of the Pullman Company.

As was noted earlier, the fact that a superior body functions as the decisive factor in the negotiation of the agreement does not necessarily serve to exclude the local union from involvement in the negotiations, if there exists continuing representation machinery in the choice of officers of the higher body and in the supervision of the negotiations. And LMRDA now makes this mandatory for the union within the commerce jurisdiction of the law. Characteristically, the officers of the superior bodies on the order of the joint councils and joint boards are elected by a constituency consisting of delegates from the constituent local unions. But this has not been universally true. Before LMRDA the chief officer of the Teamster conferences was appointed by the international union president, and after appointment became an employee of the international union, functioning under the authority of the president and the executive board. Officers other than the chairman of the conference were elected. Until 1959 the key official of the Amalgamated Clothing Workers Joint Board, the manager, was designated by the general executive board of the international union for an indefinite term.[14]

Several observers have called attention to a wave of rebellion among locals refusing to accept settlements worked out by internationals. The rebellious spirit, it has been suggested, may

[12] L. A. O'Donnell, *op. cit.*
[13] Brailsford R. Brazeal, *The Brotherhood of Sleeping Car Porters: Its Origin and Development* (New York: Harper, 1946), pp. 176–177.
[14] L. A. O'Donnell, *op. cit.*

be attributable at least in part to the impression, if not the law, of Landrum-Griffin. According to David Cole, an experienced mediator in difficult union-management conflicts:

> We find a certain degree of rebelliousness and non-conformance within the labor movement that we did not see as recently as five years ago. I could illustrate this by so many incidents in the last few years—let me just mention just one or two. . . . When the machinists, a fine, well-organized, old established union has negotiated settlements in certain key industries or key operations, like the airline industry, we have seen repudiations repeatedly on the part of the locals, or the chapters, of the negotiations or the settlements worked out, even by Mr. Hayes, the president of the union. It took dramatic form in the fall of 1959 when the Machinists working for the Capital Airlines, one of the weakest of the airlines financially, declined to agree with the settlement along the lines worked out with the other airlines. Mr. Hayes took a hand, because two years earlier there had been an unnecessary strike, it was felt, on Capital Airlines and Mr. Hayes and his associates worked to negotiate what they thought was a fair settlement, and when it was submitted for ratification it was fought by a local chapter leader—a strong-willed man—who had perhaps personal motivations, I don't know. In any event when this large meeting took place there were placards around the room—"Hayes go home"—and the settlement was repudiated. The strike took place and went on for six or eight weeks—the settlement was very close to the one Mr. Hayes had negotiated, there was some face-saving additive, but it didn't amount to very much.

> Consider the settlement of the International Harvester strike last year, which was negotiated by the International UAW, also a union to be reckoned with. When ratification was considered by some of the locals, its large Local 6 was represented by a very important local official. And his attack on the settlement was in terms of Reutherism. . . . The settlement was finally ratified but it took a great deal of effort. . . .[15]

According to *Business Week* in the late spring of 1960:

> Almost every [Federal Mediation and Conciliation] region reported in one way or another, the weakened position of the big internationals.
> A report from one described the situation as "amazing" and another said that the softening of union control over bargaining

[15] *Current Trends in Collective Bargaining,* University of California, Los Angeles, Institute of Industrial Relations, May 11, 1960, p. 2.

can be found even where the internationals are pouring substantial sums of money into strikes in the form of strike benefits.

A mediator on the West Coast commented that "the problem seems to be that too much democracy within the union seems to prevail. . . . It is no longer what the leadership wants, many times it is what a minority of the membership wants" that causes trouble. There is wide agreement on this among mediators.[16]

Short of being actively involved in the negotiation of the agreement, the international union or the intermediate bodies—but more particularly the former—can achieve a measure of influence through the setting of contract standards or through other general determination of policy. In the nature of things, this will not have the same force as the direction of individual negotiations and the local unions, depending on their strength and other characteristics of the situation, can frequently alter or even disregard such general policy.

The pattern bargaining of the UAW—as an example of direction through national policy—has been applied with flexibility to local union situations. There was considerable pressure by the national UAW to enforce the economics or the cost of the agreement package, but not the particular form of the settlement. There were many situations in which

. . . Wages were substituted for pensions because of the dominant influence of younger men in the shop, or wages were substituted for insurance because a large percentage of women were already covered in their husbands' policies, or insurance was preferred to an SUB plan because of steady employment experience, etc. It is true that in practically all instances the international representative was expected to push for adoption of the major fringe programs of the UAW. In many plans, however, considerable substitutions occurred as a result of the preference of the particular group involved.[17]

In the national job classification program developed by the Steelworkers national union and the steel industry there has been

[16] *Business Week*, May 21, 1960, p. 149.
[17] Harold M. Levinson, "Pattern Bargaining by the United Automobile Workers," *Labor Law Journal*, September 1958, pp. 672–673. A later version is to be found in "Pattern Bargaining: A Case Study of the Automobile Workers," *Quarterly Journal of Economics*, May 1960.

substantial room for maneuverability on the part of the local union.

> [In two specific instances] local union autonomy has been extensive. Although the two classification manuals were negotiated at an industry-wide level, local unions have been allowed wide operational freedom in applying them to their local situation, particularly in Local Union 504, substantive as well as procedural deviations from the manual were made when necessary. The method for administration established by this local differs significantly from those of other locals in the same company and (to the extent of the author's knowledge) are probably unique within the international. In addition, provision for resolving disputed classifications at the company level outside of the grievance machinery, and the introduction of a new "4½ step" are marked variations from the industry-wide procedural pattern.[18]

There is an implication, however, in a "mandatory" policy adopted by the Oil, Chemical and Atomic Workers National Policy Committee for the Petroleum Industry that this policy is meant to be something more than perfunctory. The "mandatory" policy in this case was ratified by 75 per cent of the bargaining units affected, and in this instance required all local unions to adhere to a policy of a general wage increase of 18 cents an hour.[19] Also true of the large industrial unions is that where a contract is negotiated by an international union or an arm thereof it is rare that the multilocal agreement will apply equally to all terms of employment. Typically, such matters as seniority and incentives are left to local determination. A UAW–GM agreement left the following issues for local determination:

> Disputes as to whether employees are members of the union; districting of bargaining units; negotiation of local seniority agreements; reducing work-week before making layoffs; setting of production standards; shift preference; wage payment plans; change from an incentive to hourly rate basis.[20]

The work rules of the printing trades craft unions are set by national policy. In the International Typographical Union, its

[18] Robert Dean Garton, "Job Classification in the Steel Industry; the Experience of Two Local Unions," *ILResearch*, vol. 5, Fall 1959, New York School of Industrial and Labor Relations, p. 11.
[19] Bureau of National Affairs, *Collective Bargaining*, July 22, 1960.
[20] Harold Davey, *Contemporary Collective Bargaining* (New York: Prentice-Hall, 1951).

president, Woodruff Randolph, said: "The ITU general laws state the minimum basis upon which collective bargaining may be had by employers who want to make agreements with our local unions. These minimum requirements are accepted as axiomatic, without challenge or questions by either party because they have come into being and remain an absolute necessity by the natural joint experience of both proprietors and employees."[21]

Writing from his experience as an employer association representative in Philadelphia, John W. Seybold has said of the ITU: "The authority of the local union group has been successively curtailed. It is now contrary to the union's laws for the local even to *present* to the employer a contract proposal which has not been previously scrutinized by the international's contract department, or to sign a negotiated contract which has not been previously found acceptable to the international."[22]

This rigid conformity to international union law, however, is not universally true of the other printing trades unions. The Pressmen's laws "are not so onerous in practice and they are not observed so scrupulously. In the case of both unions, the extent to which such regulations prove burdensome or present an inflexible barrier in bargaining will depend upon the degree to which local unions are inclined—and are permitted—to deviate from these provisions."[23]

Another manifestation of direction by national policy is the considerable number of jurisdictional agreements negotiated at the union summit in recent years. These agreements are intended to bind the locals of the signatory internationals. Their purpose is to resolve some of the more irksome problems of rival unionism. The Building and Construction Trades Department has sponsored a National Joint Board for Settlement of Jurisdictional Disputes; individual national unions have entered into bilateral pacts with each other; a no-raiding agreement is explicitly incorporated in the AFL–CIO constitution; the Building and Construction Trades Department and the Industrial Union Department have negotiated a pact relating to industrial union-craft union conflicts of the contracting-out variety; and, finally, the

[21] "Reproduction in the Printing and Publishing Industry," *Labor Law Journal*, May 1953, p. 378.
[22] *Philadelphia Printing Industry: A Case Study*, University of Pennsylvania Industry-Wide Collective Bargaining Series, 1949, p. 51.
[23] *Ibid.*, p. 55–56.

Industrial Union Department has taken over the old CIO Organizational Disputes Agreement which is the most far-reaching attempt at resolving rival union claims.[24]

These treaties have worked with varying degrees of effectiveness. When they have not worked a large element has been the unwillingness of local unions to accept nationally determined settlements. This has been a special problem in the agreements worked out under the Building and Construction Trades Disputes Agreement. The problem has been to get compliance at the local level.

The enforcement of the agreement through a grievance procedure or through informal adjustment procedures is overwhelmingly in the precinct of the local union; the railroad unions, as has been noted, are a significant exception. In the locals that are part of a multi-employer or multiplant corporation agreement, the exclusive control of the local over grievance-handling may stop at the point of arbitration or at highest management level. The international union may intervene at this final point to provide for the most effective presentation before the arbitration tribunal, and even more importantly, to guard against the local's impairment of national precedents.

STEEL

One of the most interesting aspects of the Steelworkers' organization is the contrast between its approach to negotiation and to administration. Over the years it has become highly centralized in its approach to negotiation, but it is still highly decentralized in its approach to administration. Contract administration for all plants of all companies in a district operates through the district director's office. An international representative from this office will typically handle the contract administration problems for a given plant. This leads to a high degree of local autonomy with no strong unification on the union side with respect to the various plants of a given company. On the union side, there is a considerable gap between leadership in negotiation and leadership in contract administration. Although this is filled to some extent by staff guidance, as illustrated by

[24] Jack Barbash, "Jurisdiction," *Industrial Bulletin*, State of New York Department of Labor, November 1957; John T. Dunlop, "Structural Changes in the American Labor Movement," *Proceedings*, Industrial Relations Research Association, 1956; Mark L. Kahn, "Recent Jurisdictional Developments in Organized Labor," in Harold Davey, *et al. New Dimensions in Collective Bargaining*, Industrial Relations Research Association Series (New York: Harper, 1959).

the new arbitration handbook, locals most certainly are masters of their own destiny in living under the contract.[25]

John Dunlop's judgment that "local bargaining predominates in the American industrial relations system" represents the consensus.[26] The Bureau of Labor Statistics estimates there are 150,000 agreements in effect exclusive of negotiated insurance and pension plans.[27] By European standards, certainly, the American system is highly atomized. The drift—it would be wrong to characterize it as a trend or tendency—is probably away from exclusive local control of the negotiation of the agreement. The enforcement of the agreement is subject overwhelmingly to local control, particularly in the lower stages of the grievance machinery in the case of stratified or graduated grievance systems prevailing in industry. The probabilities are that the intermediate bodies rather than the international union headquarters are the strategic element in the negotiation of the agreement; but in most instances the constituent local unions can exercise a large measure of influence through duly constituted, representative mechanisms, through local self-determination of uniquely local problems, and ultimately through open defiance of the international.

Wherever the "locus of power" in bargaining rests, the burden of facts suggests that the distribution of collective bargaining authority as among the levels of union government derives from an assessment of operating realities and not primarily from a heedless drive for power for its own sake. The latter exists, of course, but it is not a paramount force.

INTERNATIONAL DIRECTIVE—TRUSTEESHIP

The local is subject to the direction of the international if it is put under trusteeship. Trusteeship is a procedure by which the self-government of a subordinate body is set aside. It is also known as receivership and supervision. The trustee is likely to be a representative of the international, although there are instances in which a local officer becomes the trustee in behalf of the international. In these circumstances the local union officer is responsible to the international. The trusteeship is the ultimate sanction by which the national union secures compliance with its laws and directions by subordinate bodies.

[25] U.S. Department of Labor, *Collective Bargaining in the Basic Steel Industry* (Washington: January 1961), p. 123.
[26] Dunlop, *op. cit.*, p. 16.
[27] BLS, *Directory*, p. 15.

In 114 international union constitutions studied by the U.S. Bureau of Labor Statistics, 67 were found with explicit trusteeship provisions. All of the 114 constitutions provided for suspension and revocation of local union charters. The main characteristics of trusteeship provisions found in this survey may be summarized as follows:

1. Trusteeship is dealt with briefly in many of the constitutions. The constitution grants the president or the union's supreme governing body the power to impose trusteeship in their discretion: "to protect the interest of the members," "to protect the union's jurisdiction," "a local union fails to perform the duties imposed upon it by this constitution," "an emergency imminently affecting the interest of the international union or subordinate body."

2. Union constitutions frequently define the reasons for trusteeship. Characteristic reasons included, among others: "failure to comply with union directives, violation of union laws, dishonesty or incompetence in the affairs of local unions, membership indifference, and the threat of secession movements."

3. A large majority of constitutions containing trusteeship provisions lodged the final authority to designate a trustee in the general executive board or its equivalent in the international union.

4. The large majority of constitutions did not require a hearing procedure "which could be construed as relating to trusteeship cases."

5. The rights of the local union under trusteeship were only rarely specified.

6. The scope of authority of the trustees was specified in detail in virtually all of the constitutions.

7. The overwhelming majority of the constitutions did not specify the conditions under which self-government for the local union could be restored.

8. In all of the constitutions the line of appeal from a trusteeship action was to the international union convention.

9. A majority of the constitutions provided for three major procedural safeguards: hearing, appeal, and automatic termination in one combination or another.[28]

[28] BLS, *Union Constitution Provisions: Trusteeship,* Bulletin No. 1263, 1959, pp. 3–20 *passim.*

Trusteeship is regarded as a safeguard against: (1) control of the local union by dishonest persons; (2) extravagance or mismanagement of local union affairs by local union officers; (3) refusal of local union officers to conform to the financial standards of the international union; (4) control by a local union officer of the local union contrary to constitutional provisions; (5) disruption due to communist control, internal schisms, or secession movements, (6) irresponsible behavior in collective bargaining and strikes on the part of local union officers; (7) disintegration of the local union and the consequent failure to perform its proper function.[29]

The LMRDA regulates the trusteeship relationship by prescribing: (a) the broad purposes for which trusteeships may be imposed; namely, to deal with corruption, to insure the performance of collective bargaining agreements, to restore democratic government, and for otherwise "legitimate objects"; (b) the terms under which trusteeships may be litigated; a presumption of validity if the trusteeship has lasted for eighteen months or less, a presumption of invalidity if the trusteeship has lasted longer than eighteen months; (c) periodic reporting during the life of the trusteeship; (d) the preservation of assets of the trusteed locals; (e) the conditions under which the convention representation of trusteed locals may be voted at international union conventions; votes of trusteed locals can be counted only if the delegates were elected by a secret ballot vote of the members in good standing; (f) authority to the secretary of labor to investigate allegedly illegal trusteeships on complaint.[30]

The state of union trusteeships as reported under LMRDA may be summarized thus:

1. Forty-five internationals—39 AFL–CIO affiliates—have reported 508 trusteeships over subordinate bodies.

2. The Carpenters, Teamsters, and United Mine Workers were responsible for over half of the trusteeships, with the last-named accounting for more than one-third of the total. The large

[29] See George Meany's testimony in U.S. Senate, Committee on Labor and Public Welfare, Subcommittee on Labor, *Union Financial and Administrative Practices and Procedures*, 8th Cong., 2d Sess., pp. 63–65; also Archibald Cox, "The Role of Law in Preserving Union Democracy," in *Labor in a Free Society* (Berkeley: University of California Press, 1950), p. 77.

[30] Title III.

number of Carpenters' trusteeships is due to the technicality that the constituent locals of a "trusteed" district council are automatically included under the latter's trusteeship even though the autonomy of the locals as such is not in fact affected. The reports suggest that LRMDA overstates in general the number of genuinely functioning trusteeships since many internationals play it safe and file if there is any doubt at all as to the status of a subordinate body.

3. The major single reasons given—multiple reasons were given in some—for the establishment of trusteeships were "'caretaker' operations pending dissolution of local" and assistance to subordinate bodies.[31]

OFFICIAL JUSTIFICATION FOR ESTABLISHING TRUSTEESHIPS

Reason		Single Reasons		Multiple Reasons
Total reports*		453		25**
"Caretaker" operations pending dissolution of local		88		
Assistance to subordinate bodies		135		18
Ineffectiveness of local leadership	32		6	
Members unwilling or unable to assume leadership	19		1	
Failure in collective bargaining	14		6	
Reason for need of assistance not specified	70		5	
Wildcat and other strikes		7		
Failure to pay per capita or other violations of constitution		19		6
Financial malpractices		22		4
Corruption and other undemocratic practices		17		8
Dual unionism		40		2
Factionalism and dissension		37		10
Chartered under trusteeships		61		
"Conditions warranted"		14		
No record of reason		13		

* Excludes sixty-three Carpenter reports dealing with local unions placed under trusteeships together with district councils, thirty reports by Railway Supervisors and Maintenance of Way filed erroneously and twenty-four Canadian trusteeships.
** Details do not add up to total because some reports stated two or three reasons.

Source: Sar A. Levitan, "Union Trusteeships: The Federal Law and An Inventory," *Labor Law Journal* (1960) 11, 12, p. 1079, Table 3.

[31] Sar A. Levitan, "Union Trusteeships: The Federal Law and an Inventory," *Labor Law Journal*, vols. 11, 12 (1960), p. 1067. See also BLMR, *Report,* p. 32 ff.

In a systematic study of trusteeships imposed by the International Chemical Workers Union, it was concluded that "the ICWU's record with respect to trusteeship is not unblemished [but] it does not conform to the pattern described by the McClellan committee. A few abuses were noted but some of these situations were rectified before the commission of irreparable harm, and together they do not present a general picture of illicit or unethical behavior. . . . It is clear that the power of trusteeship has afforded the international president the degree of flexibility and freedom necessary for effective trade union administration in the face of internal or external threats to the stability of the organization."[32]

In general, trusteeships are indispensable to effective union administration; they have been used sparingly and under constitutional sanction. The trusteeship principle has been abused where it has been used as a device for systematically throttling local union self-government. Specifically those abuses include attempts at eliminating local union elements in conflict with the international leadership, the authoritarian ambitions of international union officers to control important locals, or to control a local's financial resources.[33]

INTERNATIONAL REVIEW—BARGAINING

There are three functions of the local union which are routinely subject to review by the international union in most international union constitutions: (1) the collective agreement, (2) the authorization to strike, and (3) the financial administration of the local union.

The state of union law on the question of contract authorization procedure has been studied by the National Industrial Conference Board, and it found:

1. Thirteen constitutions, covering a declared membership of 2,181,277 grant the international union the power to make all collective bargaining contracts or state that the international may assume this power in instances where it is deemed necessary.
2. Eighty-three constitutions covering a declared membership of 8,035,980 give the international the power to authorize

[32] Arnold Weber, "Local Union Trusteeship and Public Policy," *Industrial and Labor Relations Review,* January 1961, p. 203.
[33] Cox, "The Role of Law," *op. cit.,* p. 76; Sar Levitan, *op. cit.,* p. 1091.

collective bargaining contracts negotiated by local unions.
3. Eleven allow the locals to make contracts on their own authority. These constitutions cover a declared membership of 655,553.

NICB points out that "two or more methods of assuring international control of contracts may be used by the same union." For example, "a union's constitution may require the use of a standard contract but may also state that the local is to obtain the approval of the international executive board."[34]

There is reason to believe, however, that there is a wide gap between constitutional doctrine and actual practice. Leiserson's observation on this point is that "a local which can successfully handle most of its business and all its internal affairs is largely self-governing despite the supervisory authority the constitution vests in the upper governmental units."[35] For most contracts the review of the national union tends to be superficial, and only in the most extraordinary circumstances does a national union override a locally negotiated contract because there has probably been consultation with the international on doubtful agreements prior to consummation. This is notably true for unions that bargain in a local market situation.[36]

STRIKE AUTHORIZATION

The constitutional provisions with respect to strike authorization have been summarized by the National Industrial Conference Board:

1. One hundred and three constitutions (53.1%) covering a declared membership of 10½ million (60.5% of the total) vest final authority to approve locally authorized strikes in the international union.
2. Two constitutions covering a declared membership of 612,000 require international approval of important strikes, but allow purely local strikes if the local union bears the entire cost.
3. Twenty-three constitutions covering a declared membership of 2.8 million (16.2%) allow local unions to strike without international union approval but declare that in such cases they will receive no financial support from the international union treasury.
4. Ten constitutions covering a declared membership of 720,255

---

[34] NICB, *Handbook,* pp. 49–51 *passim.*
[35] Leiserson, *op. cit.,* p. 288.
[36] Robert R. France, *Union Decisions in Collective Bargaining,* Princeton University, Industrial Relations Section, 1955, p. 21 ff.

(4.1%) allow local unions to strike without any international union approval.

5. Nine constitutions covering a declared membership of 681,395 vest sole authority to authorize strikes in the international union.

6. Thirteen constitutions of unions of government workers, covering a declared membership of 598,438 (3.4%) prohibit strikes.

7. Twenty-nine constitutions covering a declared membership of 1.4 million (7.8%) do not contain any provisions governing strike authorization.[37]

The increased possibility of international union liability for local union strike action under law has prompted unions in recent years to tighten strike authorization procedures. The Teamsters, for example, use a "Form P2028 Request for Strike Sanction"— filled out in quintuplicate by the local requesting strike sanction. The president, the vice-president in charge of the district, the local, each one gets a copy and two copies are required for the files of the appropriate Teamsters joint council. The strike authorization procedure involves four investigations "with reports and referrals."[38]

INTERNATIONAL AUDITING

The extent to which the international unions are required to, and do in fact, audit the books of their subordinate bodies including the locals is not known precisely, but it is substantial. A special committee of international union secretary-treasurers of the AFL–CIO adopted a code requiring in part that each "affiliate should require, at least annually, that an audit be made of the accounts of its subordinate bodies by competent persons. A summary of such audit approved by such competent person should be made available to the membership of such subordinate body." The Ethical Practices Committee of the AFL–CIO believes that "almost all unions . . . comply with the minimum controls set forth" in the code.[39]

APPEALS

The constitutional basis for the international union's appellatory function with respect to the local unions are known. As summarized by the National Industrial Conference Board:

[37] NICB, *op. cit.*, p. 42.
[38] *Business Week*, August 8, 1959, p. 99.
[39] U.S. Senate, *Union Financial and Administrative Practices and Procedures,* pp. 103–105.

Almost all the union constitutions which contain disciplinary provisions also provide for appeals by members dissatisfied with the local union verdict. Only eighteen of the constitutions covered by this study fail to list appeals procedures among their provisions governing local union discipline. These unions have a declared membership of 469,074—only 2.8% of the total covered by this study.

The appeals procedure laid down in most union constitutions guarantees international controls over local disciplinary power. Even if the international union has absolutely no right to take original jurisdiction in a disciplinary case against an individual member, the member if dissatisfied with the local unit's verdict, can appeal to the international under the constitutions of almost all the unions in the study. The international may set aside the local's decision, reverse it, alter the penalty, dismiss the case, or take any other action it deems necessary. The appeals procedure described here relates the serious cases in which the member has been expelled or punished in other severe ways. A few union constitutions state that cases involving small fines and other mild punishment may not be appealed so high within the union organization as cases involving more serious punishments.[40]

There are conflicting views as to whether the international union renders a genuinely independent judgment in exercising its appeal function. Philip Taft concludes from a study of international union records:

> It is obvious that the appellate machinery offers real protection in most unions, and that central organizations do not freely allow unreasonable penalties or unwarranted convictions. . . . Those who review [a member's] case usually are concerned not only with the defendant receiving a proper trial, but with the appropriateness of the penalty. Unions have sometimes found that there is a tendency for local members to be too lenient rather than too severe, although the latter is not unknown.

> On the whole, there is no evidence that the appellate machinery does not function effectively, that it is vain or useless, or that it would be improved by government supervision. Given the

[40] NICB, *op. cit.*, p. 70. See also chapter on "Judicial Process Within Unions," in William M. Leiserson, *American Trade Union Democracy* (New York: Columbia University Press, 1959); Leo Bromwich, *Union Constitutions*, A Report to the Fund for the Republic (New York: 1959), p. 29 ff.

special and frequently difficult problems dealt with by unions, the available information shows that disciplinary machinery functions, on the whole, justly and effectively.[41]

Clyde Summers, whose raw material comes out of litigated court cases and the analysis of constitutional provisions renders a less favorable assessment:

> The ability to appeal may give some protection, but here, too, the procedure is dominated by the elected officers. An international president may hesitate to uphold an individual's appeal from a local whose support he needs in order to retain office. Throughout the whole procedure an individual discipline case is in danger of becoming a political football and being decided on the relative strength of opposing factions within the union rather than on the merits of the case.[42]

In order to enhance the independence of the appeals procedure, two international unions have set up outside review boards composed of people who have no connection with the union. These unions are the United Automobile Workers and the Upholsterers' International Union. A study made of the UAW Public Review Board indicates that it has taken its functions seriously and has been an autonomous court within the framework of the UAW constitution.[43]

SERVICE RELATIONSHIPS

The local union as day-to-day enterprise deals with the international union most characteristically in a service posture; that is, the international union representative works with the local in the negotiation of the agreement, processing grievances, assisting with technical problems beyond the competence of the local union officers, and in a variety of other relationships or functions.

The variations in the service relationship between the local and the international seem to turn on whether the local is a dependent partner in the relationship or an independent partner in the relationship. The dependent relationship is frequently due

[41] Philip Taft, *The Structure and Government of Labor Unions* (Cambridge: Harvard University Press, 1954), p. 180.

[42] Clyde Summers, "Disciplinary Procedures of Unions," *Industrial and Labor Relations Review*, vol. 4, chap. 1 (1950), p. 19.

[43] Jack Stieber, Walter E. Oberer, and Michael Harrington, *Democracy and Public Review*, Center for the Study of Democratic Institutions, Santa Barbara, California, 1960.

more to the insistence of the local union on service for its per capita than it is to the bureaucratic impulses of the international union representative. The local union argument usually runs that "we ought to get something for our money."

DEPENDENCE

Here are examples of dependent relationships in the factory situation:

GRAIN PROCESSING LOCAL—"ILLINI CITY" AND REGIONAL DIRECTOR

The regional director was the chief organizer and planner of organizing strategy for the region. In the early days of the region, he participated in most of the organizing campaigns and even during the period of the study, with his increased staff, he kept in close touch with the organizing work. For a number of years, the regional director personally undertook the close supervision of the newly-formed locals. However, that function was later delegated to subordinates. The regional director was the chief negotiator for the region. At first he negotiated most of the new contracts and wage demands, but as the region grew and more staff members were added, he handled only the most important and most difficult negotiations. He was a general troubleshooter in the region for any difficult problems concerning internal union affairs or any problems which the locals had with employers. His functions also included those of being chief advice-giver and consultant for local union officers, supervisor of the regional staff, leader of regional political action, chief public relations man for the region, office manager, and many other lesser tasks.[44]

METAL PRODUCTS LOCAL—"ILLINI CITY" AND REGIONAL REPRESENTATIVE

The local union was represented in bargaining by the five members of the bargaining committee and the president, with the assistance and supervision of one or more regional representatives. The experienced regional representative usually acted as spokesman. The constitution of the union made it necessary to submit each contract to a check, theoretically by the international president but practically by the regional office. Any strike action also was subject to regional and international approval. Aside from these general checks however, the local representatives were free to determine their relationships to the

[44] *Labor-Management Relations in Illini City,* University of Illinois, Institute of Labor and Industrial Relations, 1953, vol. 1, p. 165.

company. The regional representative was available as advisor and troubleshooter but appeared only when important grievances were in process or when grievance negotiations seemed in danger of failure.[45]

METAL WORKING LOCALS, MIDWEST AND JOINT BOARD

As in any joint board structure . . . the local unions have formal autonomy on purely local matters and, in this union, shop bodies have the final say on shop matters such as contract negotiations. . . . Again the business agent comes into the picture. It is the business agent assigned to the local or shop who makes recommendations to the unit and meets dissenting remarks or requests for clarification that come off the floor. Usually his recommendations are not solely as a result of his own thinking, however. They tend to be either based upon established joint board policy (formal or informal) or to have been brought up at the business agents' staff meetings for discussion and decision in cases where policy is not clear. . . . As a consequence there is a definite margin in favor of the original decision made by the business agent group.[46]

TEXTILE LOCALS, NEW ENGLAND AND INTERNATIONAL UNION

In a New England situation involving the Textile Workers Union, the local unions moved from an attitude of hostility to and independence of the international to a posture of dependence when it found that the problems involved in an accommodation to technical change were beyond its resources. In the past the local union had "rarely sought aid from the parent union in local matters. . . . In fact, outside help was resented." On various occasions the local had in fact threatened to withdraw from the international: in 1936 over the critical attitude of the international union toward Father Coughlin; in 1946 over an international union requirement that each local had to affiliate with a joint board. As one local confronted a drastic change in technology,

The formal structure of the local union underwent almost no change . . . [but] new developments in the relationship between the local, the international, and the management saw a

[45] *Ibid.,* pp. 336–337.
[46] Hjalmar Rosen and R. A. Hudson Rosen, "Decision Making in a Business Agent Group," *Proceedings,* Industrial Relations Research Association (1955), pp. 290–291.

shift in the local union's decision-making function away from the local officers in two directions—toward both the international officials and the rank and file. The international tended to frame general policies to guide the local union; while because the technical change negotiations affected the individual worker so closely, the rank and file became more active in making final decisions. The belief that the international union was in cahoots with management and that the local union officers were permitting this to happen resulted in a turnover of officers in 1947. The local turned to the international union in the persons of the international representative, the research director, and the manager of the area joint board. The role of the international then became that of a buffer between the resistance of the local union officers to the change and the interests on the part of management in developing a rational wage structure which would permit it to compete with the rest of the industry. The international union brought to bear a larger view of the industry's needs at the same time that its intervention probably caused one set of local union officers to be defeated and replaced by a new set.[47]

STEEL LOCAL AND DISTRICT DIRECTOR

The evolution of a relationship in a reverse trend is seen in the Sharon Steel local relationship with the district office of the United Steelworkers of America. The early shaping of the relationship between the union and the employer was influenced a good deal by the personal friendship between Henry Roemer, the president of Sharon Steel, and John W. Grajciar. As a consequence Grajciar "found himself receiving from ten to twenty telephone calls a day from members at the Sharon plant requesting that he bring up some particular grievance at his next meeting with management. He was fast becoming not only the first, but virtually the only step of the grievance procedure so far as the union was concerned. It was quite evident that such a situation was both unworkable from a practical standpoint and undesirable in its effect upon local union officials. Consequently an effort was begun to encourage a higher degree of participation by officials in the local. This effort is producing noticeable results which bode well for the long-run stability of the relation-

[47] Solomon B. Levine, *Union-Management Relations and Technical Change, A Field Study of the Experience in Woolen and Worsted Textile Mills*, Ph.D. dissertation, Massachusetts Institute of Technology, 1951, p. 64 ff.

ship." It is still clear, however, that the district director is an important element in the union-management relationship at Sharon Steel.[48]

INDUSTRIAL LOCALS AND INTERNATIONAL REPRESENTATIVES

International representatives in three industrial unions are "formally employed by the international president . . . [but the] appointments are normally made at the request of regional directors, who are thus able to reward local officers who have worked with them effectively." The duties of the international representatives consist of "supervision of local union affairs" although this is not part of their constitutional authority since the local union officers are "not formally responsible to the regional directors of these unions or their staffs." These "staff men" play a leading role in formulating the demands of their local unions in preparation for negotiation and in representing them at the bargaining table. The representative tries to conform in general to the pattern that may have been set by the international union, but "representatives do not adhere rigidly to instructions from the international. Variations in incentive programs, job classification systems, age distributions, and other local characteristics make it impossible simply to adopt a standard agreement on money issues. . . . International representatives automatically gain some flexibility in setting goals for individual negotiations."

> His relative freedom from membership pressure enables the staff man to provide a stabilizing influence in contract administration through the elimination of nuisance grievances and the resolution of conflicts of interest within the locals. Since the turnover of local officers is rather high, the representative provides a degree of continuity which permits more consistent contract interpretation and the carryover of experience in dealing with employers. An incidental role which the staff performs as a result of conferences with the local committees in preparing for negotiations and discussing grievance matters is to educate local officers in the meaning and application of the contract. Although it is not their purpose, these meetings are probably important in gaining acceptance for new contract provisions and pave the way for a more stable administration of the agreement. . . .

[48] J. Wade Miller, Jr., *Sharon Steel Corporation and United Steelworkers of America,* Causes of Industrial Peace Under Collective Bargaining, Case Study No. 5, NPA, April 1949, p. 21.

Although the representatives are considered to be important as political workers in international union politics, their influence is limited as long as the rank and file have a free vote. Their role in union politics depends in large measure on their relations with local officers and on the existence of factions within the locals that could be used by their opponents or by themselves in some circumstances, to gain access to the general membership.

Representatives have the means, depending in part on their relations with management, to exert influence on local union elections, but the obstacles in the way of success, and the risk which such interference in local affairs involves, indicate that this is not an important problem. There is no evidence that staff representatives are a threat to local union democracy. . . .[49]

Patterns of dependency have been observed in nonfactory situations as well.

BUS LOCAL AND INTERNATIONAL REPRESENTATIVE

In a Rochester local of the Amalgamated Association of Streetcar Employees with a full-time but weak business agent, the international union representative was frequently active in local negotiations but there was a measure of independence in that the local, on one occasion, asked the international union to withdraw one international representative and the international complied. During a six-week period studied by the investigator the international representative's services were requested on three different occasions by the local. The issues involved were the eligibility of a nominee to the presidency of the local, a grievance over abolishing the title of janitor, and the avoidance of a strike.[50]

UTILITY LOCALS AND INTERNATIONAL
REPRESENTATIVE

The Chicago Commonwealth Edison Company bargains with a joint council comprised of locals of the IBEW who had previously been independents. It is the joint council that bargains

[49] Myron L. Joseph, "The Role of the Field Staff Representative," *Industrial and Labor Relations Review,* April 1959, p. 368 ff.

[50] Donald W. Hill, *Labor-Management Relations between the Rochester Transit Corporation and the Amalgamated Association of Street, Electric Railway and Motor Coach Employees of America, Division 282, AFL,* unpublished M.S. thesis, New York State School of Industrial and Labor Relations, 1955, p. 62 ff.

with the company on all issues. In this situation the international representative of the IBEW is the dominating personality in the joint council, mediating differences between the locals. This position which the international representative occupies is attributed to his personality rather than to his position.[51]

INDEPENDENCE

Illustrations of the independent, nonfactory local are seen in the following situations:

RETAIL CLERKS LOCAL

A 450-member local of the Retail Clerks largely dominated by the business agent: According to that same business agent, most of the authority was in the local union itself and "as long as a local does a good job and adequately services its members the international stays out of the picture and the local runs all its own affairs. Although the international union makes spot checks to find out whether the local is doing its job.[52]

TEAMSTERS LOCAL—"ILLINI CITY"

In the Illini City Teamsters' union the 900-member local union was part of a network of international union relationships which included membership in the national over-the-road conference, the central states drivers' council, the Teamsters joint council for downstate Illinois, the central states conference of Teamsters, and the Illinois Teamsters' conference.

> The relations of the business agent to the international leadership—especially the international representative in the area—ranged from routine business to disagreements over matters such as local control, organization, and jurisdictional disputes. It is perhaps accurate to say that the business agent recognized his "legal" obligations to the international and also recognized the need for some control by the international in order to improve the total union service to the working man. However, he

[51] James C. Hogue, *An Exploratory Study of the Union Structure and the Relationship of Commonwealth Edison and the International Brotherhood of Electrical Workers,* unpublished M.S. thesis, University of Illinois, Institute of Industrial and Labor Relations, 1958, p. 27 ff.

[52] Wayne Lawrence Inks, *Unionism in the Retail Food Industry: A Local Case Study of Structure and Function,* unpublished M.A. thesis, University of Illinois, Institute of Labor and Industrial Relations, 1959, p. 55.

felt that the international authority should be largely limited to giving legal advice, interpreting laws and lobbying. Matters like organization and bargaining should be left to the local unions and their joint councils.

If the business agent felt that an action was justified in the best interests of his men, and if the membership was behind him on the action, he did not hesitate to oppose the international officials. The international office had asked him on three different occasions to show cause why his charter should not be revoked. In his own words the international looked at him as a "bad boy" because he had bucked them.[53]

The factory local that maintains an independent posture in relationship to the international is seen in a number of cases.

MILLMEN'S LOCALS (CARPENTERS)

"Barring intra-union dissension or financial difficulties or interunion jurisdictional disputes, a local union may run all of its affairs to suit itself. The writer estimates that 90% of decision-making regarding union affairs is done at a local level." The ways in which the international union was most helpful in aiding the locals was to provide the services of international representatives for negotiations, furnishing statistics, assistance in organizing workers, strike benefits, and legal aid and counsel. The advantage of belonging to the Carpenters' Union has been for these locals the maintenance of a relationship between the workers on the product in the mill and the craftsmen installing the end product. But this advantage was not always apparent.[54]

STEEL LOCALS

The two locals of the United Steelworkers of America which bargain at the Minnequa plant of Colorado Fuel and Iron Corporation are characterized as enjoying "wide freedom . . . in spite of the centralized structure of the United Steelworkers of America."[55]

[53] *Illini City,* vol. 1, p. 574.
[54] Walter Miles Allen, *Bargaining Problems in Industrial Locals within a National Craft Union; Case Study of the Midwestern Millmen,* unpublished, M.A. thesis, University of Illinois, Institute of Labor and Industrial Relations, 1956, pp. 21–22.
[55] George W. Zinke, *Minnequa Plant of Colorado Fuel and Iron Corporation and Two Locals of United Steelworkers of America,* Causes of Industrial Peace Under Collective Bargaining, NPA, Case Study No. 9, October 1951, p. 15.

CHEMICAL LOCAL

A local of the International Chemical Workers Union at the Dewey and Almy Chemical Company

> . . . is self-reliant and reasonably competent in conducting its affairs. As a matter of fact, it is sufficiently competent to conduct its negotiations without aid. The current Agreement was successfully negotiated without the presence of an International representative. Actually, the only time it has required and accepted any considerable amount of outside aid from the A. F. of L. was during the period of strained relations [with the company] in 1933–44. That aid was provided, and it strengthened the union's self-confidence at a critical time.[56]

GLASS LOCAL

The Libbey-Owens-Ford Glass Company and the Federation of Glass, Ceramic and Silica Sand Workers of America:

> The rights of the local are rigorously safeguarded. Strong feelings of membership control and local autonomy appear to stem from an early experience with one-man unionism in the person of the first International president who had a somewhat unsavory reputation within the union for dealing privately and secretly with the companies. The Glass Workers have since taken constitutional precautions to prevent a recurrence of "top-down" unionism.[57]

STEEL LOCAL

The independence of the Atlantic Steel local in relation to the United Steelworkers of America stemmed from an oversight. It was the local that was certified as the bargaining representative rather than the Steel Workers Organizing Committee. The company was therefore under no obligation to recognize the international representatives or to permit them to be involved in any way in the bargaining conference. Although this never became an issue directly, during a period of abrasive relationship between the company and the union the management was careful

[56] Douglas McGregor and Joseph N. Scanlon, *The Dewey and Almy Chemical Company and The International Chemical Workers Union,* Causes of Industrial Peace Under Collective Bargaining, NPA, Case Study No. 3, December 1948, p. 45.

[57] Frederick H. Harbison and King Carr, *The Libbey-Owens-Ford Glass Company and the Federation of Glass, Ceramic and Silica Sand Workers of America,* Causes of Industrial Peace Under Collective Bargaining, NPA, Case Study No. 2, October 1948, p. 8.

to remind the international representative that he was there by sufferance of the company.

The effect of this situation on the local union spokesmen was psychological. It gave them a feeling "of ultimate responsibility that would have been absent had the international possessed the final word on the contract."

> From 1941–1950, in other words, the international office stood in a staff rather than in a line relationship with the local so far as bargaining was concerned. It could and did offer advice and services, but the final decision was up to local leadership.

> The habit of years is not easily shaken, and the local still regards bargaining over the contract as a local affair, rather than as something that is merely local affirmation of an agreement, in which the basic points have been worked out in the Pittsburgh area. Its contract is so untypical of the usual collective bargaining agreements signed in the steel industry that for the local to follow more than the broad lines of national bargaining in the steel industry would require a major revision of its whole contractual relationship.

> The local's relationship to the International is one of voluntary cooperation rather than of dependency or compliance. The rank and file members think of the local as an organization of their own creation, not merely as a branch of a national association. They consider their present relationship with the International very much like that of one sovereign body joined with another in an alliance for mutual benefit, rather than of themselves as in any way subservient to the international office. They answer a national strike call, not because they are taking orders, but because they believe in collective bargaining, and in the necessity of a united front on the part of labor when important issues are to be resolved between labor and management on a national strike.[58]

NASHUA GUMMED AND COATED PAPER COMPANY AND SEVEN AFL LOCAL UNIONS

The freedom of locals in handling their own affairs and in negotiating their own contracts without real interference from the internationals results from a deliberate policy of the international unions represented in the company. Let some of the international representatives explain it in their own words:

[58] Glenn W. Gilman and James W. Sweeney, *Atlantic Steel Company and United Steelworkers of America,* Causes of Industrial Peace Under Collective Bargaining, NPA, Case Study No. 12, November 1953, pp. 23–24.

"I don't believe any outsider like myself knows what people in a particular local should have. What would work well in one plant would not do well in another. The locals are happier with local autonomy, and it makes for a better local labor-management relationship too."

"I have enough to do servicing all of the locals in my region, especially the newer ones without asking to get into every situation, but I stress to the local people that I'm here to help them and they should feel free to call on me for assistance or advice."

"The local president called me in frequently during the first year or so. I went up to several of his meetings when he anticipated problems with the radical minority you always find. Later, he developed skill handling problems like this himself, and after about two years he could get along on his own. He still called me on the phone if he felt he had a problem he wanted to discuss with me but he built up such a fine relationship with management and with his own membership that he called me less and less in later years. They can settle most of their own problems now."

"At first the local people up there were uncertain as to what unionism was all about, and I had to go up from Boston a good deal. Now they have local autonomy, and this is the policy of all of the printing trades' unions. The international comes in only on request, despite all this bunk you hear about the labor bosses. What pleases them, pleases me."

The role of international representatives in contract negotiations is similar in all of the locals except the engineers and the firemen. Since so few of the members are involved (4 in each), they are attached to the Lowell, Massachusetts, locals (12 miles away) of these unions, and the business agents of the Lowell locals come to Nashua each year to conduct contract negotiations. In the other locals, the local negotiations committee generally handles the first bargaining sessions without assistance from international representatives and the latter come into the picture when bargaining reaches an impasse.

As pointed out earlier, initial contract proposals may be "cleared" with the international representative, but this is for the purpose of getting his suggestions and advice, rather than his approval as a necessary step before proceeding further. Later, after agreement has been reached locally with management, it is a requirement of all the internationals that the contract be signed by the international president (or his representative) as well as by the local committee, but this approval is always given if the local committee is satisfied; there has never been an occasion when the local union voted to accept an agreement then later it was rejected by the international.

On the contrary there have been a few instances in which the international representative cautioned the locals against going "too far" or have advised them to accept an offer which the local people felt was not good enough. Speaking of his union's international representative, one former local officer said: "He suggested several times that we shouldn't get too far out of line (with other firms). He held us back more often than he pushed us, but there was no dictation."[59]

STEELWORKERS, CHICAGO

[A Chicago area local of the Steelworkers] has a record of independence in its relation with the United Steelworkers of America that matches its militancy in its dealings with the company. In a union in which controls from the national office have traditionally been strong, the local is conspicuous in its opposition to the policies of the national officers. The international representative assigned to service the local—and incidentally to help guide and control it—has always had one of the more difficult administrative assignments. The local has given so little cooperation to certain international representatives that the national union has been forced to transfer them.

The local has generally regarded the national officers, along with the particular international representatives assigned to it, as too inclined to compromise, and has preferred to control its own relations with the company whenever possible. In turn, the influence of the international representatives, and therefore of the national union, has usually been exerted on the side of the more moderate faction in local union elections. . . . In the 1957 election for president of the United Steelworkers the members of the local voted overwhelmingly for Donald C. Rarick who headed a protest movement against an increase of union dues, over the incumbent, David J. MacDonald.[60]

UAW LOCAL, BUFFALO—BELL AIRCRAFT

In the years when the control of the local was in the hands of

[59] Charles A. Myers and George P. Shulz, *Causes of Industrial Peace Under Collective Bargaining, Nashua Gummed and Coated Paper Company and Seven AFL Unions,* Case Study No. 7 (Washington: NPA, 1950), pp. 32–34.

[60] Joel Seidman, Jack London, Bernard Karsh, and Daisy L. Tagliacozzo, *The Worker Views His Union* (Chicago: University of Chicago Press, 1958), p. 70.

the so-called "left-wingers" there was relatively little inter-course between the local and the sub-regional office, mainly be-cause the faction in control of the sub-regional office was from the "anti-left-wing" sector of the organization. It was only when serious collective bargaining problems developed with which the local leaders could not cope that they turned to the interna-tional representatives for help. One such problem developed shortly after World War II. A major issue concerning seniority rights with respect to lay-offs arose when employment was cut sharply. The corporation gave preference to veterans for all re-maining jobs available. Those laid off complained about what they considered to be arbitrary notice of the dismissals. Finally the matter came to a head in the form of a one-day sit-down strike in 1945 which was quickly ended when the company agreed to send the disputed cases to arbitration, thanks to the intervention of an international representative.

When, in 1949, the Reutherites gained control of the local the relationship between the local and the international improved immeasurably. Since then, the international representatives have helped in contract negotiations, in the settlement of grievances, and even in arbitration. This is not to imply, of course, that the local leaders have relied on the international representatives to do all their work for them. On the contrary . . . the local leaders have handled most of their problems on their own hook. The point made here, however, is this: thanks to the fact that the factional leanings of the local leadership and of the sub-regional staff are of the same type, a mutual trust has been built up between the two groups, and this trust has enabled the local in many instances to handle some of its problems in a more successful fashion.[61]

UE LOCALS AND INTERNATIONAL UNION

Two locals of the United Electrical Workers managed to main-tain a high degree of control of their own affairs largely because they wished to minimize their attachment to this Communist-influenced international union. In the first case the report was written prior to the schism between UE and IUE.

Pennsylvania

There has been little coordination of union activities in the [industrial instrument] industry, and Local 116 at Brown has maintained a rather independent and autonomous position in the UE. This policy stems largely from the political situation within

[61] Joseph Shister and William Hamovitch, *Conflict and Stability in Labor Relations: A Case Study,* University of Buffalo, 1952, pp. 14–15.

the international, which is controlled by a left-wing group toward which Local 116 has not been sympathetic. The dominant UE locals in the Philadelphia district favor the present administration in the international and, therefore, have succeeded in electing to district offices representatives sympathetic to the international's administration. A former district president, who has been a leader of the right-wing faction and is now secretary-treasurer of the Pennsylvania State CIO, is retained by Local 116 as a sort of business agent, and since 1945 has played a leading role in annual negotiations at Brown.[62]

Wisconsin
UE 1111 represents production workers at the Allen-Bradley Company. . . . The union is the largest local affiliate of the United Electrical Workers—UE-Independent—in the Milwaukee and Wisconsin area. In the recent past, the local union had survived several raiding efforts which attempted to move the workers into other international affiliations. Only small groups of highly skilled employees have switched their union allegiance to craft-organized locals. In general, the membership derives great satisfaction from the real measure of independence which they secure from their present national leadership. Because of their affiliation with the UE, the union has been considered "communist-led" and "communist-dominated" but these charges are without weight in the local union situation.

As a matter of fact, the local seems similar to a number of the AFL federal labor unions. That is, the local retains a sense of complete autonomy. The UE international representative has relatively minor influence in local union affairs. The UE district organization takes a hands-off attitude toward the local. Hence, the locus of power is centered on the level of local union leadership, particularly in the hands of its top officer.[63]

LABOR MOVEMENT RELATIONSHIPS
The orbit of external pressure to which the local union is obliged to conform does not necessarily stop at the boundaries of its own international union. The union with jurisdictional problems is likely to find that its position within the labor movement of the community, particularly where that labor movement is well established, is of material value. The legitimacy of a jurisdictional

[62] Lester and Robie, *op. cit.*, p. 50.
[63] Sidney M. Peck, *The Rank and File Leader*, unpublished Ph.D. dissertation, University of Wisconsin, 1959, pp. 128–129.

claim can be substantially strengthened if it bears the stamp of approval of a powerful central labor body. The Chicago Federation of Labor is an authentic example of the importance of status within the local labor movement as a factor in the strength of the local in respect to its collective bargaining affairs.

For the building trades local unions, the local building trades council composed of the locals of the standard building trades internationals, looms important as an element in the local union's freedom of movement with respect to the pulls and tugs of jurisdictional legitimacy. The position of a local union within the building trades labor movement can at times be more important to it than its position within its own international union.

Where the dimensions of a bargaining relationship transcend the boundaries of any specific international union interest, the local union finds itself exposed to, and confronted with, another complex of interests. Hotel trades councils are cases in point. Here the council is composed not only of locals of the Hotel and Restaurant international but in the case of the New York Hotel Trades Council, locals of the IBEW, Operating Engineers, Firemen and Oilers, Building Service, Painters, Upholsterers, and Office Employees.[64]

For local unions in public employment or quasi-public employment—Teachers, AFSCME—dealing with public bodies is a part of their central bargaining process. For these locals the labor movement as a pressure group is of critical importance. This circumstance, therefore, involves the standing of the local within the central labor body as an important factor in its fortunes as a collective bargaining agency.

FACTORS

Whether a local union is independent or dependent in relation to the international is likely to be influenced by history, by the attitudes of the union parties, by economics, by the functional requirements of the situation, and by management strategy. Historically, it matters a good deal as to whether union organization evolved out of the efforts of the local people or whether the local union was established in a broadly based, international union-directed organizing campaign. This will have much to do

. [64] Morris A. Horowitz, *The New York Hotel Industry: A Labor Relations Study* (Cambridge: Harvard University Press, 1960), pp. 70–71.

with whether there has developed a tradition of self-reliance rather than a tradition of calling in the international representative.

The quality and outlook of leadership, both in the international and in the local, will influence the character of the local union-international union relationship. Power aggrandizement by a strong leader on either side will have an effect on the relationship. By way of contrast, the inability of formal leadership in the local to carry on its leadership function is likely to increase the influence of the international union; or sentiment on the part of the international union leadership that a local must find its own way, and an accompanying educational program to achieve this end may force the responsibility of independence on a local union leadership.

Economics will influence the posture of the parties. A local union functioning in a national product market will necessarily rely more on the international union than will a local operating in a local or regional market. The obverse of this sort of situation is that the international will be pressed to intervene more regularly in order to maintain a viable balance of interests. Economic facts will also be relevant where an industry or a plant is undergoing rapid technological change or rapid change in consumer tastes. The impact of change is likely to set in motion forces which the local union may be incapable of dealing with on its own power.

The pressures exerted by the employer in a specific situation can veer the local union in one direction rather than in another direction. Part of the price which the employer may exact for a livable relationship with the local union is the exclusion of the international to avoid the injection of "international policy" into the bargaining. From another vantage point the employer may find the international more "responsible"; this will bring the international union *into* a situation.

In sum the local union is part of a web of organizational relationships in which it acts and is acted upon. This web is the product of a complex interweaving of interests—with the international union, with intermediate bodies within the international, with the city and state labor movement, and with locals outside of its own international who bargain with its employer or its industry.

This web is, of course, much simpler for a local union that is not a part of an international affiliated to the AFL–CIO; or for the local that has no ties of any kind—the independent, unaffiliated local that is sufficient unto itself. But even in these situations the relationships are not as simple as they may appear at first impression. Despite the formal separation of the Teamsters from the AFL–CIO, Teamster local union relationships still persist on an informal but substantial basis. The locals of the unaffiliated operating brotherhoods must, in the nature of things, maintain workable relationships with the other railroad craft unions. The independents in the petroleum industry are involved in clearing-house relationships with other petroleum independents, at the same time that it is regarded as fair game for invasion by AFL–CIO affiliated locals.

Overwhelmingly, the impact of all of these interrelationships on the local is a consequence of function—or at least of the diverse ways in which reasonable men see function—not of a priori ideology or of sheer quest for power.

9

CONFLICT AND
CONTROVERSY IN LOCAL UNIONS

This chapter deals with the organized expressions of diversity in the local union—the issues, instrumentalities and forums of diversity.

The issues involved in diversity in the local union center around (1) internal union problems; (2) policies and attitudes toward management and collective bargaining problems; and (3) ideologies. Almost any issue in controversy will partake of characteristics of all of these categories. There will be, for example, considerable overlapping between (1) and (2). But it is the dominant theme that will determine its grouping for the purposes of this discussion.

INTERNAL ISSUES

The most pervasive issues in controversy probably have to do with the management of internal union affairs. Local union members are likely to divide here over: (a) contending job interests; (b) ethnic interests; (c) "ins" *vs.* "outs"; (d) control of the international or of intermediate bodies; (e) the quality of the union leadership performance.

Illustrations of the kinds of job interests that are likely to confront each other are set out below:

"REGULAR" *VS.* "DE LUXE" SPRAYERS

Edge-setters and sprayers were each subdivided into two groups, "regular" and "de luxe." Until about ten years ago the de luxe workers in both groups received 5¢ an hour extra. In 1943 the union executive board (predominately regular workers) filed a grievance and won an arbitration award equalizing wages between the two groups.

The two types of edge-setters were located in different buildings. After a short period of unrest the de luxe edge-setters accepted their loss of relative wage superiority without too many regrets.

On the other hand, the two groups of sprayers worked next to each other. Today the 1943 arbitration award is still a sore subject for them. In fact for a period of seven years the de luxe sprayers provided the nucleus for every anti-administration movement within the union. Finally in 1950 they were successful in overthrowing the old administration and installing one which they controlled.[1]

INCENTIVE VS. DAY WORKERS

During the war years the earnings of the incentive workers far outstripped those of day workers of higher skill. This condition smoldered for six years while the officers promised that something would be done. Finally, when a recently-negotiated contract failed to provide adequate adjustments, the day workers united for the first time and elected a completely new slate to the negotiating committee.[2]

EMPLOYED VS. UNEMPLOYED (MUSICIANS)

The issue as to whether "royalties" paid by the recording companies for recorded music would go to the performing musicians or to a general trust fund for the benefit of all the members divided the Hollywood Musicians local. This ultimately resulted in an NLRB election in which a newly organized Musicians Guild displaced the American Federation of Musicians as the bargaining representative for the Hollywood professional musicians.[3]

ESTABLISHED LEADERSHIP VS. NEWCOMERS (CONSTRUCTION CRAFTS IN KENTUCKY)

The construction locals engaged in the construction of an atomic plant at Paducah, Kentucky, divided politically as between old-timers and newcomers. The newcomers resented what they regarded as the entrenched position of the old-timers. This resulted in "a very high rate of turnover of local union leadership in both construction locals and many industrial plant unions. The turnover was in part due to the dissension created by "the

[1] Leonard R. Sayles and George Strauss, *The Local Union: Its Place in the Industrial Plant* (New York: Harper, 1953), pp. 135–135.

[2] *Ibid.*, p. 136.

[3] Arthur J. Goldberg, American Federation of Musicians, Chicago, *Report and Recommendations of Referee, In the matter of John TE Groen, etc.*, May 4, 1956. See also *Business Week*, July 19, 1958, p. 70.

great influx of new members" and "large membership blocks striving to overturn local leadership," at the same time that they sought greater freedom of action from the parent internationals who had established overriding collective bargaining arrangements."[4]

Other divisions observed have been based on over-the-road versus local cartage in a Teamsters' local, steamfitters versus refrigeration men in a Boston plumbers' local, skilled versus production workers in a Machinists' lodge.[5]

Ethnic loyalties will form the grounds of controversy within the local union just as it does in politics and in many other social groupings. Frequently the situation will stabilize itself under a rough ethnic proportional representation in the distribution of offices and perquisites. Absent this sort of compact, ethnic rivalry for offices are likely to occur, as for example happened in a steel local among Jewish and Italian groups.[6] Other examples:

LOS ANGELES LABORERS' LOCAL

Up until this year the different races came out about proportionately to our elections, but this year we had a Negro guy run on a race ticket—just plain Negro, nothing else for anybody else and you know, the Mexicans and the whites really came out—the most whites I've ever seen, I guess. The Negroes, they didn't like it on the whole; many didn't come for that reason I think. Few voted for him. But usually you get a fairly average proportion, about the same for each group. Occasionally we have a Mexican guy try it on his being a Mexican. He can get a lot of support just because of those big families they have. But this sort of thing doesn't usually work.[7]

MEXICANS AND NEGROES

In one massive local where there is little participation in general membership meetings there is nevertheless a large turnout for

[4] L. Reed Tripp, J. Keith Mann, and Frederick T. Downs, *Labor-Management Relations in the Paducah Area of Western Kentucky*, January, 1954, University of Kentucky, Bureau of Business Research, pp. 68–69.

[5] Respectively—Robert Hammer, *Industrial Relations in the New York City General Trucking Industry*, Ph.D. dissertation, Harvard University, 1951, p. 96; Edward W. Murphy, *A Study of a Building Trades Local Union*, unpublished M.B.A. thesis, Northeastern University, 1956, p. 40; *Business Week*, August 24, 1957, p. 141.

[6] Sayles and Strauss, *op. cit.*, p. 217.

[7] Scott Greer, *Last Man In* (Glencoe: Free Press, 1959), p. 90.

elections. This local predominantly ethnic, was "lily white" in staff and office personnel until recently. In the past few years a temporary dispatcher, a man of unusual sensitivity and intelligence, has risen to a position of leadership. In the process, the face of the local's leadership group was changed.

"We have a pretty well-mixed staff but that's just in the last two years. It used to didn't work that way. Why, when I came in three years back, they had a window in the front and one in the back. The Mexicans, which was most of that membership, would come in holding their caps and sneak around to that back window, pay their dues and leave without saying anything. I asked them, 'What the devil's going on here? Is this the way things are done?' and they said, 'Yes sir, that's the way we do it; we're supposed to come in and pay our dues and get out.' I asked them how it was as far as working, 'Oh, we get work but sometimes the directions are not too good and we have trouble reading a new work order.' I asked them if it would help if they had a man who could speak Spanish and explain things better. They thought so, so I asked the Boss to change the arrangement. He said, 'Hell, are you crazy? You don't have Mexican dispatchers!' And that's the issue I ran on for manager of the local."

The campaign was waged on ethnic lines and, since a majority of the local was ethnic, the new candidate had an advantage. He won by a handy margin; however, in destroying the old leadership's control of the local he created self-conscious ethnic factions. This resulted in a large number of Mexican and Negro candidates for the staff jobs—60% in the last election. The staff of the local is now dominated by Negro and Mexican leaders.[8]

By the "in" vs. "out" I mean to suggest that the issues which divide interest groups in a local union do not seem to go beyond the fact that the outs would like to be in, or the ins would like to stay in. From the standpoint of the majority of the members who vote the "outs" in, it is frequently put as "time for a change," or "they've been in office long enough."[9] "Much of the sound and fury," Sayles and Strauss concluded from their studies, ". . . signifies nothing more than the personal ambitions of one

8 *Ibid.*, pp. 138–139.
9 George S. Paul, *Causes of Industrial Peace Under Collective Bargaining, American Velvet Company and Textile Workers Union of America,* Case Study No. 11 (Washington: NPA, 1953), p. 19.

active union member conflicting with those of another. They all see themselves as inestimably qualified for the office."[10]

The amorphousness of the issues involved is illustrated in the following colloquy. The respondent is the secretary-treasurer of a very large federal local.

QUESTION: Have you ever had large internal factions within the local organization?

ANSWER: Oh yes, we've had several times where groups of people wanted to wrest the power from the groups of people who've had it. They would go out and put on a regular political campaign based on something they thought were facts, and they would campaign with posters in their shop, campaign with cards and make speeches in cloakrooms.

QUESTION: Were there any large issues involved or was it simply outs wanting to be ins?

ANSWER: Well, there was some criticism of the present officers and they would take it in and they would correct the situation. Nothing that was controversial. The fellows on the in would argue themselves that what they did was the best for the organization. But the fellows on the outside felt that if they had done something else it would have been better.

QUESTION: Like what for example? What kinds of criticisms were brought?

ANSWER: Well they felt as though we should not have fines for not going to meetings. . . . There seems to be an opinion here that a man should not be given the office without a run for it, to get what the people think about him, whether or not he should get it back. If he has no opposition it's hard to say whether the people wanted him or just because there was nobody else.[11]

The internal issue that divides a local union may have little to do with the local union but with the use of local union power

[10] Sayles and Strauss, *op. cit.*, p. 139; Arnold S. Tannenbaum and Robert L. Kahn, *Participation in Union Locals* (Evanston: Row, Peterson, 1958), p. 20; Joel Seidman, Jack London, Bernard Karsh, and Daisy L. Tagliacozzo, *The Worker Views His Union* (Chicago: University of Chicago Press, 1958), p. 70, come to the same conclusion.
[11] Personal interview.

to control a superior union body of which the local union is a part.

In the Teamsters union, control of a local union is sometimes of consequence because it provides a power base for control of a joint council of teamsters with the latter's great power in respect to strikes and teamster assistance to other unions.[12]

> Opposition within the local was engendered by another local because of a political situation which existed at the joint council level, and which because of disagreement at the joint council level Local A wanted to get rid of the officers of Local B, and therefore it went into Local B and built a campaign—by the way, an unsuccessful one. The interest at controlling the joint council stemmed from the importance of the council in recommendations for jurisdictional allocations.[13]

The issue of sustaining or opposing Walter Reuther's leadership in the UAW has in the past figured as a source of difference in UAW locals, notably in the giant Local 600 of the UAW where Carl Stellato has taken an anti-Reuther posture and in consequence stirred up the election opposition of pro-Reutherites.[14]

When quality of the leadership performance is the source of internal dissension the particular defect in leadership objected to is hardly ever articulated clearly. A characteristic formulation of the motivation where this is the issue is to be found in the observation of the leader of a large local union who ousted an incumbent.

> We thought that our union was becoming a little stale. It was just repeating itself and not progressing into what we should do. . . . And a group of us got together one day and said why don't we do something about it. Why don't we run a set of candidates against these fellows who we think are now kind of stale, growing stale, and get a little more life in there, some new blood. And boy, we put on quite a campaign. We were successful in knocking off the president and we were successful in knocking off a couple of trustees and we got some inroads made.
>
> [The old leader] gave the impression that nobody else could run his job, and by God, you fellows have to take me, and this and that, and then he would nonchalantly take care of the job

[12] Hammer, *op. cit.*, p. 64.
[13] Personal interview.
[14] *Business Week*, May 18, 1957, p. 157.

because he had a business on the outside. . . . So I ran against him and I was successful in beating him. . . . I beat him pretty bad. We campaigned on the slogan that we had to have a full-time secretary. . . . He was a good qualified man. He was one of the men, if I had to pick an individual who was more responsible than any other for the success of his organization in its infancy, I'd have to say it was he, and that's the truth. He had good sound thinking, he was sincerely behind the people. He wouldn't sell out when he got in front of management. . . . He talked the same language to management as he talked to the people and you don't find that kind of representative too often.[15]

The employment function of the business agent makes him a special target for member dissatisfaction when the business agent runs for re-election. As a close observer of labor affairs in a large Midwestern city put it:

It's difficult in terms of the building trades contests to really determine what they are arguing about. The general complaint is that things aren't being run right. A lot of this has to do with real or fancied personal injury. Of course the building trades run hiring halls. In fact, this quite often can be a source of complaint.

The motivation for discontent and contest stem from a variety of sources: from a discontent with the scarcity of jobs; with the presumed failure of the local union to protect or extend its jurisdiction; with perhaps what is regarded as the unfair operation of the hiring hall—that is certain people being favored over the others—and that would be most conspicuous in appearance when there weren't enough jobs. . . .[16]

The power of the building trades business agent is most seriously challenged when the opposition can charge him with inefficiency. One business agent told how he ousted an incumbent:

"Old Jim had been business agent for fifteen years. When he started out, he was bright, aggressive, and able. But gradually he took to the bottle. . . . In meetings he would yell at the people to sit down and shout abuse at them. . . . There were times when you just couldn't find him when you had a problem. . . . His books were in miserable shape.

"Three years ago he was elected by a 13-vote majority. A lot of the men voted for him just out of loyalty. They didn't like the

[15] Personal interview.
[16] *Ibid.*

176

old man to lose his job. . . . Well, in the last election I knew that someone was going to beat him. I just had to run."

Almost identical stories could be told in two other locals. Even where alcohol was not a problem, elections were often close.[17]

BARGAINING ISSUES

Differences in the local union are likely to turn on the proper role of the union or union leader in relation to management or in relation to the collective bargaining demands of the union. Collective bargaining issues rarely are sharply drawn.

> The voter was rarely in a position to select between real alternative objectives. On the contrary, just as in national political struggles, there was much more mud-slinging than discussion of issues. Each side claimed that it could do better—but almost no one was specific as to the exact changes of policy he would make.

> Why do candidates neglect these collective bargaining issues? One obvious reason is their general unwillingness to campaign for lesser benefits. With the exception of periods of extreme economic hardship, when the firm faces bankruptcy, no candidate would conceive of criticizing his opponent for asking too much.[18]

The president of an industrial local was opposed during an election but he was re-elected because many of his supporters felt that he was "an intelligent and responsible person." In the words of a chief steward who voted for the incumbent, "Most locals are getting educated to the fact that a man has to be good—make wise decisions—can't be radical."[19]

Most characteristically, the issue in conflict is "hard" *vs.* "soft" in dealing with management. In a Steelworkers local there was a "factional alignment . . . based partly on personality and partly on a right-left split, on the difference between those who advocated a more cautious and conciliatory policy as against those who demanded more militancy in dealing with the employer."[20] Building trades business agents in upstate New York were criticized in elections for "being insufficiently militant in protecting the members' legitimate rights or so militant as to jeopardize

[17] George Strauss, "Control by the Membership in Building Trades Unions," *American Journal of Sociology,* May 1956, p. 529.
[18] Sayles and Strauss, *op. cit.,* p. 133.
[19] Tannenbaum and Kahn, *op. cit.,* p. 35.
[20] Seidman, London, Karsh, and Tagliacozzo, *op. cit.,* p. 70.

their chances of employment (and sometimes of both faults at the same time by different factions)."[21]

700-MEMBER INDUSTRIAL LOCAL

There appeared to be two schools of thought within the local on the extent to which the union should use these mechanisms [overtime *vs.* no overtime] against management. Differences of opinion on this issue have led to a kind of factionalization in which members of one group feel that they should push management harder, and the other feels they should be more moderate. One relatively active member expressed the view that the union had taken advantage of management in the past .to the ultimate detriment of the workers. In answering the question of why he missed some of the union's meetings he said, "I get a little burned up and then I don't go. . . . Some of the things they pull against the company. I go around and see how other companies work and then I see the kind of things they pull at National. They get away with murder. I have the feeling that the union is going to blow up some one of these days. . . . Take the scooter job of a couple years ago. The union would not go along with turning out one more product a day. The union would not go along and the company lost the job. . . . If the men couldn't do it that would be different, but they could. The union says that isn't why the job was lost."[22]

CLIQUES IN A GYPSUM LOCAL

Byta's clique:
1. Identifies with management
   a. sees authority as impregnable
   b. therefore seeks security by conforming to management expectations
2. Defines workers' grievances as non-legitimate
3. Workers disapprove Byta's clique's role in grievance committee—management views them as "reasonable" and "cooperative," i.e., approves
4. Byta unable and unwilling to lead strike

Izzaboss's clique in contrast:
1. More identification with workers
   a. sees authority as vulnerable
   b. seeks security in peer ties and by conforming to peer expectations
2. Defines workers' grievances as legitimate

[21] Strauss, *op. cit.*, p. 527 ff.
[22] Tannenbaum and Kahn, *op. cit.*, p. 34.

3. Workers approve of their grievance policy—management disapproves, views them as "hotheads"
4. Izzaboss able and willing to lead strike[23]

IDEOLOGY

Ideology as a source of difference in the local union stems most frequently from the presence of an organized communist group in control or seeking control. Contemporary examples are to be found in the attempts of the IUE to wrest control away from UE elements in several local unions.[24] In a Midwest UAW local:

> During the war period the factional alignment reflected the split in the national UAW, with the Reuther adherents—socialist and other non-communist radicals together with non-politicals who supported aggressive union action—in one caucus and a combination of more conservative unionists and a small number of communists in the rival grouping. Socialists, though few in number, have played an important role as leaders in the Reuther caucus which has been in control during most of the local's history. It has always had opposition, either concentrated in a single faction or divided into two groups; since personalities and issues have undergone numerous changes these factions are difficult to characterize except for their steady opposition to the incumbents.[25]

The communist—anti-communist conflict in the local union, as in the international, is only rarely a conflict over pure trade union issues, but is more a conflict over control. In an earlier period the communists may have sought power to use the union for revolutionary purposes; in the present generation, that is since the forties, communists have recognized that they need to carry on a basic trade-union job, whatever else they do. The anti-

[23] Alvin W. Gouldner, *Wildcat Strike* (Yellow Springs; Antioch Press, 1954), p. 101.
[24] See Dalton E. McFarland, *Leadership in a Local Labor Union Undergoing Organizational Stress,* unpublished Ph.D. dissertation, New York State School of Industrial and Labor Relations, 1952; "Left-Wing Domination of Labor Unions: A Case Study of Local Union Leadership," *ILResearch,* New York State School of Industrial and Labor Relations, vol. 1, June 1955; Robert W. Ozanne, *The Effects of Communist Leadership on American Trade Unions, UAW Local 248,* unpublished Ph.D. dissertation, University of Wisconsin, 1954, on the conflict in the Allis-Chalmers Local of the UAW; Greer, *op. cit.;* Joseph Shister and William Hamovitch, *Conflict and Stability in Labor Relations: A Case Study,* University of Buffalo, 1952.
[25] Seidman, London, Karsh, and Tagliacozzo, *op. cit.,* p. 95.

communists became critical of the communist faction's use of the union as a public front and source of financial support for communist propaganda causes.[26]

There has been an ideological element in the activities of the Association of Catholic Trade Unionists. ACTU, which operates on a city chapter basis, has been mostly active in the anti-Communist fight within the UE, the anti-Communist fight in the UAW primarily in Detroit, and the fight to oust racketeers from control of certain locals. ACTU appears to have derived most of its impetus as a counterforce and there is little evidence that it functioned as a religious bloc in an affirmative way. The most systematic account available of ACTU functioning in a specific context is its activity in the UE.

> . . . The Actists in the UE generally acted without national coordination and . . . often contradicted each other on important questions of policy. . . . Where the ACTU did appear to function as an organized group—primarily in those cases where a few individuals were engaged in an intensive activity— the data indicate that it did not favor Catholics. The one exception to this statement occurs in 1949, after the UE split and during the formation of the IUE. There one can find evidence . . . that Actists tried to advance their own people within the new union. But during the struggle itself the ACTU did not. The confidential memo to the ACTU priests and the public statements of the organization emphasized over and over that ACTU should not become a religious caucus.

> Indeed, one of the most striking aspects of ACTU involvement is precisely the extent to which the Actists were affected by the charge that they were trying to form a religious bloc. . . . Father Rice believed that the UE administration charges [impropriety of a Catholic faction out to capture power] were, on the whole, successful and that they destroyed the impact of the ACTU where it worked in its own name. Even if this extreme analysis is not true, it is clear that throughout the UE fight, ACTU was concerned with allaying the fears of those who saw it as an agency for religious factionalism. . . .

> The fact that ACTU had a "special appeal" to Catholic workers did not, as far as we can tell, give it any real basis for operation. The Catholic workers were most interested and likely to

[26] See Jack Barbash, *The Practice of Unionism* (New York: Harper, 1956), chap. 14.

join ACTU in those periods in which workers in general were on the move; and once the mood of militancy subsided, Catholicism was not a sufficient motivation to bring any sufficient mass of workers to the ACTU. What this suggests is that Catholic workers are primarily moved by *trade union* issues and by those political attitudes which they share in common with their fellow workers. They do not, if the experience of the ACTU has general importance, constitute a separate conscious group. . . .

One might, in brief, summarize ACTU'S work much as Father Rice did: "We battle the UE and strike a blow for progress every once in a while, but we are not the men the commies think we are. . . ." This undramatic description more or less fits the facts. Individual Actists were important in various situations—but the ACTU, as an organization was constantly and systematically overrated, often enough by friends as well as by enemies.

The ACTU, as we have seen, did not attempt in any meaningful way to build a religious faction in the UE. But more than that, the evidence seems to indicate that it could not have done so had it tried. The reasons for this are clear enough and they have already been indicated. The key to the UE struggle was not religion, or even the political issue of communism.[27]

This view generally is confirmed by earlier investigations. Philip Taft does not believe that the ACTU record supports the likelihood that ACTU could "lead to the splitting of labor unions on religious lines. . . . ACTU has attacked labor officers of the Catholic faith; it has supported candidates for union office who were socialists and Protestants against Catholic aspirants when the ACTU was convinced the interests of the union were better served thereby."[28]

The ACTU does not seem to have grown in strength, and in fact seems to have declined. Discussion with professing Catholics active in the labor movement suggests that many Catholics ques-

[27] Michael Harrington, "Catholics in the Labor Movement: A Case History," *Labor History*, Fall 1960, pp. 259–261 *passim*.
[28] Philip Taft, "The Association of Catholic Trade Unionists," *Industrial and Labor Relations Review*, January 1949, p. 218; See also "Ethnic Factors in the Development of the American Labor Movement," *op. cit.*; L. A. O'Donnell, *Bibliography, American Unionism in the Catholic Church, with Special Emphasis on the Association of Catholic Trade Unionists*, April 1959, University of San Francisco, Labor-Management School (mimeo.).

tion the propriety and wisdom of any Catholic power grouping in the American labor movement, however limited it professes its objectives to be.

PARTY

The organizational forms through which special interests in the local assert themselves may be identified as (1) the party or the "club," (2) the faction or caucus, (3) the cadre or fraction, and (4) the slate.

The party or "club" as political bodies in their local have the characteristics of permanency, openness, and formality. The party system as such is rare. The only significant example is in the ITU which has been described in detail by Lipset and associates. The "ideological differences between the two parties" in the ITU "revolve almost entirely about internal union issues. . . . The Progressives have favored a militant policy of complete non-cooperation with provisions of the [Taft-Hartley] act, and of strikes to maintain all the rights of the union men enjoyed before it was passed. The Independents appeared to support the position of most other national unions of attempting to work within the act's provisions."[29]

The "club" is not as formal nor as much in public view but it has the quality of permanency, of the party. The use of the term "club" is frequently intended to serve as a recreational cover for political objectives. After a while if the initial reason for the political objective disappears, the recreational activities may indeed become its real purpose. An "institutionalized" club system exists in a large plumbers local in Chicago. The "social club" is composed of a group of Jewish plumbers who started the club originally to increase their work opportunities outside of the Jewish section of the city. As recalled by a club member:

> Years ago the business agent had much more power than he has now. That was when the union was run by crooks. I remember when the only place a Jew could work was in his own district, the ghetto. . . . If you got a job with a plumber or contractor who had work outside of the Jewish district the business agent would come around and ask: "How many sheenies on this job?" And if there was more than one or two,

[29] S. M. Lipset, "The Two Party System in the ITU," *Labor and Nation* (Inter-Union Institute, New York City), Fall 1950, p. 32.

he'd tell the boss to fire them and put some of his own people on the job. . . . That's why we organized the Jewish club inside the union—the social club. It was started originally so that we could have a block of votes at the meeting and get rid of the officers that set up and controlled that practice. Now they know we have an organization and could get active if that ever starts again.[30]

In the same local there exists a "Pot and Ladle" club which started as an antigangster alliance, and a "Craftsman's Club" composed of Masons.[31] Within Machinists Lodge 1487 there exists a "United Aircraft Mechanics' Club, Inc." organized to push the interests of the skilled employees of United Airlines as against the industrial workers.[32]

FACTION

The faction or caucus is less formal and less permanent than the party or club. "Factions are groups organized on the basis of issues; they may be relatively permanent or they may be quite temporary. The latter kind of issue is exemplified in the chronic question: 'How militant can we be in negotiations?' Of the more permanent issues, ethnic issues are prominent."[33] The faction is also likely to concern itself with a specific event like a strike or an election and then remain dormant until the next time. Cases in point of factional organization:

A LARGE MIDWESTERN STEELWORKERS LOCAL

Following an election held every other year, the factions tended to be quiescent, permitting the victorious officers to run the local with only a moderate amount of strife. About six months before the next election, however, factional alignments formed again, with the leaders of each group meeting informally to agree upon major candidates and prepare for their more formal caucus meetings. At these meetings, in turn, slates of candidates were worked out, care being taken that the various departments were represented by candidates with wide popular appeal, and that large minority groups such as Negroes and Mexicans were also represented. The position of vice-president of the local is one which traditionally has been held by a Negro. Sometimes dissident slates appeared, made up primarily of minority groups

[30] Seidman, London, Karsh, and Tagliacozzo, *op. cit.*, p. 49.
[31] *Ibid.*
[32] *Business Week*, August 24, 1957, p. 141.
[33] Greer, *op. cit.*, p. 89.

or organized by an independent candidate for president or another leading office.[34]

BELL AIRCRAFT LOCAL OF THE UAW (BUFFALO)

In 1949 the factional complexion of the Union underwent significant change. Partly as a result of a series of articles run by a Buffalo newspaper exposing certain leaders as "left-wingers," partly as a result of the discharge of the so-called "poor security risks" in connection with the 1949 strike . . . the "left-wing" factions disappeared completely. Two basic factions emerged: the Reutherites and the rank-and-filers. Since 1949, as before it, the allegiance of the members to one or the other factions is not a fixed one; it varies in accordance with the ability of the leadership to produce satisfactory results. But the leadership of each of these factions, in contrast to the leadership prior to 1949, does not display any "ideological leanings."[35]

LOCAL 807 OF THE TEAMSTERS UNION (NEW YORK CITY)

[Here factionalism refers to] fairly well-defined opposition groups in the union [who] . . . seek to overturn the present leadership through methods declared illegal by the union constitution and by-laws. These activities include illegal efforts for union reorganization; discussing union affairs outside of official publications; outside of official [meetings]; publication of unauthorized newspapers and circulars. . . . Union reorganization was fostered through the issuance of unauthorized petitions calling for a separate charter for over-the-road drivers—secret meetings have been held outside the union hall and cards sent to members asking their attendance. Several unauthorized newspapers have been and are being printed. These include the "IBT News," "The Clutch," "The Wheel," "The 807 Teamster Speaks," and "The 807 Truckdriver." They carry no names of sponsors or origin of publication and are distributed to union men outside the meeting hall.[36]

CADRE

The cadre is the most tightly organized and highly disciplined instrumentality through which diversity is given expression. The cadre, a term of military derivation, has long been a classic organizational weapon in the communist arsenal and, as applied to union work, means a tested group of loyal communists within

[34] Seidman, London, Karsh, and Tagliacozzo, *op. cit.*, pp. 70–71.
[35] Shister and Hamovitch, *op. cit.*, pp. 13–14.
[36] Hammer, *op. cit.*, pp. 96–97.

the union who can be relied upon to follow orders irrespective of content.[37]

The power of the cadre (or fraction) is in its ironbound discipline and in unity of purpose, enabling the cadre to place loyal followers on the key committees and in the key offices of the union, and to exert vastly more influence than would be justified by the weight of sheer numbers alone. A disaffected communist, Lee Lundgren, an officer of a Chicago local of the UE, testified:

> In all cases where matters of importance were going to come up before the local membership meeting, those matters were discussed at the Communist Party meeting prior to the union membership meeting, and that also included the selection of delegates to conventions, and any official business like that, always the names of these people were selected at the Communist Party meeting first. Then it was brought to the attention of the people at the regular membership meeting. This is, of course, a situation in which the fraction was the controlling element in the local union.[38]

Or in the words of an opposition leader of a communist-dominated local:

> Well, there are about forty active party members, but they are disciplined and they work hard. If we try to get a leaflet out it takes us a week but if they want one out they call those guys off their jobs—the union makes it OK—and they have them at every plant in a couple of hours and then, they have guys from outside the union, too, who can be borrowed.[39]

The communist technique of union penetration also provides for an outer shell, namely a caucus, for bringing together party members and nonparty sympathizers. The purpose of the coalition caucus is to provide a reputable front which will not bear the public stigma of the Communist Party—a stigma which the party has had to carry even in its relatively good times. The party frac-

[37] See Greer, *op. cit.*, p. 88; Philip Selznick, *The Organizational Weapon* (New York: McGraw-Hill, 1952), p. 18 ff.; R. N. Carew Hunt, *A Guide to Communist Jargon* (New York: Macmillan, 1957), pp. 24–29; Theodore Draper, *American Communism and Soviet Russia* (New York: Viking, 1960), p. 197 ff.

[38] U.S. House of Representatives, Committee on Un-American Activities, Hearings, *Communist Activities in the Chicago Area*, 82d Cong., 2d Sess., 1952, p. 3645.

[39] Greer, *op. cit.*, p. 89.

tion is, however, always careful to maintain the upper hand within the coalition. "Lee" Romano, a former party member in the Pressed Steel unit of the Ford River Rouge plant has described how the "progressive caucus" works:

> At Pressed Steel level we had our Communist cell and then we had what we call . . . a progressive caucus. The party cell would meet on the question of discussing different problems relative to elections in the local building of Pressed Steel officers, and also, for the election of delegates to conventions and we would pool our strength in terms of electing the particular delegates.
>
> The cell was a core of this particular caucus and they mastered the situation at all times, and the fringe pro-communists and the fellow-travelers and a few disgruntled people who were part of the caucus were led by the central core.[40]

SLATE

The "slate" is transitory and is generally limited to a specific election. The members on the slate are likely to have nothing more in common than that they can help each other's election chances.

There were three slates in the 1960 elections held by a large UAW local in Milwaukee: the Union Solidarity slate, the Rank-and-File slate, and the Union Voter's Guide slate. The Rank-and-File slate represented the group in office. The program of the Union Solidarity slate read: "Restore the local union finances on a sound financial basis, without a dues increase. Reactivate the union children's Christmas party. Maintain local union autonomy. Active local union participation in county and state labor programs." The Union Voter's Guide program read: "Working towards more local control of its own affairs. Maintain our union on a sound financial basis. Posting of the time spent on union business. Teamwork with the executive board and bargaining committee on all problems. Working with all groups for the best interest of the membership." The administration Rank-and-File slate pledged "support to the executive board in a program to represent all members at the grievance table. Our new 3-year contract must be protected to the best interests of our people in

[40] Un-American Activities Committee, *Communist Activities in the Detroit Area, Part II,* p. 3045.

a democratic manner. We endorse the full employment program of Walter Reuther and the international union."[41]

Perhaps the most common form a grouping takes to express diversity is the *ad hoc* alignment altering its composition from meeting to meeting or from occasion to occasion. Here there is no organization, no preparatory meetings; they may be moved by a mood, by an eloquent speech or by shock, to group together. As exemplified by the situation in a southern Steelworkers local:

> There are always opposing points of view with regard to any major issue that may be brought before the membership, and debate in the union hall quite often becomes vehement. The important point, however, is that as the issues being debated change, so do their proponents; and men who were bitter vocal adversaries a half an hour before find themselves united in defense or attack with regard to some new proposal. There does not appear to be any group within the local that consistently aligns itself on one side or another of an issue, or that is consistently in opposition to the elected officials.[42]

FORUMS FOR CONFLICT

The forums in which diversity is expressed are the union meeting, the union election, the National Labor Relations Board representation election, court litigation, the "wildcat" strike, and the disciplinary proceeding.

The local union meeting is the most common forum for the airing of differences within the local union. This has already been discussed in detail above. Leiserson's observation is (to repeat) that "one outspoken critic [at a union meeting] is often enough to hold officials to account and to prevent them from abusing their power. A corrupt officialdom has to suppress meetings to get away with booty."[43]

The election campaign in the local union is another powerful forum for the airing of difference. The Sayles and Strauss assessment of the election campaign will hold up generally.

[41] Campaign leaflets.
[42] Glenn W. Gilman and James W. Sweeney, *Atlantic Steel Company and United Steelworkers of America,* Causes of Industrial Peace Under Collective Bargaining, NPA, Case Study No. 12, November 1953, p. 20.
[43] William M. Leiserson, *American Trade Union Democracy* (New York: Columbia University Press, 1955), p. 286.

When there is a contest, local-wide elections are conducted with considerable ballyhoo and all the trappings of an American political campaign. There are distributions of circulars, wild charges, mud-slinging, campaign stunts, and all the rest.

"Personalities" and vituperative attacks fly back and forth. The "ins" point with pride, the "outs" view with alarm. The ins are accused of being too conservative, the outs of wrecking and irresponsibility. Each charges the other with playing into the company's hands.[44]

ELECTIONS

Here is a firsthand report of an election campaign in a large industrial local. Most of the traditional implements of politics were used: slates of rival candidates, handbills, buttonholing, rallies, and free beer. There was a noticeable absence of profound differences in the programs of the rivals. The campaign was rather unusual in the formality with which the rival groups were organized and the techniques they brought to their politicking. There were three formally organized caucuses participating in the campaign (we have observed them in action earlier): (1) the administration group; (2) the "unionist" group led by a former financial secretary again seeking that post, and a bargaining committeeman running for president; (3) the "union voter's guide" caucus whose chairman won a bid for recording secretary of the local in the primary election.[45]

The slates held meetings regularly at which they mapped the strategy to use in local union meetings, plan programs, and endorse candidates. All the slates distributed four-page flyers containing pictures and brief biographies of their candidates and other literature.

One group held meetings at which free beer and lunch was served to potential supporters. One such affair drew about seventy persons—donations of $356 to support the caucus's campaign were made. The free beer and lunch sessions prompted the administration group to ask the international union to investigate where the money was coming from, to which the response was that many of the caucus's bills were unpaid and what money it had came from workers in the plant and candidates the caucuses endorsed. That the administration group had raised the question was, it was said, a sign of their desperation. Incumbent candi-

[44] Sayles and Strauss, *op. cit.*, p. 139.
[45] Personal interview.

dates did not fare too well on the whole in the primary.

The programs offered by the three groups did not appear to be vastly different. Each group asserted basically that its candidates could do the best job of representing the workers in the union's dealings with the company. The printed literature contained no references attacking the recently concluded seventy-seven day strike of the local, but there appeared to be resentment against it among some of the workers in the plant. The election had many of the earmarks of a popularity contest. A lot of highly personal charges were made. Despite the bitterness with which the contest was being waged, however, the candidates appeared to feel that it was healthy for the union and would not weaken the union in its dealings with the company. The election was held at the plant during working hours—an arrangement worked out by the company and the union to insure maximum participation. There is ample evidence that the spirited election campaign is a common occurrence. If the election is held at a union meeting, this meeting will bring out a greater attendance—substantially greater—than is true of the routine meeting.[46]

We do not now have any general data as to the extent of competition for local union office. It is possible to approach an estimate of turnover in local union officers for all causes based on extensive data collected by Taft. My very crude estimate is that there is an annual average turnover from 20 to 25 per cent. If, as my investigation indicates, the average term of office is on the order of two years for local union offices, this suggests that roughly 40 to 50 per cent of the local union offices change hands from one term to another. The probabilities are that business agent turnover is on the lower end of this range or perhaps slightly under it.[47]

LAW

The representation machinery of the National Labor Relations Board provides a government forum for the airing of difference.

[46] See Strauss, *op. cit.;* Greer, *op. cit.,* p. 85 ff.; Seidman, London, Karsh, and Tagliacozzo, *op. cit.,* p. 192 ff.; Tannenbaum and Kahn, *op. cit.,* p. 56; Lipset, Trow, and Coleman, *op. cit.,* pp. 43–47.

[47] Professor Philip Taft of Brown University has generously made available to me a study of turnover in local union offices based on data distributed by international union and by locality. My "guestimate" is based on these data. It should be noted that Taft does not derive an average turnover rate for the total of his sample. This latter which I have calculated very crudely is solely my responsibility.

When the CIO chartered the IUE as a rival union to the UE, the battleground for resolving the question as to where the local unions would go was resolved in a series of hotly contested NLRB representation elections. UE has sought to counterattack with somewhat limited effect—but again through the channels furnished by the NLRB. The same kind of battleground has been used by the American Bakery Workers to wrest control of locals from the Bakery and Confectionery Workers expelled from the AFL–CIO for corruption.[48] The Hollywood local of the American Federation of Musicians first gave a substantial majority to the anti-Petrillo group in the local. This group then led the Hollywood professional musicians out of the American Federation of Musicians into a newly organized Musicians Guild of America by an NLRB vote of 580–484.[49] The decertification election as a phase of the NLRB representation procedure offers additional opportunities for differences within the local union to be resolved.[50]

The courts provide a similar forum for the airing of intralocal differences. As in the UE–IUE schism cases, it is likely to take the form of a contest for the control of the physical assets of the local union. Litigation is used with considerable effect in contesting expulsions of members.[51] It is now possible, in addition, to use the statutory election requirements of the LMRDA. In the first nine months of the operation of the law, 369 allegations of illegal election procedures were made, of which 338 were made by union members. Most of the allegations related to local union elections.[52]

LRMDA prescribes the maximum term of office for officers of local unions at three years and lays down standards with respect to the nomination of candidates, the election, and the election

[48] See the series of articles in 45 *Virginia Law Review* 2 (1959) Richmond.

[49] *New York Times,* May 28, 1958; *Business Week,* July 19, 1958, p. 70.

[50] Joseph Krislov, "Union Decertification," *Industrial and Labor Relations Review,* July 1956.

[51] Archibald Cox, "The Role of Law in Preserving Union Democracy," in *Labor in a Free Society* (Berkeley: University of California Press, 1950), pp. 56–57.

[52] American Bar Association, Section on the Development of the Law of Union Administration and Procedure, Report (1960) (mimeo.), p. 17; BLMR, *Report, Fiscal Year 1960* (Washington, D.C.), p. 66.

campaign. The most common violations of the election provisions reported were the blocking of nominations and the refusal to allow secret balloting.[53]

When elections are manipulated or rigged they may take the form of buying off a faction,[54] loading the election meeting, or of tampering with the ballots, as instanced by the allegations of the Secretary of Labor against an independent union.

> Ballots being printed in substantial excess of those required for the elections; ballots being removed from the printer's packages before the time necessary for mailing; ballots being returned to the union's post office lock box which was freely accessible to anyone possessing the correct combination to the lock and to anyone purporting to be authorized to open the box; ballots being taken from the post office box by representatives of the winning candidates before the arrival of the observers for the losing candidates and prior to the agreed time for collection of the ballots.[55]

In an election of a Meat Cutters local in New York City investigated by the McClellan committee, it was found that no notice was given to the membership of the proposed balloting "and . . . those in attendance cast open ballots based upon continuing the incumbent administration in office for another four years." When opposition to the ruling administration developed later "the administration forces improperly used funds from the union treasury for propaganda purposes and spent $3300 for 'poll watchers' from the dues money of the members."[56]

WILDCAT

The wildcat strike not infrequently serves as a weapon for a group that feels itself disadvantaged by the local union leadership. The wildcat has been put to this use most frequently by groups within Teamsters locals. One hundred and forty members of Local 147 of the Teamsters went out on a wildcat strike of warehousemen. "Negotiations between the company and union of-

[53] *Business Week*, February 20, 1960, p. 150.
[54] Theodore V. Purcell, *Blue Collar Man* (Cambridge: Harvard University Press, 1960), p. 25.
[55] U.S. Department of Labor, Release #4184, Thursday, July 28, 1960.
[56] McClellan Investigation, *Second Interim Report* (1959) op. cit., p. 372.

ficials over renewal of a contract had been concluded amicably last Friday but recommendations that the proposed contract be approved were voted down. A strike vote then was taken without executive consent."[57] One hundred and fifty drivers participated in a wildcat walkout refusing to haul new Buicks from Flint to dealers in other cities as required by contract. "The drivers quit after protesting against the alleged loss of their rights to negotiate their own wage agreements. They charged that the Teamsters union recently negotiated a contract covering drivers for a number of hauling companies."[58]

The wildcat as an instrument of intra-union rivalry is not limited to the Teamsters. Several hundred members of a New York City local union of the then AFL Longshoremen went on a wildcat that lasted twenty-five days in protest against an agreement signed for them by then President Ryan of the ILA.[59] Transport Workers Union Local 100 has also experienced wildcats as an expression of intra-union dissension because of the diversity of crafts and interests which are represented in this large local union. A recent wildcat involved a four-day strike of 1,500 bus drivers as a way of protesting a previously agreed to rescheduling of buses. This it was alleged would result in the transfer of seventy-seven men to another branch of the service and hence impair their seniority standings.[60]

The prevailing attitude of union leadership at all levels of responsibility is against the public airing of diversity and disagreement. The reason given is that such open controversy impairs the union's solidarity. Another reason commonly given is the unfairness and irresponsibility of much of the criticism.

In general local union leadership, like other kinds of leadership, seeks to compose differences if they can before the differences come into public view. The differences get discussed in the executive sessions of the executive board or over a beer before the meeting begins—or in a private conversation in a corner of the hall.

Another element in the situation tending to minimize open

[57] *New York Times,* August 23, 1950.
[58] *New York Times,* December 17, 1948.
[59] Barbash, *Practice of Unionism,* p. 219.
[60] *New York Times,* July 2, 1960, and June 29, 1960. See also Leonard Sayles, "Wildcat Strikes," *Harvard Business Review,* November–December, 1954.

controversy is the impatience of the rank-and-file member with bickering and haggling and what he calls "union politics" in the union. He wants his union to be run smoothly and without incident. Except for the crisis controversy—that is, the ratification of the contract, the calling of a strike, or the increase in dues—the noncommitted, that is noncommitted factionally or ideologically, member is repelled by controversy.[61]

DISCIPLINE

Conflict and diversity within the local union will take place in the forum provided by the union's disciplinary procedure. The issues involved in local union disciplinary proceedings are primarily of two sorts: (1) violation of union work rules or strike discipline—essentially job-centered infractions; (2) issues relating to the conduct of individuals and groups in the internal affairs of the local union. Within recent years a new type of disciplinary case has emerged, namely, that of the union member who invokes the fifth amendment in a legislative hearing.

Very little is known, as a matter of fact, of the role of discipline in the routine day-by-day administration of the local union. The consensus is that discipline is exceedingly rare and "a minor matter in the administration of unions."[62] The disciplinary procedure comes mostly into public view in what is essentially an aggravated form. Our knowledge of discipline in the union is derived almost exclusively from court litigation, complaints handled by public agencies—most notably the National Labor Relations Board under the Taft-Hartley law, and the LMRDA—and finally, from studies made of the appeals procedure as administered by the international union or the convention; or as in the case of the United Automobile Workers, by a public review board. The effect is to expose to public gaze only the most stubborn problems.

Taft's study of the appeals handled by the international union show the issues arising most frequently to be on the following order (the number in parentheses represents the number of cases handled in the period for which information was available to Taft):

[61] See Donald H. Wollett and Robert J. Lampman, "The Law of Union Factionalism—The Case of the Sailors," *Stanford Law Review,* February 1952.
[62] Clyde Summers, "Disciplinary Procedures of Unions," *Industrial and Labor Relations Review,* vol. 4 (1950), chap. 1, p. 19.

Union	Period	No. of Cases	Infractions
Carpenters	11 mo. 1952	(8)	Violation of trade rules: worked on Saturday afternoon, overtime, or holidays without permission.
Hodcarriers	1941–1953	(52)	Work rules
		(16)	Causing dissension
Intl. Ladies' Garment Workers Union	1948–1952	(12)	Complaints against conduct in shop
		(11)	Violation of provisions of contracts or shop rules
Machinists	1951	(6)	Neglect of office by local officers
National Maritime Union		(8)	Leaving ship shorthanded
Asbestos Workers	1948–1950	(4)	Nonunion job or crossing a picket line
Bricklayers	1942–1950	(9)	Assessments by locals
Order of Railway Conductors	1941–1946	(16)	Dispute over local elections
IBEW	1949–1951	(2)	Working below wage
Hotel & Restaurant Workers	1948–1952	(23)	Misappropriation of funds
American Federation of Musicians	1951–1952	(81)	Failure to submit contract to local union where an engagement is played
Painters & Decorators	1948–1951	(19)	Disputed elections in locals
Brotherhood of Railway Trainmen	1946–1948	(81)	Elections in locals challenged
International Typographical Union		(31)	Application for membership
Operating Engineers	1944–1948		

Source: Philip Taft, *The Structure and Government of Labor Unions* (Cambridge: Harvard University Press, 1954), chap. 4 and supp.

In Summers' investigation of reported cases cited by courts, administrative boards, and arbitrators (1890–1950), the issue most frequently involved out of 171 cases in which specific conduct was punished were: criticizing officers or union policies (43), aiding rival union or dual unionism (23), violating union work rules (19), refusing to strike or strikebreaking (12), bringing suit or testifying (14).[63] In a random sampling of NLRB cases involving individual charges of union members, out of 56 cases violation of rules figures in 26, 14 involved charges of rival unionism.[64]

The cases handled in one year by the UAW Review Board involved: (a) a union member who lost her job because of complaints lodged against her with the local union by fellow employees; (b) suspension of two members because they resorted to a civil court suit; (c) an election dispute; (d) release to the press of an item damaging the local union without first clearing it with local officers, and utilization of membership mailing lists for his own political purposes; (e) local election irregularities; (f) three cases involving the handling of shop grievances by local union and regional officials.[65]

There are, to be sure, many individual accounts of abuse of the disciplinary procedure. But these are not very useful for a general assessment of the problem, however much they illuminate particular cases of injustice.

The available facts, admittedly meager for a balanced judgment, warrant the following generalizations: (1) The disciplinary procedure is rarely invoked. (2) When it is invoked the issues are prevailingly work rules problems for the nonfactory unions, and internal union "politics" for the factory unions. (3) The disciplinary procedure has been used to suppress diversity and criticism. (4) The disciplinary procedure is just as likely to be used by a member or a group of members seeking protection from the acts of a ruling administration as it is by a ruling administration against a member. (5) Disciplinary actions do not necessarily end within the local union; they can be appealed to the international. (6) Intervention by the courts on equity grounds and more recently through instrumentalities created by LMRDA will become increasingly characteristic.

The Congress thought the disciplinary problem was of sufficient public interest to warrant public intervention by a federal statute setting out the rights of union members and a broad union procedure for dealing with discipline.

---

[63] *Loc. cit.*

[64] *Business Week*, August 10, 1957, "NLRB Sustains Rights of Union Members."

[65] UAW Public Review Board, *2d Annual Report*, 1958–1959.

A PROFILE
OF THE RANK-AND-FILE MEMBER

There can be no question of the basic loyalty of the rank-and-file union member to his union. Every test demonstrates that the overwhelming majority of union members support their unions— whether the test is a survey of attitudes, a government-supervised strike poll, or a union shop authorization referendum.[1] Indeed, the government polls are probably as indicative of the union member's underlying loyalty to the union as they are of his position on the issues on which he is being polled, since the setting of the poll is invariably one in which the member is, in effect, being asked to repudiate the union leadership.

Union members vary in the intensity of their identification with the union and in their perception of union purpose. Within these variations there are cross-variations which turn on the circumstances in which their commitment to the union is being put to test.

STRONG IDENTIFICATION

The union member who identifies strongly with the union can be one for whom, like the miner or the seaman, the union is the major and the most vital attachment to a meaningful society. This, for example, is the way a group of southern Illinois miners saw their union:

[1] See *Union Security: The Case Against the "Right-to-Work" Laws*, American Federation of Labor–Congress of Industrial Organizations, 1958; U.S. Senate Labor Committee, *Report No. 646*, 82d Congress, 1st Sess. (1951), p. 1; John A. Hogan, "The Meaning of Union Shop Elections," *Industrial and Labor Relations Review*, vol. 2, no. 3, April 1949; Fred Witney, "Union-Shop and Strike-Vote Elections: A Legislative Fallacy," *Industrial and Labor Relations Review*, vol. 2, no. 2, January 1949, p. 248; Herbert S. Parnes, *Union Strike Votes*, Princeton University, Department of Economics and Sociology, Industrial Relations Section, 1956, ch. 4.

For most of the miners unionism was a normal and natural part of the environment in which they grew up, an institution to be accepted and identified with in almost the way that one's church is accepted. Loyalty to the union developed much as did loyalty to one's country, as a result of accepting and internalizing the standards of behavior, the values and ideals, to which one is exposed in one's family and community. In the mining areas a boy grew up expecting to go into the mines when he reached the appropriate age, and going into the mines involved joining the union, which he had already learned to accept. It was not a choice to be made, as many factory workers may make a choice, but a step to be taken automatically and inevitably.

The typical miner raised in a union miner's home in a community in which almost every man was also a miner and a union member, had heard a great deal about the union from a very early age. He had heard his father talk about the union, he had also heard strike stories from other relatives and friends, he had witnessed union-management conflicts or fights between members of rival unions, and he had attended burial services at which union leaders officiated. "All my life I heard about unions," a miner in late middle-age said. "I would always hear speeches about how our forefathers lived and died and fought for unions." For men such as these there is an emotional quality to their attachment to the union that stories of non-union days, or even personal experience of non-union conditions, can seldom bring to factory workers. For such miners, moreover, their union is part of an identification that includes the community and the occupational group, a view that can have no counterpart in the case of a worker reared in a metropolitan area.[2]

Or the view in "Coaltown":

"When I was 14 years old I joined the Hodcarriers Union, a grown man. I didn't have to do this because my family was quite prominent in the community. I know that I was the happiest man alive when I joined the Hodcarriers Union because at last I was a union man. As I mentioned to you before if you are not a union man in this community you are actually nothing."

. . . A son of a merchant claimed "whether you were like others or not was mostly based on whether you were union or non-

[2] Joel Seidman, Jack London, Bernard Karsh, and Daisy L. Tagliacozzo, *The Worker Views His Union* (Chicago: University of Chicago Press, 1958), p. 24.

union and this included merchants and their children. You see they did not belong to the union and if you did not belong to the union you were out. You could tell about the feelings. I know that I wished many times that my father was a miner because I was on the outside."

. . . [And still another view.] "You see the miners' kids were proud of their families and if your family didn't fit the pattern they really let you know about it. The kids would draw off in their own group to say something about the mines or else the union and this was considered a secret and not for the ears of us other children."[3]

Thus we find for example, too, that the Miners are almost the only union group with anything resembling an indigenous union culture, as reflected say in a folk-song tradition. [The] "combination of isolation, singing tradition, and bitter struggle has provided what might be called the perfect climate for the production of protest songs."[4]

The hypothesis has been advanced by Kerr and Siegel that the strong union solidarity of the Miners, and the hypothesis applies equally to the longshoremen, sailors, and loggers, "form isolated masses, almost a 'race apart.' "

They live in their own separate communities: the coal patch, the ship, the waterfront district, the logging camp, the textile town. These communities have their own codes, myths, heroes, and social standards. There are few neutrals in them to mediate the conflicts and dilute the mass. All people have grievances, but what is important is that all the members of each of these groups have the same grievances. . . . Here you do not have the occupational stratification of the metal or building craft, of the hotel or restaurant, or of the government bureau.

. . . The union becomes a kind of workingclass party, or even government for these employees, rather than just another association among many. Union meetings are more adequately attended and union affairs more vigorously discussed; and, as one consequence, personal and ideological factionalism and rival unionism are more likely. Strife within and between unions is a sign that the union is important.[5]

[3] Thurman R. Lantz, *People of Coaltown* (New York: Columbia University Press, 1958), p. 260.
[4] Edith Fowke and Joe Glazer, *Songs of Work and Freedom* (Chicago: Roosevelt University, 1960).
[5] Clark Kerr and Abraham Siegel, "The Inter-Industry Propensity

The women's garment cloakmaker is as far removed ethnically, temperamentally, and industrially from the coal miner as anybody can be; neither does he live in an isolated community. Yet the cloakmaker is a union member for whom the union has been a central life-interest attributable, I think, to a socialist environment and a living tradition of struggle. The cloakmaker is a product of urban society and his attachment to the union has had to weather the competing interests of the large city. The cloakmaker was the prime mover in the development of unionism among the immigrant garment workers—a Jew, invariably a radical (perhaps today an unattached radical) and a self-educated man.

The early cloakmakers' unions were always torn by doctrinal disputations and eschatological refinements. They forever debated and fought about how many ideological angels could stand on the point of a cloakmaker's needle. Unlike the cutter or presser, the cloakmaker is a philosopher. The average cutter or presser is a trade unionist "pure and simple" without any theoretical undertones or Utopian overtones. But the cloakmaker is the eternal Sartor Resartus, trying to fit society into new patterns.

He is highly oral, racy and curious, a born kibitzer and folk commentator, full of yarns and stories to illustrate his point. In the early days he was way on the left: it was the cloakmakers who formed the bulk of the militant rank and file of the socialist and anarchist movements. But time has mellowed him: today he is usually a devout New Dealer. Yet for all his beliefs in some sort of collectivism, he is an incurable individualist. Authority does not impress him, and he knows no sacred cows. You've got to tell him the reason why—and then he has a better reason. He believes not only in free speech but in free vituperation, which doesn't make for a docile rank and file. In the course of their history the cloakmakers have followed some leaders through thick and thin but even their fanaticism was voluntary and democratic; it was never of that mystical sort which is bred by demagogy and terror and [democracy in the International Ladies' Garment Workers Union] is largely due to the tradition created by the cloakmakers.[6]

---

to Strike—An International Comparison," in Arthur Kornhauser, ed. *et al.*, *Industrial Conflict* (New York: McGraw-Hill, 1954), pp. 191–195.

[6] Benjamin Stolberg, *Tailor's Progress* (New York: Doubleday Doran, 1944) pp. 16–17.

Cast in different shapes and molds than the miners or the cloak-makers, but sharing with them the union as a vital if not a central interest, are the printing trades union members.

> A member of a craft union of the type to be found in the printing industry will generally have stronger ties to his union than is frequently the case with the so-called industrial union. To a craft union member his "card" is not only proof of union membership but also of "journeyman" status. The card is regarded by the union as an indication that the holder is a craftsman, proficient presumably, and specifically trained by diligent unions to carry on its skills and traditions. The card represents not only a "prestige factor" but also a badge of craftsmanship which entitles the member to greater security and to greater ease of employment.[7]

Strong union identification is also characteristic of the building trades unionist. To one union plumber, for example, the idea that a plumber might not want to join the union was incredible. "I think a guy who doesn't want to join is a psycho. If he stands on his constitutional rights and doesn't want to join, then I think he is un-American because a good union organization is an asset to the country and not a detriment. A guy is crazy to refuse to join." My impression is that the railroad unionist is also close to his union judging by the frequency with which the union enters even casual conversations among railroad employees.

UNION AS FUNCTION

For perhaps the largest number of union members the union serves a function, not a mission. The primary function of the union as these rank-and-filers see it is protection from the unbridled rule of management. If he is not totally involved in the union, he does not, however, lack a deep-rooted perception of the protective function of the union. Responding to a question as to whether or not they would be better off without a union, rank-and-file members of a Teamsters local responded—as did Machinists and Auto Workers—variously but to the same effect:

[7] Thomas E. Dunwoody, "State of Our Industry," quoted in John Warren Beckwith, *A Comparative Study of the Political Attitudes of a Printing Pressmen's Local and a Group of Non-Union Employees*, M.A. thesis, University of Illinois, Labor and Industrial Relations, 1955, p. 4.

TEAMSTERS

Worker never had it so good without a union. . . . Without the union we would not have what we have today. . . . If we didn't have a union we wouldn't have anything. . . . The wages and conditions wouldn't be worth talking about. . . . If it wasn't for the union we would be working for wages like the WPA was. . . . I am a union man and always will be. . . . There are times when the company's decisions can be wrong and don't take the time to find out, where the union will and should take time. . . . Without the union you wouldn't have a leg to stand on. . . . It's overall protection of the working man. . . . In the 24 years I've been a member I never had it so good. . . . The union sticks for you if you are in the right. . . . A union means protection in your job and the right to complain and arbitrate. . . . Without the union we would have no contract, the company would run things the way they wished and put drivers on trucks that are not union and the union men would set home. . . . Without a union I believe my status in life would be lowered and hardship would insure. . . . If it wasn't for the union a working person would have nothing to say. . . . If it weren't for unions we'd be working for peanuts. . . . I worked under the conditions before we had the union and I know what the hardships were.[8]

PACKINGHOUSE WORKERS

Outstanding remains the significance attributed to protection, quantitatively as well as in the manner in which most workers mention protection. It had a quality comparable to what free association may reveal as the outstanding quality of a dream. It is difficult to convey in any direct manner this feeling which I gained while interviewing but there is an interesting indirect measure, namely, the frequency with which "rights" (that means seniority rights) have been mentioned in conversations in the cafeteria. Workers talk very rarely about what is happening inside the factory gates. Sports, recreational events, local activities, and sex are the main topics of conversation. "Rights" however have been mentioned repeatedly.

There is, indeed, a new tradition growing up around the system of "rights" which is the direct result of union activity. It is a new order which supersedes and is in sharp contrast with the arbitrariness of the boss system. It is only natural that this

[8] Ronald Coyte, *A Teamsters Local*, unpublished thesis, University of Wisconsin, 1959.

new system becomes the focal point of the worker's perception of the union and of the meaning which they bestow on unionism. Security and protection are the magic words which open the gates for an understanding of unionism, more so than wages by themselves.[9]

In a West Coast shipyard during World War II, the union leadership showed little feeling for the newcomers. "Apathetic and often suspicious though he was concerning unions and their activities, the worker was nonetheless also aware of his weakness as a propertyless individual before the oppressive power of wealth."[10]

The "disinterested allegiance" of the union member can become active identification with union goals and purposes as a result of some transforming event, most frequently a strike. The strike creates the group solidarity and cohesiveness that comes of shared experience in a crisis. There is an atmosphere of adventure, of sacrifice, and of camaraderie which gives the participant in a strike a strong emotional commitment to the union, and which has a substantial carryover into later union activities once the strike is over.

Union folklore has it that women are not the material out of which strong unions are made, but the impact of the strike experience solidified this group of garment workers. As described by a picket captain:

[9] Fred H. Blum, *Toward a Democratic Work Process,* The Hormel-Packinghouse Workers' Experiment (New York: Harper, 1953), p. 42. See also Beckwith, *op. cit.,* p. 42; Milton Derber, "Case Study 1, Grain Processing," in *Labor-Management Relations in Illini City,* University of Illinois, Institute of Labor and Industrial Relations, 1953; Glenn W. Miller and James E. Young, "Member Participation in the Trade Union Local," *American Journal of Economics and Sociology,* vol. 15 (1955), p. 44; Arnold Rose, *Union Solidarity* (Minneapolis: University of Minnesota Press, 1952), p. 101; Hjalmar Rosen and R. A. H. Rosen, *The Union Member Speaks* (New York: Prentice-Hall, 1955), pp. 108, 122; Seidman, London, Karsh, and Tagliacozzo, *op. cit.,* p. 80; Constance S. Tonat, *A Case Study of a Local Union: Participation, Loyalty and Attitudes of Local Union Members,* unpublished M.A. thesis, Wayne State University, 1956, p. 105; Edwin Francis Harris, *Satisfactions and Dissatisfactions of Semi-Skilled Automotive Production-Line Workers,* M.S. thesis, Wayne University, 1950, p. 62; Helen Baker, John W. Ballentine, and John M. True, *Transmitting Information Through Management and Union Channels,* Princeton University, 1949.

[10] Katherine Archibald, *Wartime Shipyard: A Study of Social Disunity* (Berkeley: University of California Press, 1947), pp. 141–142.

I never thought that the girls would turn out the way they did and stick to it the way they did. I thought they would stop after a week or so, but as time went on, we got stronger and stronger. The company would do a lot of things that would make the girls that much madder until they said that they would walk all winter if they had to.

And another leader on the same situation:

They were brought to court, went to jail; they were out there in bad weather and good weather. I think they got more determined and militant when they saw that the company wouldn't negotiate and when the scabs went in.

And in the words of a rank-and-file striker: "Meeting all the girls on the line impressed me the most. I never knew them before—not really. We were all together and jolly on the line. We would dance together, sing together, and we are friends now."[11]

The morale-building effect of the strike is, on occasion, perceived by union leaders. In a Textile Workers local:

The most spectacular tactic used to build union morale was the short walkout in the spring of 1945. Although ostensibly a "spontaneous demonstration" to speed up the disposition of the War Labor Board case and to correct some specific grievances in the departments where the walkout started, actually it was carefully organized in order to convince the company of the strength of the union and to reassure the union members and the business manager of the local's strength. A number of the locals doubted that the walkout would be effective, but they thought the risk a necessary one and were considerably surprised with the strong rank-and-file support.[12]

The average rank-and-file member is a "business" unionist and the average in this case covers almost all members. He is interested in wages, hours, and working conditions and the union as a means of protection against management. The Illini City local union in grain processing reveals the characteristic union goals of the rank-and-file member: a strong union, good working

[11] Bernard Karsh, *Diary of a Strike* (Urbana: University of Illinois Press, 1958), pp. 141–142. See also Ross Stagner, *Psychology of Industrial Conflict* (New York: John Wiley, 1956), chap. 13, p. 414 ff; Seidman, London, Karsh, and Tagliacozzo, *op. cit.*, p. 246 ff.

[12] Richard A. Lester and Edward A. Robie, *Constructive Labor Relations*, Princeton University, Industrial Relations Section, 1948, p. 28.

conditions, high standard of living, the protection of the worker's interest in the plant, and job security.[13] He rejects total involvement or emotional commitment, or as one worker in another situation put it: "I'm not interested in the union as a social group. If you need help it's there. It seems to do a good job and if it didn't people would yell. I joined and pay my money because I had to but I still think it's a good thing if it protects the workers."[14]

DEMOCRACY

Most rank-and-file members regard their unions as being democratic in the sense of the members having the last word. But they don't want to be actively involved in running the union and most would not accept positions of responsibility even if they were offered.[15]

The union member has strong doubts about his ability to stand up and talk back to management. He tends to carry over his insecurity in the work situation to possible relationships with management as a local union officer. He is concerned too with his inadequacy in an educational way to deal with the functions of a union office. In open-ended responses to the question, "If you were nominated to office in the union would you accept and what is the reason for your answer?" here are some representative responses in a local of agricultural implement workers:

> All dirty work and no credit at local levels. . . . I have 42 miles to drive. . . . Do not think I could do a good job for the members. . . . My wife and I are both working, I couldn't devote enough time to do it justice. . . . Not enough pep. . . . I believe the international rep has too much control over union. . . . I don't know English enough. . . . Lack many

[13] *Illini City,* vol. 1, p. 235. See also William H. Keown, "Some Dimensions of Company-Union Downward Communication," *Wisconsin Commerce Reports,* University of Wisconsin, vol. 4, chap. 3, June 1955, p. 140; see also Helen Baker, *et al., op. cit.*

[14] Miller and Young, *op. cit.,* p. 39.

[15] William G. Layton, *Dual Allegiance Among Unionized Employees,* M.A. thesis, University of Illinois, 1955, p. 36; Miller and Young, *op. cit.,* p. 40; Rose, *op. cit.,* p. 55; Hjalmar Rosen and R. A. H. Rosen, "The Business Agent Looks at Collective Bargaining," *Personnel Magazine,* May 1957; Seidman, London, Karsh, and Tagliacozzo, *op. cit.,* p. 80; Raymond J. Barrett, *The Structure of a Local Union,* unpublished thesis, University of Wisconsin, 1959, p. 41; Dwight Scarborough, *The Federal Labor Union: A Case Study,* unpublished thesis, University of Wisconsin, 1959, p. 64.

qualifications needed for making a good union officer. . . . Not qualified for an officer's job. . . . Live out of town, no transportation where I live. . . . I do not speak good English. . . . No spare time. . . . Not under present set-up, too many dictators. . . . Too many other duties such as church duties. . . . Dog-eat-dog. . . . Because I couldn't think I could handle it. . . . Cannot express myself enough. . . . Have no time. . . . Do not have time due to other interests. . . . I don't understand nothing about unions. . . . I don't have time to devote to it. . . . Our union is not strong enough to do much good. . . . Too many other obligations. . . . Too many enemies. . . . Spelling. . . . They are thankless jobs, not enough backing by members. . . . No membership backing or leadership strength.[16]

There is general agreement that attendance at union meetings is important, and the average member is aware of the poor attendance which he deplores. But this is not seen as a defect in the democratic process. As one union member put it, "I don't know much about how the meetings are run but I've never heard that they weren't run right. I would have if everything wasn't all right." He thinks his officers are doing a good job but there is a pervasive suspicion of authority in general—of the possible over-exercise of authority in the form of favoritism and pushing other people around.[17]

The union member wants specific things out of his union rather than abstract, routine democratic control. If he has a say in the critical issues that affect him—strikes, ratification of contracts, participation in the grievance procedure—he feels he has enough control to suit him.[18]

The worker's loyalty to the union does not seem to be appreciably impaired by the presence of a union security provision which, in effect, compels him to join the union. In a large industrial local in Columbus, "being forced to join a union because of a union shop contract clause is not a major deterrent to union solidarity."[19]

[16] Coyte, op. cit. See also Ralph H. Bergmann, *A Field Study of Factors Determining Worker Attitudes Toward a Union Organizing Drive*, unpublished Ph.D. dissertation, Massachusetts Institute of Technology, 1950, p. 185.

[17] Miller and Young, op. cit., p. 40.

[18] Arnold Tannenbaum, "Mechanisms of Control in Local Trade Unions," *The British Journal of Sociology* (London), December 1956.

[19] Glenn W. Miller and Ned Rosen, "Members' Attitudes toward the Shop Steward," *Industrial and Labor Relations Review*, July 1957, p. 530.

The same conclusion was reached in an investigation of a large warehouse local in St. Louis.[20] In a Miners local, even though "a union shop clause had been in effect in this mine field for more than a generation, those who wish to work in the mines had no choice but to join the union. Yet it is of interest that few responses stress the compulsory aspect of joining."[21] Only in the Kansas City local of the unaffiliated National Brotherhood of Packinghouse Workers did a majority express itself against the union shop, which is ascribed to the fact that the leaders of this local are opposed to the union shop.[22]

The feeling for the union shop for the rank-and-file members is based largely on grounds of equity.

PACKINGHOUSE WORKERS
If a guy comes in and works with you, even if you get a raise he gets one. And if he's not in the union, I don't think it's fair.[23]

AGRICULTURAL IMPLEMENT WORKERS
. . . Why should there be free riders? . . . If a majority belong why not make all belong?[24]

PLUMBERS
You pay dues to a union and then work with a man who doesn't pay dues. You spend time learning the trade and then work with a man who probably didn't spend any time but just picked up a wrench. It's bad for the morale. You pay dues to the union to uphold your rights and a non-union guy will come in and get the same benefits.[25]

The union for many union members is the local union. There is no "over-loyalty" in most instances to the international union or to the federation. To the degree that awareness exists, the impression of CIO seems to have been stronger to the average member of a CIO affiliate than his opposite number in the AFL—always excepting the traditional crafts who have always had a relatively high sensitivity to their AFL status. Most union members are

[20] Rose, *op. cit.*, p. 185.
[21] Seidman, London, Karsh, and Tagliacozzo, *op. cit.*, p. 24.
[22] Theodore V. Purcell, *Blue Collar Man* (Cambridge: Harvard University Press, 1960), pp. 182–183.
[23] *Ibid.*, p. 182.
[24] Barrett, *op. cit.*
[25] Seidman, London, Karsh, and Tagliacozzo, *op. cit.*, p. 58.

only dimly conscious of the existence of these higher bodies or of the network of lateral affiliations like central labor bodies.

He generally approves involvement of the union in politics. Politics is favorably viewed by the union members; it means getting out the vote, fighting for clearly defined union issues. There is considerable disapproval of union contributions to political parties and to political candidates and union support of issues which go beyond bread-and-butter union issues. With all his reservations, however, he tends to support the union voting recommendations. There is a small group that favors a labor party, but by labor party this group does not mean a socialist party. The main reason given for support of the labor party idea is to hold the politicians to account more effectively.[26]

EMPLOYER

His strong support of the union generally does not preclude the rank-and-file member from also being well-disposed toward his employer. This is the attitude which has come to be known as dual loyalty or dual allegiance. He finds no inherent contradiction between being well-disposed to his union and to his employer. There are several probable qualifications which need to be made to this generalization: (1) There is no dual loyalty when the union is in conflict with the management. There the union member invariably takes the union side. (2) If there is no ideological commitment to the class struggle on the part of the average union member, there is what might be called a visceral class struggle reaction. (3) The union member is extremely suspicious of an inordinately cozy relationship between his officers and management.

At the same time that he looks kindly upon his employer or at least he is not unkindly, one has the impression in talking with union members that they are deeply suspicious of the power and authority of employers and big business as a class. A personal experience will illustrate this. In teaching workers classes economics, I frequently raise this question with respect to recessions: If production and employment were to go down, why would consumer income or personal income hold up? Invariably the first-impression response is: a few wealthy guys were getting

[26] Investigations carried on by Alton Bartlett, University of Wisconsin graduate student in Industrial Relations, 1960.

most of it. Or many union members are very skeptical when I advance the hypothesis that an effective functioning grievance procedure might conceivably be beneficial to both the union and the employer. "Why should the employer want to deal with workers' grievances?" they ask.

However, this visceral class-struggle reaction cannot be pushed too far. Several organizers have reported recently that wholesale attacks on the employer or attacks on a rival union for being too "soft" with the employer have boomeranged. This may be simply fear that the union will not be able to get away with open defiance or it may be due to a feeling that workers have not, in fact, been mistreated by the employer. The boomerang effect of anti-employer appeals is likely to develop where workers have developed a behavior pattern of submissiveness to the employer —as in white collar work. The tactic of building up "hostility to the boss . . . has not been notably successful. . . . Many astute white-collar organizers de-emphasize the class struggle. At times they imply that top management is really in favor of the union."[27]

Clerical workers experience the least identification with the union. Union members who also carry on part-time farming are only rarely strong for the union. Men tend to be stronger pro-union than women. The most influential determinant of union loyalty is length of membership. The longer the union member is in the union the more he cares about the union. Other suggestive determinants of union loyalty, but less certain, is the relationship between marital status and loyalty. Married men seem to be more concerned about the union than single men. And the greater activity and participation in the union, the greater is the commitment to the union; but at the same time, the greater is the degree of criticism of how the union is functioning.[28]

The absence of total commitment does not seem to stem from other demands on the union member's loyalty. For the most part he is not a joiner. The only characteristic social affiliation is a church affiliation. There is little evidence of involvement in organizations like PTAs, or political parties which have prior claims

[27] George Strauss, "White Collar Unions Are Different," *Harvard Business Review*, September–October 1954, p. 75.
[28] Walter H. Uphoff and Marvin D. Dunnette, *Understanding the Union Member*, University of Minnesota, Industrial Relations Center, 1956, p. 17 ff. See also Barrett, *op. cit.*; Rose, *op. cit.*, p. 69.

on his participation in the union. The activities that do seem to have conflicting or prior claims are family and recreational activities.[29]

HOSTILITY

Where strong reservations or outright hostility are expressed toward the union the grounds given are practical ones—the union is ineffective. Only rarely do union members say they can get as much without a union, or run down the principle of unionism. In every one of these instances, except where otherwise noted, the union generally received the overwhelming endorsement of the membership, and what are set forth here are the sentiments of the disaffected minority:

STEELWORKERS LOCAL

The union hasn't done anything for the men. It said it would improve working conditions. So far they haven't. If I were for it, I'd be a strong union man. If it were good I'd just as soon join. A lot of odd guys join it then run it down. They find everything wrong with it. Unless it's better why join?

I have the very lowest thoughts possible about the union. It is useless, the union hardly ever wins, only when the company lets them win. I think the company's more or less fair in its judgments.

The union is no damn good. Look at the ignorance of the officers. It's a racket. The international representative is a sorry character.

I dropped out of the union. The committeemen are green and don't know anything. They've got a "racket."[30]

TEAMSTERS LOCAL

They did more harm than good with some of the clauses in the contract and doing the things the way they want instead of the members. . . .

[29] See Alice Hanson Cook, "Labor's Search for its Place in the Community," *Journal of Educational Sociology*, vol. 29, no. 4; Alice Hanson Cook, "Education of Workers for Public Responsibility in Community and Political Affairs," *Labor's Public Responsibility*, National Institute of Labor Education, 1960; Bernard Barber, "Participation and Mass Apathy in Associations," *Studies in Leadership* (New York: Harper, 1950).
[30] Charles R. Walker and Robert H. Guest, *The Man on the Assembly Line* (Cambridge: Harvard University Press, 1952), pp. 131–132.

They don't do anything for us if we have a complaint, they never send out a representative. In eight years of employment I only saw one union man. . . .

If you're willing to work and improve yourself you don't need a union. . . .

The principle and purpose of a union is good, but the personnel doesn't follow these principles when a gripe is made. . . .

A union is all right if it is kept clean as far as officials are concerned. . . .[31]

CHICAGO PACKINGHOUSE LOCAL

Purcell found substantially less union allegiance in a Chicago local of the Packinghouse Workers than he did either in an East St. Louis local of the Amalgamated Meat Cutters or a Kansas City local of the unaffiliated National Brotherhood of Packinghouse Workers.

Why do we find so much less union allegiance in Chicago? Four reasons come to mind. (1) The serious failure of the UPWA's 1948 strike. (2) The fight between Local 28 and the international UPWA, creating the impression of two unions in the plant. (3) The capture of Local 28 leadership by the Communist Party. (4) The race issue. . . .

In Chicago some of the packinghouse workers were so aroused by these issues that they were actually against the idea of having any union in the plant at all (union disallegiance). We found not a single employee in the other two plants who was positively against the idea of having a union.[32]

AGRICULTURAL IMPLEMENTS LOCAL

The union is not strong enough to do much good as I said before. . . . Sold out by international long ago. . . . No good membership fight and backing. . . .[33]

Whatever workers say, the results of NLRB elections do indicate that there are groups of workers who vote in favor of no-union, or who vote to decertify an existing union as their bargaining representative.

An analysis of the decertification elections for the illumination that is cast on union "disloyalty" suggests the following observations:

[31] Coyte, op. cit.
[32] Purcell, Blue Collar Man, pp. 169–170.
[33] Barrett, op. cit.

1. Union decertification elections are very infrequent and the total numbers of workers involved are small.

2. The union decertification election runs against the union in two-thirds of the cases but no information is available as to whether there is a subsequent return to union.

3. A disproportionate share of the decertification elections are in the south, suggesting that employer anti-union sentiment is an important factor.

4. The decertified units tend to be the smaller units.

5. "Typically, the craft and departmental units decertified in the regional offices involved office and clerical employees, professional and technical employees, guards, warehousemen and service units" not the standard crafts or production and maintenance groups.

6. The decertified units are newly organized rather than well-established unions. An unsuccessful strike seems to have been an element in some of these decertifications.[34]

In summary then: Rank-and-file members are overwhelmingly loyal to their union. A small group rejects the union. The loyal member varies in the degree of commitment and strength of union identification, ranging from the union as a central life interest to the union as a protector of workers' rights. Except in a crisis situation like a strike the union is one of many other interests for most members, but these other interests are personal, not social. The strike does often evoke a total involvement in the union for the rank-and-filer. When he thinks of the union concretely he means the local union; generally the international is indistinct and central and state bodies even more so.

What the union member wants from his union is primarily economic protection. He accepts the political functions of the union, but he wants the union's politics kept close to the union's economic role. He thinks his union is democratic because the membership has the final say on issues that matter, and he believes too that his officers are doing a good job. Most union members do not want to be union officers because they think they lack the education and knowledge to do the job and because they have strong doubts about their resoluteness in talking back to management.

As for the employer, the union member is generally well dis-

[34] Joseph Krislov, "Union Decertification," *Industrial and Labor Relations*, July 1956.

posed toward him as an individual person or individual company but he will line up against him when the union-management relationship is a bitter one. To employers and business as a group —if not as a class—there is what I have referred to as a visceral class-struggle reaction, a kind of distrust, which lacks ideology to be a Marxist-model class struggle.

11

DEMOCRACY AND THE LOCAL UNION

An inventory of the conditions of union democracy derived from the responsible discussion[1] can be listed as follows:

[1] This discussion is based on the following: Benjamin Aaron, "Unions and Civil Liberties, Claims v. Performance," *Northwestern University Law Review*, March 1958. V. L. Allen, *Power in Trade Unions* (New York: Longmans, 1954), particularly "Introduction." American Civil Liberties Union, *A Labor Union "Bill of Rights," Democracy in Labor Unions, the Kennedy-Ives Bill*, New York, 1958. Warner Bloomberg, Jr., Joel Seidman, and Victor Hoffman, "Paradoxes of Union Democracy," *The New Republic*, 1959. George W. Brooks, *Sources of Vitality in the American Labor Movement*, New York State School of Industrial and Labor Relations, Cornell University, 1960: Just as I was completing this book for publication, I read this work. In many ways it is the most stimulating and provocative statement of many of the issues which are raised in this chapter. We are in agreement on many points but I suspect in disagreement on many others. I regret that I didn't get it in time to include it for consideration here. From Michael Harrington and Paul Jacobs, ed., *Labor in a Free Society* (Berkeley: University of California Press, 1959): Hugh A. Clegg, "The Rights of British Trade-Union Members"; David L. Cole, "Union Self-Discipline and the Freedom of Individual Workers"; Arthur J. Goldberg, "A Trade Union Point of View." William M. Leiserson, *American Trade Union Democracy* (New York: Columbia University Press, 1959). Seymour Martin Lipset, "The Law and Trade Union Democracy" (mimeo.) for delivery at 1960 annual meeting of the American Political Science Association, New York. C. Peter Magrath, "Democracy in Overalls: the Futile Quest for Union Democracy," *Industrial and Labor Relations Review*, July 1959. Joel Seidman, *Democracy in the Labor Movement*, New York State School of Industrial and Labor Relations, Cornell University, 1958. Benjamin M. Selekman, "Trade Unions—Romance and Reality," *Harvard Business Review*, May–June 1958. From United States Senate Subcommittee on Labor of the Committee on Labor and Public Welfare, *Government Regulation of Internal Union Affairs Affecting the Rights of Members*, Legislative Reference Service, Library of Congress, 85th Cong., 2d Sess.: John T. Dunlop, "The Public Interest in Internal Affairs of Unions"; J. B. Hardman, "Legislating Union Democracy"; Paul Jacobs, "Union Democracy and the Public Good"; Clark Kerr, "Unions and Union Leaders of their Own Choosing."

1. The important policy issues must be subject to membership determination.

2. Union officers must be responsible to the membership. Responsibility to the membership means the latter's effective right to elect these officers, criticize them, remove them for cause, and vote them out of office.

3. The legitimacy of opposition must be firmly established.

4. Basic membership rights must be guaranteed. These rights include free speech, assembly, and press, free elections and secret balloting, disciplinary due process and equal treatment of members.

5. The membership must participate effectively in the affairs of the union.

6. Legislative, executive, and judicial powers should be separated as to those who exercise these powers.

CRITICISMS

Contemporary criticism of union democracy ranges between two poles: on one side, a denial that union democracy exists at all and that the prevailing system is closer to oligarchy and control by a ruling bureaucracy. This for some imperceptibly merges into the view that the normal standards of political democracy may not be applicable at all to the union's appropriate function and purpose. At the other pole is the view that there is nothing seriously wrong with union democracy. In between these poles commentators criticize union democracy on a variety of grounds:

1. The union, if not totally an oligarchy, is moving rapidly in that direction.

2. The union's demands on the member for institutional loyalty are endangering individual rights.

3. There is an incompatibility between responsibility to the business system and industrial stability and adherence to the full range of democratic procedures.

4. Democracy prevails in the local union but is seriously threatened in the international.

5. Union leaders have only a "lip-service" attachment to union democracy.

6. There is nothing seriously wrong with union democracy since the nature of union leadership inherently requires a sensitive responsiveness to the interests of the membership.

When efforts are made to be specific about the factors which diminish union democracy the bill of particulars includes:

1. Supralocal bargaining.
2. Union security provisions.
3. The unwieldy size of unions.
4. The multiplant jurisdiction of locals.
5 The absence of rival unionism.
6. The dominant role of political machines.
7. The absence of real choice for the union member who is limited to plebiscitary approval or disapproval.
8. The lack of membership participation.

Since this is a diluted summary, I am blurring points of special emphasis, qualifications, and exceptions that shade the judgments of individual commentators. There is, for example, no universal agreement among commentators on all of the conditions of union democracy. Commentators put more emphasis on one standard or another, and frequently the stress is put where the most aggravated departure from the standard seems to them to be. Some writers stress the legitimacy of opposition to the ruling group as the most important standard of union democracy. Others, however, explicitly reject this as an indispensable standard. Still others place the weight of importance variously on individual membership rights, on the quality of membership participation, on separation of powers, and on due process in the disciplinary procedure. It is not unlikely that many of the standards were formulated with the international union in mind rather than the local, although few writers make the distinction plainly.

DEFINITION

The preconceptions with which I approach the theory of democracy as applied to the local unions are:

1. Democracy is a valid standard to apply to the union performance.

2. The application of democratic theory to the union must be related to the central role and function of the union.

The union must be democratic because the union holds itself out to be a democratic movement. The union must be democratic further because its main purpose is to represent workers in the employer-employee relationship—or to put it another way, to introduce a measure of democracy in the government of the plant community. There is a serious question as to whether this function can be discharged by an undemocratic union. If the union is not a mechanism of representation it is nothing.

If the democratic theory does not have relevance to the union as a going concern it becomes a dogma or an ideology. Democracy is not all. In the world of the living it is interwoven with all sorts of practical considerations. The starting point of any attempt to define democracy, Joseph Schumpeter says, is to recognize that "democracy is a political method . . . for arriving at political . . . decisions and hence incapable of being an end in itself irrespective of what decisions it will produce under given historical conditions."[2]

CONSTITUTION

Against this setting I am ready to formulate a kind of syllabus of local union democracy.

1. Constitutions and by-laws should conform to the principles of democratic government—I am mostly in agreement with the items in the democratic inventory opening this chapter.

a. The policy issues of the local union must be subject to formal, in addition to informal, membership determination.

b. The membership must have the right to elect all officers, criticize them, and remove them for cause.

c. Basic membership rights must be guaranteed; namely, free expression, free assembly and association, free elections and the secret ballot, due process in disciplinary cases, and equal treatment of members, subject to the rule of "clear and present danger" to the union's existence.

d. All members should have full voting rights on all issues and offices which are subject to membership approval.

2. The climate within the union should permit reasonably free and effective utilization of these instruments.

3. The goals and actions of the union must be consistent with the generally accepted democratic principles of the larger society.

On the specific side the primary instrument of union democracy is a written constitution which marks out in detail the design of local union government. This design should include: (1) the functions and purposes of the union; (2) the manner of elec-

[2] Joseph Schumpeter, *Capitalism, Socialism, and Democracy*, 1950 p. 220, quoted in H. B. Mayo, *An Introduction to Democratic Theory* (London: Oxford University Press, 1960), p. 33.

tion, the grounds and procedure for removal, the terms of office, and the scope of authority of the officers and committees of the union; (3) the questions which require formal approval by the membership; (4) the procedure by which the officers of the union are held to account by the membership; and (5) the rights and responsibilities of individual union members.

The notion that democracy is related to decision-making is critical. Vital interests are at stake in the union which engage the activities of men and women in a serious way. If the union is performing a socially approved role, then the responsible application of democratic theory must take this role into central account. "Trade union organization [V. L. Allen asserts] is not based on theoretical concepts prior to it, that is on some concept of democracy but on the end it serves. In other words, the end of trade union activity is to protect and improve the general living standards of its members and not to provide workers with an exercise in self-government."[3] A good deal of the criticism of union democracy, and many of the definitions of democracy as applied to the union, are, to use Reinhold Neibuhr's words in another context, "Simple moralisms." "A simple moralism," Neibuhr has said, "is always pathetic when it obscures the power realities which underlie moral issues."[4]

This does not mean that every practical need of the union is per se a ground for short-circuiting democracy—just as democracy is not all, neither is the union all. My view is that democracy in the union should be asserted to the point of inconvenience if necessary, but not to the point of critical impairment of vital functions. The problem in developing a theory of union democracy, then, as I see it, is to find the common ground between democracy as a significant part of the complex of values in our society and the union as a going, effective, decision-making institution in modern industrial society.

In line with this concept of a theory of democracy related to decision-making, we cannot, to use the language of A. D. Lindsay, "ask the ordinary member . . . to do more than he can or will. . . . We must, therefore, distinguish between the various processes by which the government of a country is kept responsible to public opinion from the highly technical and specialized proc-

[3] Allen, *op. cit.*, p. 15.
[4] *The New Leader*, February 4, 1957, p. 10.

esses of government itself."[5] The point is that the presence of functioning leadership is necessary in a complex government and that the exercise of vigorous leadership authority cannot properly be regarded in and of itself as a conspiracy to subvert democracy.

Major questions should be determined by the union meeting or by referendum. These major questions are, among others: recommendations for changes in the collective bargaining agreement, the approval of the agreement, the strike, increases in dues, assessments, initiation fees, etc., financial obligations beyond the routine voucher expenditures, and acceptance of executive board minutes. Sufficient latitude should, however, be given to the officers to administer the day-to-day affairs of the local efficiently and effectively. The executive officers must be given a scope of authority consistent with their responsibilities. No democratic purpose is served if the executive officer of a union becomes an errand boy.

In a union of any size there ought to be, in addition to the local-wide union meeting, representative mechanisms through which diverse interests can be reflected. Where the local is what is known as an amalgamated local—where it bargains with several employers—mechanisms should be established to provide for adequate representation and expression of all substantial interests within the local union. Even in a one-plant local with a large membership sublocal bodies on the order of departments or plans should provide for involvement of the membership in aggregates smaller than the local-wide meeting. In factory unions the stewards' body can provide an intermediate instrumentality between the top executive officers and the union meeting.

The local officers should be subject to periodic elections—two years sounds like an optimum period—by the union meeting or a referendum. Reasonable requirements for nomination to, and the holding of, union office may be set but they should not act to exclude any large numbers of people from holding office. Qualifications relating to minimum length of membership and experience in the industry, membership-meeting attendance, in addition to the LMRDA requirements, are not unreasonable.

The union needs to have available to it appropriate disciplinary sanctions to secure compliance with its duly established rules. The stakes involved are sufficiently grave so that the union

[5] A. D. Lindsay, *The Modern Democratic State*, I (London: Oxford University Press, 1943), p. 282.

should not be required to tolerate dissension to the point of destruction or serious impairment of its authority.

Grounds for disciplinary action against individual members should be specifically stated. The test of disciplinary action must be the injury to the union, rather than the injury to the dignity of the union leader. Other than the failure to meet financial obligations, reasonable minimum grounds for serious disciplinary action would appear to be: (a) active agitation in behalf of a rival union; (b) union corruption; (c) a member crossing a picket line established in connection with a strike by his local union at his establishment; (d) acting as a "spy" in behalf of the employer with whom the local deals; (e) seriously impairing the union's performance of its legal obligations under the collective agreement; (f) slander or libeling of union members and officers in the course of union affairs; (g) violation of duly authorized union rules and regulations.

Disciplinary procedures should be spelled out in detail. These procedures should include provision for making the charge, for a timely and fair hearing, for a decision, and for an appeal from decision. The defendant in union disciplinary proceedings is entitled as a matter of right: to know what the specific charges against him are, confront those who are making the charges, and he is entitled to decision and review by persons not themselves involved in the dispute. The guilt or innocence of the party and the penalty should be finally determined for the local union by the local-wide union meeting with reasonable time for presentation by the parties at interest. In the case of a large local, the governing delegate body other than the executive board should be the court of last resort within the local. In the event of conviction the punishment should fit the offense, and the constitution and by-laws of the local union should relate specific punishments to specific offenses.

The exceptions to these disciplinary safeguards can be suspension or expulsion for nonpayment of dues and other constitutionally sanctioned financial obligations. Another appropriate exception is disciplinary action stemming from disorderly conduct at a union meeting, in which case the penalty should be limited to expulsion from the meeting or a small fine in accord with the constitution.

The general scope of union functions should be spelled out in the local union constitution and by-laws. The authority of the local to carry on collective bargaining, strikes, education, political action, legislative activity, and welfare activities where necessary should be clearly indicated. Moreover, the procedure whereby binding commitments on the part of the local are made should be specified. With respect to collective bargaining this means procedural provisions for preparing collective bargaining demands and the approval of the final bargain. It should also include some responsibility, depending on the circumstances, for the officers involved in the bargaining to report back, whether in a union meeting or by some form of written communication.

The financial standing of the local should be reported in writing to the membership and should be subject to periodic audit by an elected committee, and where the local can bear the cost, by a public accountant at longer intervals. The report of the latter should also be distributed to the membership.

The constitution should establish channels and guarantees for freedom of expression and freedom of assembly with respect to local union affairs. Union experience indicates by and large that the following kinds of protected dissent can function without seriously impairing the security of the union:

(1) Sections of the official publications of the union should be open for free discussion of union policies at all times. (2) During an election period, specific portions of the official publications of the union should be equitably earmarked for discussion of pros and cons with respect to officers up for re-election, and with respect to policies. (3) The union meeting should be organized in a manner to allow free discussion of all viewpoints subject to the timely disposition of union business.

CLIMATE

The climate in which the administration of the union functions should be conducive to the exercise of these constitutional rights, otherwise there is form but no substance. The world is full of democratic constitutions that have died because they have not been rooted in fertile soil.

The first condition of a democratic climate within the union is that the union leadership at all levels must *consciously* accept democracy as an article of union faith. It is possible that departures from democracy are due more to a blunting of the democratic impulse than it is to a leadership plot to do in the rank and file.

Union leadership must be able to take internal criticism in its stride without necessarily imputing base motives to the critics. Responsible treatment of the minority by the majority also requires a responsible approach by the minority to the majority.

The democracy of the union functions within, and is subordinate to the larger democratic goals and purposes of, the larger community. Discrimination because of race, color, or creed are offensive to the underlying principle of democracy and therefore incompatible with genuine union democracy, even if all the democratic forms of the union have been adhered to in the enactment of these discriminations.

Democracy implies a respect for the autonomous right of associations to govern themselves, within the general framework of accepted values. But this right of self-determination is endangered if groups outside the union seek through conspiratorial means to subvert this autonomy and to remove the center of union authority from its legitimate sources.

Democracy in the union is affected by external acts, in particular the acts of the international union and its various instrumentalities. Since the international union is not the main interest of the present work, I deal with this question summarily. The agencies of the international union which limit the self-determination by the local in matters affecting it should be supported by a representative mechanism that permits appropriately elected delegates from the local unions to determine the outcomes.

Where receiverships are concerned, there should be an opportunity for a hearing to permit the affected local union to argue the necessity of the receivership before the receivership is made permanent. There are emergencies in which fast action is required. In such situations authority can be given to institute a temporary receivership, subject to a hearing of the sort indicated before the receivership is permanently established. The responsibility of the receiver to account for his actions to the local union membership should be no less than the responsibility of the regular officers, and the receiver should set aside only those processes of local self-government which are essential to achieve the purpose for which the receivership was installed in the first instance—always assuming, of course, that the receivership was installed for a proper purpose in the first instance. The receivership should not be a total substitute for the self-governing processes of the local union.

The appellate machinery in the international should be organized in a manner to maximize an independent judgment of the persons and issues in controversy. I am not certain, without further investigation, whether a *public* review board is indispensable—certainly it is desirable.

MISCONCEPTIONS

There are several misconceptions about the nature of union democracy. I shall deal with these as they concern the local union.

There is the small group mystique. The argument runs that the smaller the group, the more democratic it is. This is true, I suppose, all other things being equal—but all other things are never equal. Is the small group small as a device to get greater individual participation, or is it small because it wants to exclude other workers who have some claim to being in the group? If it is small in order to preserve a quasi-monopolistic interest in a given supply of jobs, or to exclude potential members on grounds of race or ethnic affiliation, then the smallness of the group frustrates, rather than advances, democratic objectives. There is no inherent virtue in smallness or bigness except as it is related to the needs of the jobs that need doing.

There are characteristics of the small group which, in fact, minimize democratic government. For example, small groups isolated from one another, even though they have a common larger objective, are much easier to manipulate and control because they lack the power of numbers to make themselves effective. The most obvious example is the communist cell or fraction in a union or a plant which is indeed small but is made to order for compact control. Small, isolated groups are also easier for management to control and manipulate. It may easily be a subversion of democracy for a small unit, because of its strategic power, to determine an issue as to prejudice the interests of a larger group which has been disenfranchised. Some are smaller than they ought to be measured against the scope of the problems which the union confronts, and continue small because a group of leaders wants to maintain its cozy control.

Then there is the participation syndrome whereby participation is equated with democracy. Democracy is a system of government and should not be confused with busy-work, largely irrelevant to the important decision-making function of the system of government. What too many union leaders with whom I have

talked are concerned about is not so much the lack of involvement of the rank-and-filer in decision-making as the absence of
busy-work participation in activities pre-planned by the leadership. There are local union leaders who use participation as a
cover for the condition that the membership does not, in fact,
have anything important to say about the way the union is run.

Participation does have by-products and merits on its own in
building a vital union. But these merits are not intrinsically related to democracy. The by-product of participation is that participants tend to have a deeper concern with issues than non-
participants. To this extent participation is an aid to local union
democracy. But participation can frustrate democracy by involving membership in the pageantry of democracy, without its
substance.

The aspect of participation that receives the most attention is
attendance at membership meetings. But candor requires recognition of the fact that the routine union meeting is a bore, just
as all routine meetings are bores, whether they are meetings of
university faculties, parent-teacher associations, precinct political
organizations, or legislatures. They are all bores even though
indispensable to the conduct of the·organization's business; and
only a handful of people can be expected to, and do in fact,
involve themselves responsibly in the routine.

Heedless attempts to get maximum attendance at union meetings, regardless of interest and concern in the business of the
union, can have mischievous consequences by bringing out people
who just do not care and have no sense of responsibility about the
union as an enterprise. On these same grounds political scientists
are taking another look at the quality of responsibility which
voters are likely to bring to the polls if it needs a high-pressure
public relations campaign to get them there.

What needs to be underscored with respect to the union meeting is that when critical issues are up, the evidence indicates that
there is substantial attendance at the union meeting. Arnold
Tannenbaum has had some very wise things to say on this subject which I think are generally applicable:

> Control in a local union is a complex process. It is exercised
> through various phases of activity: legislative, administrative,
> and sanction; and relative to many issues which differ in their
> importance to the membership. Different persons may be differ-
> entially involved in the various phases of control. Furthermore

the members often view control of their union in pragmatic terms, in terms of those issues which make a difference to them.

. . . Membership control may be maintained at a fairly high level without a corresponding involvement of the rank and file in the regular formal meetings of the union. Members exercise control through meetings, but also through other channels. Informal discussions and representational arrangements, ratification power and the power of election and recall, all represent possible mechanisms of control at the disposal of the membership.[6]

The evidence is clear that all attempts to encourage attendance at local union meetings—door prizes, fines, beer—have failed. And if they had succeeded, there is serious question as to whether the membership meeting as an instrument of democratic government would not become simply a social occasion—which is fine for union conviviality, but it is a mistake to confuse this with democracy.

Militancy as an index of union democracy is of the same temper of perspective as is participation. Both are emotively related to democracy but are not of its essence. The members of the Teamsters Union are undoubtedly among the most militant; so are the Newspaper Deliverers in New York; so are the Miners. But none of these groups has been particularly noted for the high quality of their democratic government. The Auto Workers, the Typographical Union, to pick out conspicuous examples, are also militant, but the quality of democratic government is high by any standard. In many ways the most democratic union I have encountered in the course of this investigation is a federal labor union—but militancy is not its most notable characteristic.

There is the misconception that the increasing involvement of supralocal bodies in collective bargaining—most particularly the national union—necessarily impairs democracy in the local union. On the facts the national union, and its instrumentalities, undoubtedly have more influence in the negotiation of agreements than they had a generation ago. The effects of this trend, however, have been widely misunderstood. The negotiation of the agreement is not all there is to collective bargaining, and the national union is not an undifferentiated identity.

Collective bargaining is not only an agreement, it is also the enforcement of the agreement. The local union is still critically

[6] Arnold Tannenbaum, "Mechanisms of Control in Local Trade Unions," *The British Journal of Sociology* (London), December 1956.

important in enforcement of the agreement and in the local application of terms of the master contract. Moreover, the representative mechanisms devised to secure policy consensus have injected a large element of organized local involvement even in the determination of the terms of the agreement by the suprabodies. The test in this situation is whether effective and organized methods of representation exist through which the local union constituencies can make their judgments felt.

In certain respects the national union is not doing enough in collective bargaining in terms of the job at hand. Except for slogans, only a handful of unions have a collective bargaining program in any meaningful sense. Most unions have not asked the right questions, much less evolved answers, about the effect of collective bargaining on the economics of the industries in which they are operating; nor have many unions undertaken a serious comparative analysis of their own contracts on an industry basis, or multiplant-company basis. These are all problems which are properly in the province of the national union and its instrumentalities and are beyond the capacity and resources of the locals to deal with in an effective way.

There are areas of internal union management where there is reason to believe that a *greater* exercise of authority by the national union or its instrumentalities would be desirable; for example, more detailed supervision and development of standards in health and welfare administration and bargaining, and in financial administration. This is particularly applicable to the situation in which the national union is not otherwise extensively involved in the total bargaining situation.

There is no a priori principle which can be specifically applied as to the relative allocation of authority between the national union and the local union. It is surely wrong to assume that local autonomy is always preferable without reference to the issues involved. It is even wrong if the argument is that local control is necessarily deemed to be more democratic. The test must always be the decision to which the control is being applied. It is perhaps possible to borrow the concept of the "appropriate unit" to illuminate this question. When applied to the problem at hand, the appropriate unit concept tells us that the electoral unit involved in any decision must conform (to the extent possible) to the unit which will be affected by the decision on which consensus is sought. When the local union makes a collective bargaining decision which seriously prejudices larger interests in the union, these latter are to all intents and purposes being excluded from a voice in a decision on which (democratically) they have a right to be heard. When a local union engages in discriminatory practices against Negro workers, or Puerto Rican workers, it may be imperiling vital interests of the other groups in the union, to say nothing about whether a majority decision of any kind which runs seriously against fundamental democratic values in the society can be democratic. The test of the democratic use of power, then, does not turn alone on the extent of local self-determination, but on whether the unit is inclusive enough to provide every materially affected group with a systematic opportunity for participation in the making of the decision.

When the large issue at stake under this heading is distilled for its vital essence, it comes down to big versus small. We tend to equate big with bad and small with good—and to a large extent, I suppose, this is true. But the fact is that most of the urgent problems of our society *are* big and the problems of the union society are big, too. The problem can be dealt with only by the involvement of big organizations.

In an industrial society which is constantly having to face the dislocating forces of war and peace, of movements of industry, of wholesale technological change, and of inflation and recession, only a broad, resourceful, and informed attack will be adequate to the task. This requires organizational mechanisms with the capabilities of coping with problems on a large scale. The unions cannot escape the consequences of this drive of events, and we ought not to despair in advance of our capacity to devise incentives and methods to make big organization democratically workable.

The same order of values is evident where the effect of leadership on local union democracy is concerned. Strong (big) leadership tends to be equated with impairment of democracy, weak (small) leadership with the strengthening of democracy.

It has been asserted that union leadership which is responsive to the reasonable profit-making needs of the employer must, in the same measure, be less responsive to the demands of the membership for "more"—therefore less democratic. Leadership does tend to be more "responsible," but this has nothing to do with democracy if the rules by which the dialogue, as it were, between leadership and membership are carried on and governed by democratic principles—or to be more specific, if the members have systematic opportunities to say "no" to the leader's demand for reasonableness. An illustration in point is when a meeting of over-the-road teamsters in Milwaukee by a vote of 73–38 over-rode the objective of the secretary-treasurer that the members "voluntarily give up a contract guarantee of time-and-a-half for more than 48 hours work" on the grounds that the provision "was costing them jobs."[7]

Do local union members in fact say "no" frequently to their leaders? The evidence here is that they do, and they are likely to say "no" more often on collective bargaining issues than on issues of internal union government.

The test of democracy must in the first instance rest, as we have been saying, on the effective availability of mechanisms to influence policy, to change officers, and to engage in free discussion of union policy. In this framework there can be more than one authentic character of leadership consistent with democracy in a local union—ranging from the charismatic leader to the ineffectual leader, from one-man leadership to group leadership. It happens that the bold, imaginative, creative leadership has come from strong men and large unions. The innovations in local union outreach have come from strong leaders in large nonfactory type local unions. Innovation demands maneuverability, and maneuverability seems to be a characteristic of the paid union leader. There is an obverse side to this coin. The characteristic of maneuverability that creates the bold leader within a democratic framework has on occasion, when pushed to pathological extremes, produced the corrupt, authoritarian leader.

The presence of an institutionalized party system or factionalism within the union is another index of democracy in the union upon which a high value has been put. The starting point of this judgment is sound enough—diversity, of which a party system is a reflection, is a hallmark of democracy. The facts are that organized and open diversity is endemic in the local union. To be sure, this diversity does not take the form of a party system. But we have seen diversity expressed in clubs, slates, factions, and cliques. These are the instrumentalities which the American trade union experience has yielded up, and I am unable to understand why these are less valid as channels of difference and dis-

7: "Teamsters Turn Down Bid for Overtime Cut," *Milwaukee Journal,* February 13, 1961, p. 1.

sent than is the type of party produced by the political arena in the public sector. The outlets provided by elections—both union and NLRB elections—court litigation, government-administrative agencies, and even wildcat strikes, provide ample opportunity, which is frequently realized, for the expression of diversity within the local union.

The contention that local unions are governed by oligarchies and by self-perpetuating bureaucracies cannot be sustained by the available facts. The mass of evidence I have cited here in considerable detail indicates quite the contrary. There is a substantial turnover of officers and local union officers are frequently turned out of office. Even when they experience long tenures in office the weight of the evidence is that the local union officers are highly sensitive to the pressures of competitive elections. Moreover, the evidence further indicates that by and large members do feel that they are running the union and that their officers are formally and informally sensitive to their needs on the issues that matter to them. The systematic involvement of the union member in the issues that matter to him—strikes, dues increases, contract approval—is substantial.

The idea of bureaucracy in any accepted meaning has, in fact, very little application to the local union. The overwhelming majority of local unions have no full-time officers. There is little social distance between the members and the leadership in the local union. This is even true of the very large local unions. Nor is there any substantial factual basis that there is a tendency in the direction of oligarchic control in local unions. The unsettling effects of this period of major economic transformation—as this is being written—run in the opposite direction.

The discouragement of rival unionism has been cited as an antidemocratic influence on American unionism. The question has been raised whether exclusive representation in the bargaining unit by the majority union is not at odds with the democratic principle. The line of logic, if not the intended result, which finds intrinsic democratic merit to rival unionism is only one remove from a rejection of union representation altogether. Even the most democratic union imposes obstacles in the way of competition among individual workers in the bargaining unit. Indeed, the elimination of this competition is the main objective of unionism. Now, fundamental objection to unionism on this ground, even though I do not agree with it, is not altogether untenable.

What is untenable, I believe, is the acceptance of unionism in principle and at the same time criticism on principle of union policy because it seeks to minimize competition among workers by dulling the effect of rival unionism. There can be proper objections to the lengths to which the reduction of rival unionism should go and the methods by which it is achieved, but principled objection on this score is at odds with the logic of unionism. The labor movement's own conviction of the injurious effects of rival unionism is supported by the facts.

Rival unionism has no inherent relationship to democracy in the rival unions or to the quality of the union performance. Rival unionism has hampered effective unionism in the chemical industry.[8] Rival unionism at the height of the division between AFL and CIO in the late thirties spurred effective unionism just as it seems to have been a stimulus to more effective representation in the Northwest lumber industry.[9] Rival unionism in the form of jurisdictional disputes in the printing trades and the building trades or among the seagoing unions is not relevant to democratic unionism in these situations. District 50 of the United Mine Workers is currently the most militant protagonist of rival unionism. And whatever other merits District 50 raiding has, it is without any noticeable effect on democracy in District 50, the United Mine Workers, or on the unions whose bargaining relationships it is raiding. An AFL–CIO survey of raiding, preparatory to the negotiation of the no-raiding agreement, held that there was little net gain for any raiding union.[10]

The level of propaganda discourse which the contending unions characteristically carry on in a rival union situation is depressing, barbarous, and frequently ugly. A serious question is raised as to how a movement can maintain itself as a cohesive force in the face of such disintegrating acts on the part of its constituent elements.

There are those who would accept a general sensitivity and responsiveness on the part of union leadership without more, either as democracy or as a satisfactory substitute for democracy.

[8] "Competitive Unionism in the Chemical Industry," *Industrial and Labor Relations Review*, October 1959.
[9] Margaret S. Glock, *Collective Bargaining in the Pacific Northwest Lumber Industry*, University of California, Berkeley, Institute of Industrial Relations, 1955.
[10] Arthur J. Goldberg, *AFL–CIO, Labor United* (New York: McGraw-Hill, 1956), Appendix D.

Sensitivity of union leadership to the interests of the rank and file is very important. But in terms of any verifiable test of democracy it does not, in my judgment, carry weight because sensitivity can become insensitivity unless it is checked by a democratic system. Responsiveness can become obtuseness unless there are forms of government which effectively hold leadership to account in a constitutional manner. Democracy anywhere is more than a mood or a temper; it must begin by being a system of government.

The separation-of-powers standard has practical meaning at some points and not at others. It is plainly relevant to the local union disciplinary function where the executive—business agent, president, etc.—ought not to judge disciplinary infractions which arise out of executive action. Separation of powers is not meaningful when applied to the union meeting which, in most local unions, partakes of executive, legislative, and judicial functions and validly so in the very character of the union meeting as a local union form of government. The members are physically and socially close enough to the local leaders that to enforce a separation of powers—legitimate enough in public government— would result in a sharp reduction of control by the union membership over the details of union government without any constructive results in return.

The union shop question is also largely relevant to the question of union democracy. The issue is posed this way usually: if a worker is forced into the union in the first place how can there be a democratic union. There can be no legal union shop—membership as a condition of employment after hiring—unless the union represents the majority of the employees in the appropriate bargaining unit. The Taft-Hartley law used to prescribe a special union shop election authorizing the union to make the demand on the employer but not compelling the latter to agree. The election provision proved so unnecessary that it was subsequently eliminated by the Congress on Senator Taft's recommendation. The union shop "de-authorization" election is still in the law so that workers can get rid of an unwanted union shop. In any case, once the union shop is established most workers want it to continue.

It is possible to argue that union security is inherently undemocratic since it does force some people to join and stay in the union against their will. I am unable to take this argument seriously since working for a living does involve many restrictions on individual freedom and the question becomes one of whether the restriction is a reasonable one and whether, in this form of restriction, there is a democratic choice available. It is not unreasonable from this viewpoint to compel every union citizen to pay for the union's keep if the employer agrees to as he must before it can become effective, and if the affected workers have the opportunity to reject or approve or turn out the union shop. All of these conditions have to be met in the case of a legal union shop.

DEFECTS

From the standpoint which I have set out, there are valid criticisms of the local union's democratic performance which are within reach of correction and which I believe to be related to the union's function as a union. These are not to be interpreted as proposals for legislation nor have I taken into special account the changes which are made by LMRDA. I support the changes whether or not they may be already required under law. I do not believe that except as indicated it would require legislation to meet these criticisms and in any case my thought is that these criticisms can and should be met to the extent that they apply by the internal processes of the unions.

1. The geographic jurisdiction of some locals is so broad— multistate as we have seen in certain cases—that lacking a delegate-body mechanism, the members outside of the headquarters city are effectively disenfranchised. These locals have the scope of a district or regional intermediate body but with the government of a local union. This same criticism applies to large locals with a diverse industry character that lack a delegate-body type of representation between the member and the top officers of the local.

2. Most international unions—at least before LMRDA—did not provide adequate and comprehensive guidance to the local unions in establishing their own local union constitutions and by-laws. The international unions should develop model constitution and by-laws with sufficient flexibility to take local differences into account. At the very least the international union should provide a comprehensive framework. Most local union officers have neither the time nor the technical competence which it takes to do this adequately and legally.

3. I have serious doubts as to the wisdom in terms of what I have called the larger democratic goals of the community of

barring *members* on grounds of membership in so-called subversive organizations, particularly where union membership is virtually a condition of earning a living. Carried to its ultimate it would mean that a communist for example is not entitled to earn a living, or for that matter entitled to become a public charge if he is barred from earning a living. Genuine security objections are proper with respect to the employment of communists, fascists, etc., but this is a government and employer responsibility. The union's responsibility is to see that security standards are fairly applied. In my judgment it is entirely proper for the local to bar by constitutional provisions communists or Fascists or other disreputable characters, as *officers*—the difference is that holding office in the union is a privilege whereas union membership comes close, in many instances, to being an indispensable requirement for holding a job.

4. *De facto* or formal restriction on admittance to membership limited to kinship or ethnic connections is objectionable, as is restriction based on anything else except lack of work. This raises the question of the closed shop principle. The closed shop is prohibited, of course, by the Taft-Hartley law. But it is no secret that the ban is observed more in the breach than in the conformity, in the casual employment hiring hall industries. The closed shop is a necessary requirement of any hiring hall situation. The legal ban on the closed shop should be eliminated and replaced by a legal ban on the closed *union*, except where it can be demonstrated that the labor market situation at any given time would impose an unreasonable sharing of work if new members were admitted.

5. The financial officer of the local should be required to notify members of arrearage in dues and other financial obligations and to notify the member also that he is in danger of suspension or expulsion or loss of job, as the case may be.

6. The provisions relating to disciplinary action are defective at several points.

a. The grounds on which charges may be brought are in some instances inordinately broad. The grounds should be made more specific. Such language as disloyalty, language detrimental to the association, bringing the union into disrepute, conduct unbecoming a union member—without more—illustrate the indefiniteness of the offense as stated frequently in the local

232

union constitution, and are inadmissible as a basis for union discipline.

b. The constitution should provide that the trial committee should exclude anyone as a member who has a direct interest in the case either as a charging party or as a defense witness.

c. Where the local union meeting is the court of last resort within the local then the constitution should prescribe procedures as to how the case shall be presented and as to the manner of voting. There should be some provision for equal time for the charging party and for the respondent in the disciplinary action. The ballot, which should be secret, should provide for a separate vote on whether the respondent is guilty as charged and as to the penalty.

d. Most local union constitutions appear to provide too much discretion in relating the penalty to the offense. The punishment should clearly fit the offense, and the constitution should specify the range of penalty applicable to each major category of offense.

7. The business agent and assistant business agent, where they exist, are the most important posts in the local union and they should be elected directly by the membership and not by the executive board.

8. The nomination procedure should be held at a separate meeting from the election meeting and the constitution should provide for reasonable notice for both meetings if the election is held at a local union meeting rather than in a referendum away from the meeting.

9. Election tellers should be elected, not appointed, by the executive board or a chief executive officer.

10. Candidates should be entitled to watchers of their own choice as a matter of right.

11. In addition to executive board members who are elected on a local-wide basis, provision should be made for election of members on a sublocal constituency basis, particularly for locals where there may be some material diversity of interest by way of skill or plant location, etc.

12. A serious defect in many written constitutions is their failure to set out in any detail the procedure whereby collective bargaining is carried on in the local union. The local union constitution should set forth:

a. the composition of the bargaining committee—and it should be a committee reflecting all the substantial interests, even if it is the executive board that functions ex officio as the bargaining committee;

b. the procedure for drawing up of demands, reporting of progress, and the final approval.

13. The constitution should make provision for the intelligible reporting of finances and the right of reasonable access to the supporting documents.

14. The means of communication between the member and the local union, other than the union meetings, should be strengthened. For example, a local union bulletin or newspaper, even if produced simply in mimeographed form, serves a useful purpose in keeping the membership in touch with what is happening in the union. The plant bulletin board in the factory local serves the same purpose. The evidence is that these local union sheets and bulletin board notices are read by the members.

15. The local union meeting hall can be improved in many instances which I have observed. This is no place for a temperance lecture nor am I qualified to deliver one, but I have a strong feeling that the meeting hall as an adjunct to a tavern communicates something less than the most attractive impression of the union as an institution.

16. The stewards' body can be given greater recognition and identification in the structure of the local union. Suggested forms are regular meetings of the stewards' body and status recognition along the lines of remission of dues, superseniority, and, most importantly, an accepted role that goes beyond acting as an errand boy for the local-wide officers. The other side of this coin is that the steward must know his job and this invariably requires some kind of training program by the local union.

17. Some intermediate bodies, particularly the joint-board type or joint-council type in the larger city, have gone too far in reducing the local union to nothing more than a union meeting. These area intermediate bodies should appropriate only those functions which are intrinsic to it. Many of these intermediate instrumentalities can profitably review their relationship to the local union to determine the appropriate functions and responsibilities of each.

18. Local unions frequently lack routine channels through

which criticism can function. Lacking these channels, criticism and opposition circulate through the grapevine route with all the exaggerations, distortions, and ill-feeling that normally accompany this route. Given constitutionally approved channels and guarantees within which criticism and opposition can function openly, it ought to be possible to prevent this criticism and opposition from overflowing and throwing the union into chaos. The availability of a local union periodical, even if mimeographed, which is open to all comers would be a major contribution toward creating an orderly channel for controversy.

19. Like the election campaigns in public government, election campaigns in the unions are too often among the less edifying spectacles of democracy in action. A minority that rises to power to become the majority through base and ugly appeals can so brutalize the democratic process that it is impossible to maintain a viable relationship ever between the majority and the minority. Every contest becomes a battle to the death. If democracy is to be made tolerable the minority must observe the rules of the game and participate responsibly in the government of the union. Responsible government by the majority becomes manifestly difficult if not impossible if the minority applies the maximum pressure of which it is capable, such as indiscriminate recourse to rival unionism or secession movements or court litigation, on the theory that anything goes.

20. The international and the intermediate bodies can improve their performance by providing a more meaningful research and information service to the locals, by assisting the locals in the development of useful education programs, the efficient discharge of the auditing function, and by assisting the local union to maintain its books according to some standard auditing procedure.

PROGRAM

The union member is loyal to his union—there can be no question about that—but except for crisis, it is for most of the union members a kind of disengaged loyalty. The union, as has been said, serves a function not a mission for the rank and filer and in principle this is to the good. The human purposes of a democracy are best served when there are no exclusive monolithic loyalties. But it may be that the disengagement has gone too far and that union leadership must give sober reflection as to how the tie that binds the member to his union can be strengthened by a deeper understanding of the purposes of unionism in our time.

There are several noticeable lacks in the union member's understanding of his union. First of all, there is a feeling of insularity; for many a member his local is all there is to the union. Union citizenship, however, requires an understanding of the role of constitutional government in the local and of the role and function of the international and the intermediate bodies. Secondly, it is also clear to me that the average union member does not have a clear understanding of the union purposes in politics. This is not to say that he does not support the union in politics, but I think he does not understand the real needs of the union in politics and in legislation.

Education has an important function to perform in making for more effective democracy in the local union. If education has a viable function to perform it must operate on the assumption that democracy depends on the will of human beings to achieve it—in specific here—democracy depends on how much union leaders want it. Further, the assumption is that most of them do want it but many of them need to reminded and refreshed as to what democracy really means.

The educational program for union democracy might be constructed along some of the following guidelines:

1. The educational program must differentiate between the leadership, whether in-leadership or out-leadership, and the rank-and-file membership.

2. With respect to union leadership, the educational program can stress the major themes in the democratic tradition in the United States. These themes relevant to the union are the tolerance of dissent, the legitimacy and role of controversy in a democracy, free and open discussion as the laboratory for the testing of diverse viewpoints.

The educational program must also deal with the human and administrative skills required to make democracy effective and manageable, such as the administrative skills involved in running a committee, an executive board meeting, a union meeting, and the techniques of leading a discussion which comes to a conclusion.

While it is possible that the union leadership can be seriously engaged in a formal educational enterprise because of their interest and involvement, I do not think that it is possible for the rank and file in the same degree and on the same order. The educational devices in dealing with the rank and file need to be less formal, more creative and imaginative than we have had time to think about. In a literal sense, the union must reach the rank-and-file member where he is—at home, in the shop, and at the union meeting, to the extent to which he attends. The fact that he has to be reached where he is and not through classes does not exclude educational planning. It simply means that the educational channels have to be different.

An important element in communicating a feeling of democracy to the average union member is the quality of the face-to-face relationship between leader and member. The leadership's responsibility for its side of the face-to-face relationship constitutes a large part of the human relations skills of democracy. It is idle to talk about democracy in the union if the leader's attitude toward individual union members runs counter to all the nice words about democracy. The union meeting cannot and should not give the appearance of a neatly oiled machine running the show, and where there is contempt expressed or implied for what appears to be offbeat opinions. The union's involvement in politics cannot be carried to the point where political opinions not in conformity with the union's position do not get a hearing. The newspaper of the union cannot communicate an image of democracy if it conveys an impression of being the organ of the leadership that happens to be in power. The way the office girl talks to the union member when he comes in to pay his dues or find out about union problems, the tone of voice in which the union leader talks to the rank-and-file members—all of these are among the bits and pieces that go into the making of the rank-and-file member's total impression of the union as a democratic institution.

So much for the quality of the approach. As to the content of the approach, I believe it is of primary importance that the union member understand his own union. The printed output of the labor movement in the United States is enormous, but little of it is devoted to the fundamentals of unionism and to the plain facts about what the union is, how it spends its money, and how it governs itself. The first publication that a union needs above all others is a pamphlet on what might be called "union civics" or "union citizenship"; the kind of information about the union the applicant for naturalization gets about his country, but few native-born citizens do.

The objective in all of this is to get across the idea that democracy is in large part a transaction between the leaders and the members and that the delicate balance of the transaction is distorted when one side or the other does not carry out its side of the bargain.

The important criticisms of local union democracy are then: (1) the failure of the governing documents to reflect total functioning of the union in a comprehensive way; (2) the inadequacy of the disciplinary provisions; (3) the absence of customary rules of the game for controversy; (4) the excessive disengagement of the union member from union affairs except for crisis.

All of these criticisms are understandable in the nature of the union as an institution. In origins the union began as a primitive equalitarian democracy, where conduct between leaders and members and among members was regulated by a feeling of comradeship and solidarity, not by written constitutions. The written constitution was largely a ritualistic document copied outright with minor variations from a variety of disparate sources or from "boiler plate" provided by the international and regarded as having little operating relevance to the facts of government. Indeed, why was it necessary for these unionists to rely on formal written documents as the ultimate source of government when the union had something stronger and deeper to assure honest and democratic government: their commitment to a morality of trade unionism? Although vague as words, the concept of that recurring phrase "conduct unbecoming a union member" had concrete meaning to the committed unionist. It meant the violation of a shared code which has a good deal of meaning even today where, in many respects, the informal standards have been incorporated in the AFL–CIO codes of ethical practices. This informal code was seen very explicitly in a discussion by a group of union telephone workers in response to the question, "What is a good trade unionist?"

1. Recognizes a picket line.

2. Does not discriminate between color, race, creed, sex, or minority groups.

3. Patronizes union labor: (a) advertising to other workers the benefits of belonging to a labor organization; (b) unifying effect in labor movement; (c) shows spirit of mutual aid.

4. Shows management the profits from unionism.

5. Does not report another worker to employer.

6. Abides by majority decision.

7. Does not carry internal union disputes to public.

8. Keeps union affairs from management.

9. Is sure information about union is complete and correct before it is released to members.

10. Settles disputes and grievances between members within the union.

11. Organizes the unorganized. Every unorganized worker retards the progress of organized workers.

12. Participates in civic affairs.

13. Brings the principles of unionism to the public.[11]

This spirit of trade union government evolved when the union felt itself to be the victim of a conspiracy of destruction by employers and government, and indeed by the total society—a feeling that exists strongly today, incidentally—so that the open airing of controversy within the union has been regarded as a serious breach of the union's solidarity. Robert Hoxie captured this attitude very well more than a half-century ago, "So far as workers are concerned, there is no society as a whole and no long-run but immediate need and rival social groups."[12]

Well, the situation now is that, for better and worse, the feelings that people have toward each other—even though fundamental—are not sufficient to regulate relationships and the conduct of affairs in the modern union. The modern union is a business in a literal sense—this has no invidious connotation for me—handling substantial sums of money, involved in the vital job and other interests of its members, regulated by public authority and presenting the ordinary human temptations. Conformity to explicit standards is consequently an unavoidable obligation for the union today.

The attempt to formulate these standards has the additional effect of forcing local union people to grapple with issues of democratic government which they have only vaguely confronted up to now. My experience as a teacher of unionists leads me to believe that the "instinctive" democracy of the local union al-

[11] Jack Barbash, *Labor Unions in Action* (New York: Harper, 1948), pp. 181–182.

[12] Robert F. Hoxie, *Trade Unionism in the United States* (New York: Appleton, 1923), p. 262.

luded to in the concluding paragraphs that follow makes it possible to bridge the gap between democracy as feeling and democracy as constitutional government.

CONCLUSION

A total appraisal of democracy in the local union as I understand it must recognize that these defects, significant as they are, do not critically impair the great vitality of democracy in the local union.

The superior democratic performance of the local union is due to (1) the closeness of the union member physically and socially to the governmental process; (2) the meaningfulness and concreteness of the issues which the local union deals with; (3) the highly developed state of unionism as a technique of representation evolved through a century and a half of experimentation; and (4) the great power of "instinctive" democracy in American life generally. There are, of course, the pathological types of local unions of which due notice has been taken here, but these are not altogether amenable to the processes of internal union government. To be sure, greater vigilance by members will minimize the effect of corrupt union leaders, but the best human institutions will produce evil men—this is primarily a job for the policeman's function of the state. Moreover, union pathology—and this holds true especially for corruption—has its roots, as I have said, in a complex of forces: the structure of the labor market, the nature of the work, and the economic organization of the industry.

The local union represents a tribute to the capacities of "average" people to conduct affairs of great complexity, to devise ingenious governmental forms with flexibility and imagination, and to hold their leaders to account. The quality of the achievement is heightened by the fact that the local union is primarily what somebody has called a "do" democracy; it is *action* which turns on the outcome of the democratic process here, not simply words alone.

In short, local union democracy as part of the total union system has been sufficiently effective to enrich the material and human substance of life for millions of working people.

INDEX

Beck, Harold, 89
Beckwith, Warren, 200n
Bedsole, Naftel, 82
Bell Aircraft Corporation, 164, 184
Berger, Morroe, 109n
Bergmann, Ralph H., 205n
Bertram, Gordon W., 137n
"Bill of Rights," 74
Block brothers, 97, 98
Bloomberg, Warner, Jr., 213n
Blum, Fred H., 53n, 202n
Bookbinders, see International Brotherhood of Bookbinders
Bowling clubs, 10
Brazeal, Brailsford R., 137n
Brewery Workers, see International Union of United Brewery, Flour, Cereal, Soft Drink and Distillery Workers of America
Bricklayers, Masons and Plasterers' International Union of America, 194
Brocher, Donald E., 42n
Bromwich, Leo, 42, 152n
Brooks, George W., 213n
Brotherhood of Carpenters and Joiners, see United Brotherhood of Carpenters and Joiners
Brotherhood of Locomotive Firemen and Enginemen, 43
Brotherhood of Painters, Decorators and Paperhangers of America, 25n, 167, 194
Brotherhood of Railroad Trainmen, 194
Brotherhood of Shoe and Allied Craftsmen, 123
Brotherhood of Sleeping Car Porters, 139
Building Service Employees' International Union, 167; Local 14, 19
Building and Construction Trades Department, 14, 143
Building trades, 7, 10, 43, 77, 78, 93, 176, 200; upstate New York, 126; see also Construction trades
Building trades councils, 2, 7, 137, 167
Bureaucracy, 228
Business agent, 5, 54, 76, 77, 155, 176, 189, 233; see also Chapter V.

CIO, see Congress of Industrial Organizations
CWA, see Communications Workers of America
Cadre, 183, 184, 185
Calloway, Ernest, 112n
Carpenters, see United Brotherhood of Carpenters and Joiners
Carr, King, 161n

Carter, Tasile, 20n
Case, J. I., 2, 10
Catholic workers, 180
Caucus, 182, 183
Central labor body, 103
Chairlady, 113
Chamber of Commerce, 51
Chapel, 71
Chapter, 70
Charges, 28, 219, 232
"Charismatic" leader, 108
Chasan, Will, 44n
Chatman, Abraham, 85
Chicago Commonwealth Edison Co., 158
Chicago Federation of Labor, 167
Chicago Restaurant Association, 95
Chinoy, Eli, 102n
Christie, Robert A., 138n
Christoffel, Harold, 109, 110
Cities Service Company, 87
Citizens, 26
City central labor body, 3, 4, 7
Clegg, Hugh A., 213n
Clerical workers, 208
Cliques, 227
Cloakmaker, 199
Closed shop, 232
Closed union, 232
"Club," 182, 227
"Coburn, Tom," 108
Cohn, Sidney E., 133n
Cole, David L., 140, 213n
Coleman, James, 54n, 71n, 123n, 189n
Collective bargaining, 1, 2, 3, 103, 149, 177, 218, 233
Collins, John J., 87
Collusion, 11, 95, 97
Colorado Fuel and Iron Corporation, 160
Committeeman, 113
Committees, 5; anti-discrimination, 5; bargaining, 5, 35; community services, 5; fair practices, 5; finance, 38; nominating, 32; political action, 5; recreation, 5; trial, 28
Commons, John R., 15n, 17n
Communications Workers of America, 9
Communists, 8, 68, 105, 108, 132, 165, 166, 179, 180, 185, 222, 232
Communtiy activities, 1, 3, 5, 78
Congress of Industrial Organizations, 4, 8, 44, 83, 132, 144, 190, 206, 229
Constitutions, 131, 216, 231, 238
Construction trades, 77, 113; Illini City, 126; Kentucky, 171; West

242

NICB, *see* National Industrial Conference Board

NLRB, *see* National Labor Relations Board

Nashua Gummed and Coated Paper Company, 107, 162

National Association for the Advancement of Colored People, 43, 44

National Association of Manufacturers, 51

National Brotherhood of Packinghouse Workers, 206, 210

National Industrial Conference Board, 26, 27, 31, 149, 150, 151n

National Joint Board for Settlement of Jurisdictional Disputes, 143

National Labor Relations Board, 22, 23, 43, 51, 132, 133, 187, 189, 190, 193, 210, 228

National Maritime Union, 68, 194

National Planning Association, 10

National Policy Committee for Petroleum Industry, *see* Oil, Chemical and Atomic Workers International Union

National Railroad Adjustment Board, 139

National union, *see* International unions

National Union of Marine Cooks and Stewards, 64, 68

Negotiations, 183

Negroes, 8, 27, 40, 43, 44, 52, 83, 106, 107, 172, 226

Neibuhr, Reinhold, 217

Neufeld, Maurice, 22n, 81n, 91n

Newspaper and Mail Deliverers' Union of New York and Vicinity, 43, 63, 66, 224

Newspapers, 234

Nominations, 32, 39, 233

Oberer, Walter E., 153n

O'Donnell, L. A., ix, 134n, 138n, 139n, 181n

Office Employees' International Union, 167; Local 9, 25n, 90

Officers, 32; paid, 3; part-time, 3, 34

Oil, Chemical and Atomic Workers International Union, 142

One-industry towns, 10

Operating engineers, *see* International Union of Operating Engineers

Operative Plasterers' and Cement Masons' International Association of the United States and Canada, 42

Opposition, 97, 214, 235

"Organization for Membership

Rights," 8

Organizational Disputes Agreement, 144

Organizing, 3

Order of Railway Conductors and Brakemen, 194

Ozanne, Robert W., 68n, 110n, 179n

Packinghouse workers, *see* United Packinghouse Workers of America and National Brotherhood of Packinghouse Workers

Painters and Decorators, *see* Brotherhood of Painters, Decorators and Paperhangers of America

"Paper" locals, 8, 10, 54, 94

Paperworkers, *see* United Papermakers and Paperworkers

Parnes, Herbert S., 39n, 79n, 196n

Participation, 222

Party system, 227

Patrolmen's Benevolent Association, New York, 11

Pattern bargaining, 141

Paul, George S., 107n, 173n

Pearlin, Leonard I., 73n

Peck, Sidney M., 111n, 128n, 166n

Penalty, 29, 233

Pensions, 141

Per capita, 4, 37

Perlman, Selig, ix

Petrillo, James, 8, 190

Photo-engravers, *see* International Photo-Engravers Union of North America

Picket line, 219, 238

Plasterers, *see* Operative Plasterers' and Cement Masons' International Association of the United States and Canada

Plumbers, *see* United Association of Journeymen and Apprentices of the Plumbing and Pipe Fitting Industry of the United States and Canada

Political activities, 1, 3, 5, 10, 207

Port branch, 19

President, 100, 107, 110

Pressmen, *see* International Printing Pressmen and Assistants' Union of North America

Printing trades, 200

Professionals, 9, 71

Public employment, 11

Puerto Rican workers, 8, 94, 226

Purcell, Theodore V., 52n, 53n, 103, 106n, 107n, 191n, 206n, 210n

Quill, Michael, 86

Quorum, 40

Wallace, Henry, 109
Wallick, Frank, 90n
Waterfront Commission, 41
Weber, Arnold, 80n, 149n
Welfare activities, 1, 3
"Welfare union," 82
Wharton, Hunter P., 96
White-collar, 208
Wildcat strikes, 148, 187, 191, 228
Willner, Don, 39n
Withdrawal cards, 36
Witney, Fred, 196n

Wollett, Donald H., 193n
Women, 208
"Work permit" men, 42
Work rules, 142, 193, 194
Wurf, Jerry, 86

Young, James E., 53n, 54n, 124n, 202n, 204n, 205n

Zinke, George W., 160n
Zinos, John, 86